# Technology and the Common Good

# Technology and the Common Good

## The Unity and Division of a Democratic Society

*Allen W. Batteau*

berghahn
NEW YORK • OXFORD
www.berghahnbooks.com

First published in 2022 by
Berghahn Books
www.berghahnbooks.com

© 2022 Allen W. Batteau

All rights reserved. Except for the quotation of short passages for the purposes of criticism and review, no part of this book may be reproduced in any form or by any means, electronic or mechanical, including photocopying, recording, or any information storage and retrieval system now known or to be invented, without written permission of the publisher.

**Library of Congress Cataloging-in-Publication Data**

A C.I.P. cataloging record is available from the Library of Congress
Library of Congress Cataloging in Publication Control Number: 2022016090

**British Library Cataloguing in Publication Data**

A catalogue record for this book is available from the British Library.

ISBN 978-1-80073-526-2 hardback
ISBN 978-1-80073-527-9 ebook

https://doi.org/10.3167/9781800735262

To Adam, Laura, and Benjamin,
as they work together for their common good.

# Contents

| | | |
|---|---|---|
| List of Illustrations | | viii |
| Acknowledgments | | ix |
| Observations | | x |
| Introduction. | Cultures and Countercultures of Technology | 1 |
| Chapter 1. | Worlds without Technology | 13 |
| Chapter 2. | Goods, and the Common Good, in a Liberal Society | 34 |
| Chapter 3. | Technology and the Commons | 62 |
| Chapter 4. | Beyond the Traditional Commons | 94 |
| Chapter 5. | Public Goods and Institutions in Cyberspace | 118 |
| Chapter 6. | Democratic Vistas | 137 |
| Chapter 7. | Building Institutions for a Technological World | 162 |
| Conclusion. | Reclaiming the Commons | 183 |
| References | | 206 |
| Index | | 215 |

# Illustrations

### Figures

0.1. Leonardo da Vinci, Flying Machine (c. 1488). Wikimedia Commons, public domain. — 2
1.1. Stonemason's hammer. © Osumi Akari. https://creativecommons.org/licenses/by-sa/4.0/deed.en. — 15
1.2. The Archimedes screw. Wikimedia Commons, public domain. — 18
1.3. Leonardo da Vinci, Vitruvian Man (c. 1490). Wikimedia Commons, public domain. — 21
1.4. Pont du Gard. Wikimedia Commons, public domain. — 23
2.1. Thomas Cole, *The Oxbow* (1836). Wikimedia Commons, public domain. — 45
2.2. Harley-Davidson Softail Breakout FXSB103. © Lothar Spurzem. https://creativecommons.org/licenses/by-sa/2.0/de/deed.en. — 51
3.1. The airplane flies around the world, *Le Monde Illustre* (1912). *Chronicle* / Alamy Stock Photo. Used with permission. — 67
3.2. A. J. Russell driving the Golden Spike, Promontory Point, Utah (1869). Wikimedia Commons, public domain. — 78
4.1. The RF spectrum. US Department of Transportation. https://www.transportations.gov/pnt/what-radio-spectrum. — 100
4.2. Yosemite Valley. Wikimedia Commons, public domain. — 104
7.1. International Law of the Sea. Wikimedia Commons, public domain. — 178

### Tables

2.1. Types of goods by exclusion and subtractability (Hess and Ostrom 2007: 7). — 41
5.1. Technological impact on governing the commons. Table created by the author. — 125

# Acknowledgments

Writing a book is never a solitary individual effort. Even the shortest books represent the dedication and contribution of numerous scholars and colleagues. I particularly would like to express my appreciation to Julia Gluesing, whose detailed comments on the final manuscript did much to improve it. The contributions of Maria Roti, particularly to the illustrations and figures, were also invaluable. The efforts of Danny VanZandt in completing the illustrations were also valuable. Special note goes to Carlo Cubero of Talinn University for introducing me to E-Estonia. Other colleagues who favored me with insightful comments include Kristin McGuire, Lucia Laurent-Neva, Andy Newman, Alejandro Perez, Jonathan Rauch, Carmen Bueno, Hung-Sying Jing, Inga Treitler, Lotta Björklund-Larsen, and Marc Kruman, all of whom gave the manuscript a careful reading and valuable comments. My greatest appreciation goes out to all of these; the obvious faults of the book remain my responsibility.

# Observations

There is no such thing as a free sunset.

—This volume, p. 42

During the Middle Ages, forests were sometimes over-cleared, and fields were exhausted by villagers that had not yet discovered the principles of crop rotation, but the possibility of exhausting the entire planet's resources would have to wait until the Industrial Revolution.

"Things are in the saddle and ride mankind."

—Ralph Waldo Emerson, 1847

Smart investors know that a diversified portfolio of short-term and long-term securities, bonds and equities can better withstand the ups and downs of business cycles; likewise a diversified institutional portfolio of public, private, club, and common pool resources can better withstand unexpected events, the ups and downs of wars, famines, market crashes, and pandemics.

—This volume, p. 144

"There is almost nothing, however fantastic, that (given competent organization) a team of engineers, scientists, and administrators cannot do today. ... When [builder and technicians] have imagination and faith, they can move mountains; out of their skills they can create new jobs, relieve human drudgery, give new life and fruitfulness to worn-out lands, put yokes upon streams, and transmute the minerals of the earth and plants of the field into machines of wizardry to spin out the stuff of a way of life new to this world."

—David Lilienthal, *TVA: Democracy on the March*

*Introduction*

# Cultures and Countercultures of Technology

Before there was thinking, there was making. Before *homo sapiens* developed the learned and elaborated systems of collective representations that today we call "culture," there were complex toolkits, surviving in the archeological record, enabling early hominids to hunt animals, build fires and cook food, erect simple structures, and reshape their material environment. Although archeologists frequently call these complex toolkits "technologies," the word itself did not exist before the Industrial Revolution. Earlier societies, going back to Athens and before, had a discourse of *téchnē*, but before 1612 this was never joined with *logos*, learned authority represented by written language. In the High Renaissance, an extraordinary figure such as Leonardo da Vinci might create both classic paintings and ingenious machinery such as a flying device (Figure 0.1). But in a technological age, focusing on the so-called "STEM" (Science, Technology, Engineering, and Mathematics) disciplines, such Renaissance men and women are much rarer.

Prior to the Industrial Revolution, there was a social gulf between the practical arts of toolmakers and rude mechanicals on the one hand, and the fine arts and philosophy of educated gentlemen and ladies on the other. Although Thomas Jefferson might experiment with clever furniture or an early copying machine (the "polygraph," a mechanical device for tracing handwriting), his social status had less to do with such practicalities as botany or animal husbandry and more to do with his lineage going back to the Randolphs, the Jeffersons, and other early settlers of the colony. Even well into the nineteenth century there were questions as to whether the "agricultural and industrial classes" should be admitted to elite academies. This social divide, existing for millennia, has been no less definitive of technology than the materials and purposes from which it is constructed.

2 • *Technology and the Common Good*

**Figure 0.1.** Leonardo da Vinci, Flying Machine (c. 1488). Wikimedia Commons, public domain.

How do we think about technology? In the twentieth and twenty-first centuries, there has been a vast explosion of literature describing, celebrating, questioning, and at times condemning technology. Most of the discourses of technology, we can discover, are motivated less by the practicalities of tools and other useful implements, and more by the social and political positions and purposes of the authors. These purposes range from celebrating the triumph of the nation-state, through the conquest of space, to romantic visions of perfect freedom over the internet, to a condemnation of state power as alien and evil, as embodied by world-destroying weapons. Discourses of technology link "technology" with "progress" and typically see technology as a means by which humanity can transcend its current condition. The multiple discourses of technology differ on some fundamental questions: Who leads this transcendence? How is it accomplished? What sort of good does it represent? And most importantly, what sort of narrative does this progress embody? Is the narrative of technological progress a story of man's attaining godlike perfection (Noble 1997), or is it a Faustian bargain? Is it available to all, or concentrated in core regions of the modern world system? Is it a triumph of the everyman, or a remote elite? Is it accomplished with the head or with the hands?

A "standard view" of technology, as critiqued by Bryan Pfaffenberger (1992b), understands technology in purely utilitarian terms as harnessing of the powers of nature toward human ends. This standard view is enshrined in an evolutionary anthropology that sees technological advance as driving institutional development, with values and beliefs ("superstructure") changing as a consequence (Harris 1968, for example). It acquired state approval and endorsement in the United States when Vannevar Bush, President Franklin Roosevelt's science advisor, published *Science: The Endless Frontier* (1945), presenting a linear progression from basic science to applied science to technological development as official policy. In this view, the role of the government, as represented by agencies such as the National Science Foundation, is to support basic research (typically in university laboratories), which private industry then turns into useful inventions. Practical inventions that serve state purposes, whether military weapons, surveillance technologies, architectural monuments, or code-breaking, might also be developed under state sponsorship.

Propelling this standard, official view was the decisive role that scientific discovery and technological invention played in World War II, beginning with the use of radar in the Battle of Britain, enabling the Royal Air Force to overcome the numerically superior Luftwaffe, continuing with cracking the German enigma code, and ending, of course, with the dropping of the atomic bombs on Hiroshima and Nagasaki. Technology, for a quarter-century after this, was linked to national advancement, which then set a pattern for the rest of the world to follow. The result of World War II was an unquestioned triumph of good (as represented by democracy) over evil (in the form of fascism), which in subsequent years was replaced by other evils such as communism, hunger, disease, and ignorance, and most recently terrorism. Technology, in this official narrative, finally offered mankind the possibility of escaping from these age-old ills. "Modern technology [provides] effective solutions of the problems that have troubled the human race since its beginning" (Borgmann 1984: 7), although nuclear weapons, perhaps *the* supreme technological achievement of World War II, might call this question, of escaping from age-old ills, into question.

A similar set of technological narratives is told in the corporate world, where competition in marketplaces replaces conflict on battlefields: just as in war, whichever competitor arrives at the marketplace "the firstest with the mostest" has a decisive advantage, with the firstest referring less to physical presence on the battlefield and more to product innovation in the marketplace, and "mostest" referring to features, performance, and value. Early technological advantages in the marketplace create a "path dependence" that competitors find difficult to overcome. It was in this manner that technologically inferior products such as Microsoft Windows achieved market superiority over more robust and user-friendly rivals such as Apple's OS-2, and how VHS video recorders overtook the superior Betamax: early numerical preponderance created self-reinforcing cycles where growing numbers of users attracted growing numbers of vendors and developers, whether of pre-recorded tapes or software applications, which in turn attracted growing numbers of users. Social acceptance is now recognized as a critical component of technological success, and the dream of every innovator is that his clever new device or idea "go viral" and be propagated through social media.

Propelling these dreams is an enthusiastic view of technology that has taken root in the last 30 or 40 years. Earlier technological enthusiasms, such as personal aircraft that could be parked outside one's suburban home, or wearable communication devices, were generally the substance of nerdy fascination that were found only in the pages of *Popular Mechanics*. In the current century, however, an inflection point has been reached, and such enthusiasms spilled over into broader discussions of technological utopias: package delivery via drones, regional commutes via pneumatic tubes, driverless cars, or internet displays on one's eyeglasses—all are now the objects of serious investment and promotion, and search for justification and social status. This excited, the futuristic narrative of technology is perhaps today the dominant narrative.

In the background, for well over a century, has been a dystopian narrative, whether exemplified by George Orwell's *1984* (1949) (with its accent on propaganda and surveillance), Margaret Atwood's *MaddAddam Trilogy* (2004, 2009, 2013) (describing a future where genetic engineering has created new versions of humanity), or Stanley Kubrick's *Dr. Strangelove* (1964), a film about a mad scientist in love with the destruction of humanity. These stories present a dark future in which technological devices vaguely threaten humanity, although the threat is sufficiently ill-defined that responding to it is difficult. Multiple nineteenth-century literary strains, including Romanticism (exemplified by Mary Shelley's *Frankenstein* [1818]), Nihilism, and the Gothic (for example, *The Matrix* series [Lana and Lilly Wachowski,

1999, 2003, 2003, 2021], in which technology practically obliterates distinctions between "real" and "virtual") interweave in these dystopian accounts. The 70 years since the publication of *1984* have largely borne out Orwell's narrative, only with improved technology: surveillance devices that are carried in one's pocket, and the Ministry of Truth both on network TV and internet newsfeeds and in proliferating conspiracy theories with a global reach. On the surface, these narratives present a story of technology-out-of-control and mad scientists out to reshape the world. Beneath this surface is a Romantic vision of the perfect freedom that technology affords society, marked by an absence of the restraints of time, space, authority, and sociality.

A more down-to-earth story of technology is told when engineers set down their shovels and slide rules, and pick up their pens, describing from first-person experience what it means to design, build, operate, and maintain complex systems (Florman 1976; Petroski 1985, for example). These systems always embody a wealth of tacit knowledge, which *by definition* cannot be articulated: "Here, let me show you," a message combining embodiment and direct interpersonal engagement, is frequently a technique of engineering communication. The *embodied* character of technology, the manner in which it is comprehended as much through the hands as through logical constructions, contrasts with more academic accounts in which technology is elevated to an academic abstraction.

The discursive context of these narratives is the changing social status of builders and artisans and inventors over millennia in different civilizations. In earlier civilizations, builders were often buried with their tools; on feast days in the Middle Ages, guildsmen would parade with their tools. Going as far back to the Egyptians, where unnamed artisans were revered, and to the Greeks, where Athenian gentlemen disdained the useful arts (favoring instead the liberal arts of grammar, rhetoric, logic, arithmetic, geometry, music, and astronomy), those who design and build useful devices have nearly always occupied a lower rung on the social ladder than those who commissioned them. James Watt, who perfected the steam engine over earlier efforts by Thomas Savery and Thomas Newcomen, was the son of a watchmaker. Henry Ford, arguably the founder of the American middle class, was the son of Belgian and Irish immigrants, lacking social status, a nobody, really, until his Highland Park Assembly Plant, with its innovative methods in production and industrial relations, made manufacturing a foundation for broad prosperity. With the exception of architects such as the Roman Vitruvius, whose imperial patrons and monumental achievements guaranteed them an elevated status, engineers have nearly always occupied a lower social rank than other learned professionals. This social gulf between technicians and learned professionals, each comprising separate communities, is no less determinative of the character of technological devices than the more explicit statements of "user requirements" that accompany every technological innovation.

Behind each of these narratives is a cosmology, a set of assumptions about what counts for technology and how we go about understanding it. In the futuristic view, the emphasis is on disruption, which is a "good thing": disruption propels progress. Stable objects and implements, such as cooking pots and dinner utensils, even if they might embody some of the characteristics typically associated with technology, including usefulness, standardization, engineered materials, and assemblage, are not considered technology from this point of view, unless one includes everything human-made as "technology."[1] The dystopian view also emphasizes disruption, but in a negative light, as an upsetting of settled social arrangements. The engineering view, by contrast, emphasizes practicality and problem-solving, leaving the definition of "problem"—whether hunger or illness or the width of a tunnel-bore—uninterrogated. By contrast, the "social construction of technology" sees problems, social groups, and technological artifacts as always mutually constitutive.

Every culture includes a central narrative and a small number of root metaphors. The central narrative is the story we tell about ourselves, perhaps existing in several versions but always telling the same story either of heroic accomplishment or tragic fate (or more interestingly, some combination of both). The heroic accomplishments of David Lilienthal's "dreamers with shovels" are similarly presented in Henry Petroski's *Engineers of Dreams* (1995) or popular accounts. Other stories, such as that of the "brilliant invention" (xerography, for example) or the "mad scientist" (*Frankenstein*), draw on other sets of archetypes and central characters such as the heroic pioneer. The central narrative of American culture is carving a New World out of the wilderness, a narrative that confines to a minor key tragic stories such as the fate of indigenous and enslaved peoples, whose dispossession and forced labor built the New World. Other cultures tell other stories, whether the French "City of Light," Paris, bringing enlightenment to the world, or China's Middle Kingdom as the source of harmony between Heaven and Earth, or Rome, the "Eternal City," the foundation of civilization. These narratives are a core part of the *cosmology* of their culture, a statement about "who we are" and where we fit into the universe.

Cultures are based on root metaphors, vivid images presented either in figurative language or compelling visual representations that condense centuries of meaning into a singular compelling image. In America, the pioneer is such a root metaphor, heroically conquering savage tribes and civilizing the wilderness: despite the closing of the frontier more than a century ago, this narrative has more than a bit part even in contemporary politics, with national candidates bragging about their Wild West roots, and a new cabinet member, Secretary of the Interior Ryan Zinke, in 2017, riding into Washington, DC, on his horse. "Patriots" in period costume, resisting the tyranny of an "alien" ruler, play a part even in twenty-first-century American politics. In France, the heroic narrative of Marianne at the barricades, defying tyranny, has been reenacted many times since 1789, most recently in the *Mouvement des Gilets Jaunes* (yellow vests movement). In Mexico, by contrast, the tragic narrative of *Los Niños Héroes* (the Little Heroes), cadets resisting the American invasion in 1912, is memorialized in a monument in Mexico City, and captures a sentiment felt by Mexicans in every decade since.

Cultures, in other words, are not so much "mental models" as they are shared stories and images and experiences, whether of witnessing a compelling image or reenacting a heroic role. This *shared* quality makes these experiences and retellings the basis of kinship, a fellow-feeling and common identity that goes beyond the particularities of time and place. When this sharedness breaks down, the sense that we have anything in common breaks down. America today presents us with the profound irony of a nation on the cutting edge of technological innovation that nevertheless embraces some of the strongest voices opposed to scientific findings, whether climate science, evolution, or medicine. As I will elaborate in Chapter 3, Section 4 ("The Constitution of Ignorance"), this is less paradoxical once one understands that technological devices augment only certain human capabilities (counting and tabulating, for a primitive example) at the expense of other capabilities such as creativity and artistic expression or collective effort that do not lend themselves to simple technological solutions. An excessive, naïve enthrallment with technology has the unintended consequence of leaving societies *less* capable of confronting unexpected events, whether pandemics or climate catastrophes. Other examples of challenges where technology has failed will be developed in Chapter 3.

It is my thesis that this excessive focus on technology, at the expense of other areas of human interest, poses unique challenges for the common good. Establishing what we as a society have *in common* and how this connects us one to another is a central question for the *social* sciences, yet one that is frequently lost in an individualistic society. To develop this, I will examine the interplay between private goods and privatization, on the one hand, and collective goods—public goods, club goods, and common pool resources—on the other. Building on Elinor Ostrom's *Governing the Commons* (1990), I will demonstrate that "the commons" (a shorthand for collective goods and values, potentially embracing not simply open spaces like parks and public squares, but also intangible resources such as identities and attention), like private goods, always has a foundation in the tools, architecture, and instrumentalities of civilizations. Different civilizations have radically different understandings of what their members share, whether the open fields of preindustrial England, the *agora* of the Athenians, the language of l'Académie Française, or the imagined community of the nation-state. David Bollier and Silke Helfrich, in *The Wealth of the Commons* (2012), present multiple examples of "commoning," the embrace of common goods. In contemporary discourse "the commons" is both a concept and a trope, both a designation of certain types of goods and different types of values, and it is also a figure of speech for what the members of collectivities *share*, whether spaces or identities. The act (or imagination) of sharing creates a sense of kinship, and the homology of "kin and kind" suggests a basic foundation of society. The overvaluation of private goods for the past 250 years, going back to Adam Smith's *The Wealth of Nations* in 1776 (Smith 1970), has blinded societies and governments to the centrality of what they have *in common*, including public goods and common pool resources.

Examining these issues through an anthropological lens, taking into account the full range of humanity and the role of culture in defining both humanity and human variation, is central to my thesis. Culture, in the standard anthropological formulation, is understood as a learned system of shared understandings, although technology often adds complexity to cultural simplicity. The *shared* aspect of cultures is central to defining what human groups *have in common*, and hence a shared sense of the good. The "common good" is a cultural formation, different in every tribe, village, and nation.

To develop this viewpoint, I will first examine the subsistence patterns of societies lacking in "technology" as contemporarily understood (Chapter 1), noting that these societies, while often having sophisticated tools, nevertheless did not fetishize them as "technology." In Chapter 2, I will examine the emergence of private goods and the eclipse of the common good consequent to multiple developments creating the modern era, including European expansion, the Industrial Revolution, the rise of the factory system, and the rise of liberal economics as reflected in Adam Smith's *The Wealth of Nations*. In Chapter 3, I will examine the interplay of technology and shared goods, whether common pool resources, public goods, club goods, or toll goods. Drawing on Elinor Ostrom's *Governing the Commons*, I will describe how critical features of technology, including independence of locality, scalability, and translation and compression of energy and information, pose challenges to some of the aspects of commons governance, including "gatekeeping" and "monitoring."

Chapter 4 will examine some of the newer commons emerging in a technological society, including the radio frequency (RF) spectrum, airspace, and branding, a commons that did not exist before the twentieth century. Chapter 5, "Public Goods and Institutions in Cyberspace" (also a commons that was only recently invented) examines attention and desire as a new commons. Beginning in the seventeenth century, the commons, the fields that villagers shared, were enclosed (as described further in Chapter 2); today, the commons of shared public spaces, shared identities, and shared aspirations are fragmented by technology. The new enclosures of advertising and social media undermine the common good, splintering the nation into market segments and tribal attachments. The increasing tribalism of American culture is adequate testimony to this. "Democratic Vistas" (Chapter 6) considers the different "-scapes" (not only landscapes but also ethnoscapes, mediascapes, and technoscapes) that define a democratic society, while Chapter 7 examines several case studies in the successful governance of technologically created commons, including the high seas, airspace, and the global circulation of capital. My conclusion, "Reclaiming the Commons," builds on the idea of reclamation as an appropriate management strategy not only for worn-out lands, but also for worn-out institutions.

Cultures are not limited to national cultures; they can include cultures of the arts, of industries, or of technology. The importance of cultures of technology is that they frame the questions of institution-building: they outline the possibilities (including some options and excluding others) for bounding and legitimating institutional power and identity, and focus attention on a few central questions. In the "endless frontier" narrative, for example, institution-building means funding research and training, and then getting out of the way, allowing the scientists and engineers to build a better tomorrow. In the dystopian, "mad scientist" narrative, technological expertise must be kept in check by institutional authority. In the "innovation imperative" narrative, the hero-entrepreneur assembles new devices with new routines of work and leisure to create a durable business. Other prudent steps that might not fit into the narrative, whether a fact-based assessment of a technology's capabilities and limitations and its long-term sustainability, or a reflection on its ultimate purposes, are passed over: in the mid-1990s, as America was on the verge of a technological upheaval, Congress eliminated the Office of Technology Assessment, because its fact-based, technocratic assessments were incompatible with the triumphant narrative of heroic technology. The cultures of technology, that is, the shared narratives about what technology is for and where it should go, frame the vectors of technological development in a more fundamental way than either the laws of physics or statements of "user requirements": in the twentieth century, multiple nations sought to overcome the law of gravity, whether through the German V-2 rockets raining down on London or the space race between the United States and the Soviet Union.

It is generally accepted that technology is *socially constructed*, that it constitutes a human project rather than a deterministic unfolding of the laws of nature. "social construction," however, begs the question of what sort of project technology presents, its unique character, and its ultimate purposes. The cultures of technology outlined here present contrasting answers to these questions, particularly the question of ultimate purposes. Both the official view, as represented by the "endless frontier," and the dystopian view are in agreement that the ultimate result of technology is to advance the power of the state; they only differ in whether or not that is a good thing. The dystopian view presents a nihilistic understanding of the state as fundamentally evil, and technology as the instrument for accomplishing that ill will. By contrast, both corporate and enthusiastic views adopt a utilitarian perspective, seeing technology as creating more leisure, abundance, and enjoyment, where leisure and abundance are assumed to be ultimate goods. As I will demonstrate in Chapter 2, utilitarianism represents intellectual laziness, a retreat from the stubborn facts of cultural variety that were being discovered around the world in the seventeenth and eighteenth centuries: Finding differing beliefs about the good in Africa, Asia, and Latin America, European philosophers created a version of the good that everyone could agree upon: individual enjoyment.

In contrast to all of these views, the culture of technology of those who actually design, build, operate, and maintain the devices is far more pragmatic: "are we accomplishing our goals?" Most engineers are conscientious professionals, yet in their professional capacity they are not expected to question the ultimate purposes of their devices. Such questions are more typically dismissed as "philosophy."

With all of these differences in how to make sense of technology, there is nonetheless an overall consensus that "technology" is removed from public negotiation. In the design and construction of a technological device, certain imperatives must be met. Some of these, called "user requirements," are negotiable; other imperatives, such as the stresses that can be borne by connecting structures of a bridge or the storage capacity of a memory chip, are not. Just as we cannot vote on the laws of thermodynamics, so too such technological issues as the geometry of a structural member or the memory requirements of a desktop computer are beyond popular negotiation. In resolving such issues, the arbiters are the engineers who design and build the bridges and boxes, and not the public that buys them. In sum, all of these cultures present technology as a force or entity disengaged from the social realm, a beneficent (or maleficent) force beyond negotiation that can only be handled by a technological elite: the engineers.

Technology, as a named class of cultural objects and as a subset of the universe of useful things, is an instrument of state formations: state authority is required to create the standards and other autonomous representations needed to turn local tools into broadly accepted toolkits. As I will elaborate on in Chapter 2 ("Goods, and the Common Good, in a Liberal Society"), the term "technology" should be properly restricted to artifacts of the modern era, inasmuch as the term itself was coined only in the seventeenth century to describe the emerging instrumentalities of the Industrial Revolution: applying the term "technology" to preindustrial toolkits, while at times a convenient archeological shorthand, is in fact an ethnocentric imposition of numerous assumptions onto cultures and societies where they demonstrably do not fit. An interrogation of technology is as much an interrogation of state authority and purposes as it is an interrogation of form and function, and the discourse of statecraft, including coalition-building and authority-formation, is present, even if *sotto voce*, in all discourses of technology.

But, as presented here, these multiple discourses of technology and the commons cannot all be right: when is technology beneficial or malevolent, when is it something that can be controlled, or something out of control, something that brings people together or divides them, something that liberates or enslaves humanity? Whether the commons is shared by all members of a community (and what that commons is), or is a resource for the strong to prey on the weak, are pressing questions as technology races forward, creating new commons and erasing the old. Resolving issues such as these, or at least suggesting a new discourse in which they can meet, a more complex narrative within which the many parties interested in technology can agree to disagree, is the objective of this book.

### Note

1. "Fernand Braudel has written that '[in] a way, everything is technology'" (Adams 1996: 11). This proclivity to universalize what I hope to demonstrate is a time- and place-bound cultural practice, culturally derived and culturally bound, is contrary to the spirit of social anthropology: the very definition of ethnocentrism. The *place*, as I shall discuss in my first two chapters, is less a geodetic space, bounded with lines on a globe, and more a topological and semantic space, bounded by a dominant discourse unique to the modern world. Although many technological systems ramify around the world, most conceptions of what is and is not technology have an identifiable structure. Cultures assign meaning to the artifacts and practices that we call "technology," and then act on it accordingly.

Chapter 1

# Worlds without Technology

Human tribes have survived for millennia without depending on technology as we understand it today. The toolkits of earlier societies, whether the bone tools of the Innuit or the stone tools of the Athabaskans, represented local adaptations to the opportunities of their ecosystems, the materials at hand, their subsistence strategies, their cosmological outlooks, and their relationships with their neighbors. The Innuit and Athabaskan tribes of the North American Arctic, despite inhabiting adjacent environments, are distinguished not only by differences in their hunting practices but also by the materials and shapes of their tools, and their fundamental conceptions of the universe. Technology, in the sense of instrumentalities severed from the possibilities or opportunities of the immediate environment, has been a fairly recent development in human history.[1]

In this chapter, I will outline the productive strategies of tribes and civilizations that existed for millennia without elevating their useful arts to the object of learned discourse that today we label "technology." These strategies include not only productive strategies of food-getting and shelter-procuring, but also strategies of coexisting with their neighbors: through warfare, trade, or careful avoidance. In so doing, I hope to make clear that the instrumentalities of earlier societies had a decisively different character from those of modern society: less in the simplicity or sophistication of their design and more in the local character of their adaptation. Technology as we know it today combines engineered sophistication and a *disengagement* with immediate environmental opportunities and constraints, together with new paths and media of circulation into distant lands and environments. *Commons* are distinguished not only by their boundaries and resources, but also by the possibilities for circulation within them. The *discourse* of technology in the contemporary world is part of this circulation.

To demonstrate these differences, I will first examine the local adaptations of tribal societies that have been well-represented in the ethnographic and archeological record, showing how their toolkits embodied multiple values: instrumental values—what the tool accomplishes—are obvious, and social values—the ownership of the tool, in multiple senses including the tool as an identity object—are likewise obvious. Scholars have paid less attention, however, to cosmological values—that is, statements that the tools make about *who we are*, the nature of the universe, and our place in it. Although the emphasis of modern technology—man's mastery over nature[2]—is obvious, simpler tools such as arrowheads make similar statements. I will then examine the accomplishments and social status of the useful and mechanical arts in classical antiquity and the Middle Ages, demonstrating that while there was a discourse of the useful arts, it did not require its own unique term. Architects and artisans in ancient Rome, for example, had a respected status, and their guilds were part of the emerging civil order. The cities of the Roman Empire maintained communal order, in which the guilds were the beginnings of civil society.

The rise of "technology" as a named practice, as I will develop in the following chapter, resulted from the confluence of three major currents in the fifteenth, sixteenth, and seventeenth centuries: the corruption of the feudal order, European expansion and the colonization and conquest of indigenous peoples, and the consequent Industrial Revolution. The Industrial Revolution, as I will introduce at the end of this chapter and develop in Chapter 2, was first and foremost a *social revolution*, an upending of a stable social order.

## Borderland Adaptations

A tool is a total social fact, embracing numerous values. Never as simple as they may seem, tools always encompass multiple social, instrumental, and cosmological discourses: a simple stonemason's hammer, for example (Figure 1.1), presents multiple, layered meanings. There is the identity of the hammer as a specific kind used by stonemasons, who formed a separate guild from the carpenters, who used a different hammer, and then there is the metallurgical refinement in the steel alloy of the hammer's manufacture and its polymer grip, not to mention the legal claims in the intellectual property in its design and the practicality in its two faces, one flat, one pointed, which are used for different masonry tasks. "Reading" the stonemason's hammer requires that one be conversant with the separate discourses of guild traditions, construction tasks, material properties, and patent law.

**Figure 1.1.** Stonemason's hammer. © Osumi Akari. https://creativecommons.org/licenses/by-sa/4.0/deed.en.

The tools of indigenous societies are as much of this character as those of today. In every case that is documented, the design and selection of tools and techniques are closely tied not only to the materials at hand and the practical objective, but also to religious and cosmological assumptions, social relationships with kin, colleagues, and neighbors, and the meanings of multiple tool traditions. Any choice of tools can be analyzed from all of these perspectives, if the relevant data are available.

For a classic example, we might consider the hill people of Burma (today Myanmar) during British colonial times. Edmund Leach, in *Political Systems of Highland Burma*, described the ecological situation, modes of subsistence, social structure, and military relations of two seemingly distinct ethnic groups, the Kachin and the Shan. The Kachin practiced hillside cultivation, clearing hillsides and planting them with rice, whereas the Shan practiced wet rice cultivation with irrigated, lowland fields. Aside from a few cooking implements acquired from trading posts, these two separate populations had almost no common implements or tools. The wet rice cultivation of the Shan permitted the use of buffalo-drawn plows and harrows (Leach 1954: 32), whereas the Kachin dry rice cultivation required a system of shifting cultivation or crop rotation with hoes and other hand tools. Yet the dynamic of political relationships between and within these two groups included (for the Kachin) an alteration between *gumsa* hierarchical and *gumlao* egalitarian political organization, with historically some *gumsa* Kachin adopting Sinified ritual practices, moving to the lowlands, and presenting themselves as Shan. In other words, differences between Kachin and Shan were rooted less in ancestry and more in adaptive complexes of environment, subsistence techniques, and external relationships. Their technical ensembles of different rice cultivation techniques were adapted to their immediate ecological situation and their relationships both with neighboring tribes and with the British colonial authorities, who sought to suppress warfare between the two.

Similarly, the Innuit (or Eskimo) and Athabaskan hunting bands of the Canadian Arctic occupy adjacent ecological zones, with the Innuit, who subsisted on sea hunting, using bone tools and the Athabaskans, living within the forests, using wood and stone tools. This ancient separation, definitive of these two peoples, represents two separate adaptive strategies, with environment, toolkits, and social structures tuned to each other, the Athabaskans organized into matrilineal clans and the Innuit into nucleated bands. The toolkits of these two peoples reflected their separate cosmologies as well, with separate conceptions of the heavens above and the earth below.

For a final example of adjacent ecological adaptations, there are the Plains and Woodland tribes of North America. Ten thousand years ago, dramatic climate change resulted in the expansion of grasslands into forested regions, and adaptive complexes suited to the forests gave way to other strategies and techniques. Although we have no ethnographic data from these patterns, the archeological record reveals variation in mobility, tool design (arrowheads), raw material sourcing, and adaptive patterns adjusted to local "microenvironments" (Jennings and Wyckoff 2009). As populations shifted, mobility patterns shifted as well, favoring interaction with other bands in similar ecotones. New projectile designs reflected shifting tribal boundaries. In short, something as fundamental as the design of an arrowhead represents a local adaptation as the Plains–Woodland border shifted.

What all of these have in common is that the boundary between two "tribes" is expressed in the ecological zones, the different toolkits with which they exploit their environments, their different ritual practices, their different social structures, *and* their different tribal identities, which are typically indicated by various totemic objects such as tools and tribal dress. Identity is a people's fundamental statement about "who we are" and "where we fit into the universe," embracing tribal (and other social) distinctions, networks, roles, cosmological assumptions, and identity objects such as tools. When this sense of identity is threatened, there is a "cosmological crisis," a collapse of sensemaking. Many contemporary examples include emergency workers being ordered to drop their tools (Weick 1993), or racist citizens convinced in 2009 that the leading symbol of their nation, the chief executive, was an alien from Kenya, or established, educated elites seeing in the first figure of their nation a carnival pitchman. The way we make sense of the world is not simply an act of mental cogitation, but an enacted performance involving social networks and constructed artifacts, in addition to an act of mental construction. In other words, as I will elaborate below, tools are not simply for altering the world, but are also crucial for the ongoing human project of making sense of the world.

As identity objects, tools are much more than just useful implements, built and valued on utilitarian bases (what works best). Efforts to introduce improved, modern technologies, whether steel axes among the Yir Yoront, or snowmobiles among the Innuit, always have unforeseen consequences, and they are not always beneficial. Among the Yir Yoront, for example, a tribe of Australian Bushmen, making stone axes had been the exclusive domain of men until missionaries in the 1930s began giving away (obviously superior) steel axes. This was not so much a technological improvement as a cosmological crisis, as relationships between the sexes changed dramatically with men's importance diminished, and the tribe ultimately died out (Sharp 1960). Similarly, the introduction of snowmobiles for reindeer herding among the Skolt Lapps of northern Finland, which are obviously superior to dogsleds, had several unforeseen consequences: the tribes became dependent on external sources of energy (a process that Pertti Pelto [1973] includes in "delocalization") and because of the requirements of snowmobiles, several smaller herders were unable to survive and the remaining herdsmen, while fewer, had larger herds. An increased sociopolitical differentiation was reflected in greater participation in the cash economy. The traditional toolkit represented a balanced adaptation with the social and natural environment. In a similar fashion, in a technologically sophisticated industry, air traffic controllers' use of *paper* "strips" to exchange information within the control tower is as much a *social* exchange, reinforcing relationships, as it is an operational utility (Gras et al. 1994); these strips contain critical flight information, including aircraft identification and route, and are *manually*

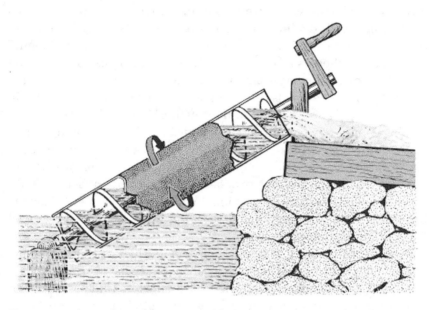

**Figure 1.2.** The Archimedes screw. Wikimedia Commons, public domain.

passed back and forth among controllers. Likewise, the mark of a good computer programmer is that the source code is "commented," a metalanguage explaining the logic of the code. In both cases, a sophisticated system uses unsophisticated utilities to reinforce social relationships through which we understand the world.

The toolkits of indigenous peoples lacked instruction manuals. This, of course, is not surprising in societies lacking written language, but it points to the fact that the joining of *tékhnē* (craft, skill) with *logos* (the authority of the written word) is a recent yet profoundly consequential invention. Prior to the invention of written language, knowledge of how to use tools was transmitted through the hands and voices of the elders, with the consequence that this knowledge and its transmission was a valuable property and token, binding elders and juniors together, much as critical knowledge today binds together mentors and protégés. It was only with the development of literacy and long-distance trade, carrying useful ideas and objects around the world, that tool fabrication and use became severed from its immediate surroundings. "Tools" no longer required immediate, local utility. This *recontextualization* of instrumentalities gave them new meaning, often with profound consequences.

In antiquity, engineers left us marvelous drawings and documents of ingenious inventions for solving classical problems, whether the raising of water, the fortification of walls, or the navigation of the Mediterranean. The Archimedes screw, for example, invented in the third century BCE and pictured here (Figure 1.2), was an improvement over earlier pumping systems. Likewise, wheeled vehicles were an improvement over horseback, and embodied at least local conventions for their design. As transport and trade extended, there was an ongoing traffic in such ingenious devices and solutions: some of the most notable of premodern devices were introduced less through direct import and more through a process of stimulus diffusion or local adaptation, the copying of devices borrowed from the neighbors and the adaptation of these devices to local circumstances. The Middle Ages, lasting (very roughly) from the tenth to the sixteenth century, saw a great growth in production and distribution instrumentalities, which in the seventeenth century would provoke a semantic innovation, the coinage of the word "technology."

Far more typical, however, has been the selective borrowing of techniques and implements among neighbors, a process of diffusion that optimally "tunes" the local toolkit to the local situation. Borrowings can include not only physical implements and tools such as grinding mills, but also symbolic devices such as the alphabet and numerical notation, the diffusion of which are well documented (McCarter 1975; Chrisomalis 2010). This process of local adaptation accounts for the great variety of Greek, Greek-influenced, and Roman scripts across Europe.

In sum, the array of peoples around the globe is mirrored by an array of cultural assumptions *and* an array of toolkits, and, with the rise of cities, with an array of linguistic and cultural devices such as written language. Before the Industrial Revolution, toolkits were adapted to immediate challenges and opportunities, whether procuring food, appeasing the gods, or defending against neighboring tribes. Improvements in transportation gradually extended the meaning of "neighbor" while still preserving an (ever-diminishing) separation. This had profound consequences: "Cultural difference," in the words of Claude Lévi-Strauss, "depends less on the isolation of the various groups than on the relations between them" ([1952] 1968: 20). As human tribes ranged over expanding territories, defining "who we are" and "how we are different from our neighbors" became an increasing challenge. In these challenges, tools were used not only for taming the natural environment but also for sorting out the social environment, as well as making sense out of it all.

## The Useful Arts in Rome and the Middle Ages

The rise of cities, beginning in Mesopotamia in the fourth millennium BCE, and in the Western world climaxing in Rome in the first century BCE, was a technological and architectural achievement. Unlike the aggregation of huts, tipis, igloos, and yurts that are typical of the settlements of foragers and pastoralists, cities embrace multiple architectural and engineering and ultimately monumental feats, which build upon earlier settlements and are later built upon by successive populations. These include sturdy dwellings, roads, city walls perhaps, and public squares. They also include monumental palaces and houses of worship, imposing edifices intended both to edify and intimidate the citizens. Roman cities included sewers and aqueducts, although these fell into disrepair with the decline and collapse of the Roman state.

These engineering feats were central to their civilizations. An examination of some of the documents left behind by the Romans can give us an appreciation of the status of the useful arts in Rome. For example, a military engineer, Marcus Vitruvius Pollio, in his volume *The Ten Books of Architecture* (*De Architectura libri decem*; dedicated to the emperor Augustus), discusses soaring subjects such as the plans for theaters and basilicas, as well as more mundane subjects such as slaking lime and color preparation. *De Architectura* provides both practical insights into construction and more abstract insights into the cosmological principles of arrangement, order, eurythmy, symmetry, propriety, and economy as the fundamentals of true architecture, as well as the purpose of public buildings toward which these were employed. The nobility of architecture, in other words, has always been not simply in its usefulness, but in its capacity to inspire and order. Vitruvius was providing not only an instruction manual for public construction, but also a promotional tract for public spaces. Vitruvian Man, Leonardo da Vinci's well-known fifteenth-century drawing (Figure 1.3) based on *De Architectura*, expresses the principles of order and symmetry.

When one considers technological implements as condensing numerous social interests and motivations, not only those of the designers and the users but also those that authorize the form and function of the implements through standards, then one can see that technological objects compress a broad range of meaning into discrete packages, including not only the motivations and interests of the users, but also the authority of the state as represented by standard-setting bodies. This authority can be patrimonial, as in that of the Roman emperor (and

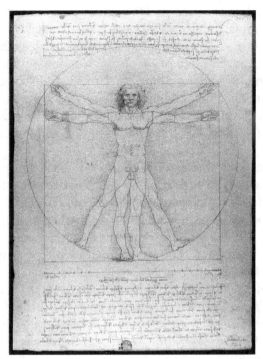

**Figure 1.3.** Leonardo da Vinci, Vitruvian Man (c. 1490). Wikimedia Commons, public domain.

patron of Vitruvius) Augustus; today, it is more typically bureaucratic, such as that of the standard-setting bodies authorized by the National Institute of Standards and Technology (NIST) to set standards for electrical current, radio transmission, and the internet. These representations are no less definitive of the technology than the actual physical object or implement.

For a technology or any practical implement to be adopted, users need to be convinced that it is worth their while to learn to master it. This is often a decision taken on faith, and the importance of "early adopters" in promoting a new technology is well documented (Rogers 1995: 252ff.). Early adopters are persuaded that a new technology can work wonders—improve productivity, connect them with new friends, or please the emperor. Numerous technologies, whether for communication or transportation or office automation, are typically in their early years *less* efficient or effective or reliable than their precursors, until the early adopters work out all the kinks and difficulties that were not evident to the designers.

Promotional tracts such as *De Architectura* are also definitive of what would in the modern era be called "technology" (a word that did not exist before 1612). By joining the mundane, such as the preparation of materials or the direction of streets, with sublime properties of symmetry and harmony and eurythmy, Vitruvius established a template for technology, which combined the exalted and the practical. The Romans clearly had both sophisticated tools and a learned discourse of tools, but not until 1612 was this linked to *logos*, the authority of the written word.

These tracts and representations are no less definitive of technology than the actual physical implements and accomplishments. Technological authority and prestige ramify around the world in the form of representations, whether in words or images. whether in the Lighthouse of Alexandria, which was constructed in the third century BCE and reproduced in painting and sculpture for many centuries since, or Roman chariots, which have been reproduced in multiple images for many centuries. Very few had an embodied relationship with the events of 20 July 1969, when Apollo 11 landed on the moon. Yet on this date, hundreds of millions, if not billions, witnessed the event, either live on television or in newspaper headlines, affirming American supremacy over the Soviet Union in space.

Taken together, promotional tracts, standards, instruction manuals, celebrations, and other documents constitute *autonomous representations*, descriptions of the technology that can circulate more widely than the actual physical implement. Autonomous representations mean that the different social values compressed within a technological object—authority, sociality, sacrality, awesome power—are free to compete with other values. Of equal importance with autonomous representations, technological values are embedded in new arrays of relationships: in the Middle Ages, craft skills were carefully guarded by the guilds, and one could learn the skills only by apprenticing in the guild. Only much later, with the rise of trade schools, did the craft become more democratically accessible, although in some fields, notably the learned professions, skills and crafts are still closely guarded.

Another example of classical discourse on technical subjects is provided by Frontinus's *De Aquaeductu*. Frontinus was a Roman engineer and an administrator who was concerned with a problem—delivering a safe and adequate water supply—that even two millennia later vexes advanced industrial societies. *De Aquaeductu* concerns itself both with design matters such as the diameter of pipes and the adequacy of arches for supporting aqueducts such as the Pont du Gard in southern France

**Figure 1.4.** Pont du Gard. Wikimedia Commons, public domain.

(pictured here in Figure 1.4), as well as administrative matters such as determining who is allowed to draw water from the municipal source. By committing these concerns to a book, Frontinus elevated them from simply practical problems to the discourse of learned society. In time, architects and engineers would become some of the leading figures of civil society.

The decline of Roman achievements in architecture and the useful arts represents an important theme for us: the close relationship, the mutually reinforcing relationship, between state formations on the one hand and imposing technological achievements on the other. The aggregations of power and information and connection contained in awesome technical constructions, whether Roman aqueducts or Silicon Valley microchips, depend on state-level aggregations of power and resources, either directly through instrumentalities of the state or indirectly through state-chartered guilds or corporations. Some of the leading firms in Silicon Valley, such as Hewlett-Packard and Intel, got their start as defense contractors, and the internet, initially conceptualized in the 1950s by the defense contractor RAND Corporation, was launched in 1969 as a government program (DARPAnet, a creature of the Defense Advanced Research Projects Agency). Early cults, such as that of the Celtic priests who built the Stonehenge, an observatory-cum-burial ground, represented similar aggregations of power, in this case the ability to command thousands of laborers to move stones weighing hundreds of tons to a central site more than two hundred miles away. Stonehenge was a singular achievement, with few other traces of the architects, the builders, or the priests who commissioned it. More lasting technical achievements depend on lasting political authority—that is, state-level formations.

Classical and medieval civilizations had impressive engineering and architectural achievements, and produced numerous tracts describing these and other useful arts, such as Mariano Taccola's *De Ingeneis* and *De Machinis*. The useful arts, however, occupied a lower rung on the social ladder than both the liberal arts and military and governing arts. As a consequence, toolmaking and tool-using lacked the status of an autonomous force that they have acquired in the modern world.

In the Middle Ages, these state-level formations promoting and conserving technological knowledge were primarily craft guilds, bodies chartered by the Crown and given a monopoly on the production of different crafts, whether spinning, weaving, locksmithing, shoemaking, or any number of other crafts. Craft guilds and their uneasy partners in merchant guilds were city formations that, typically like cities, existed with royal charters and varied in their character from city to city and from country to country.

Merchant and craft guilds had precursors in the Roman *collegia*, bands united to regulate and protect their trade. The character and privileges of guilds varied from city to city, with some having an exclusive monopoly and others being a less formal association. Terms of apprenticeship varied, as did the privileges of the masters. In all cases, the central body comprised the masters or syndics, with journeymen—aspiring masters—having limited privileges, but typically itinerant either for a day (*une journée*) or for months on end. As the journeyman improved his skills, eventually he could create and present a "masterwork," which, if approved, admitted him into full membership in the guild. Aspiring to the status of journeymen were the apprentices, who were indentured for a period of a few months to as many as seven years. The terms of indenture might include a payment to the master, paid or unpaid labor, and compensation consisting of room and board and perhaps shoes and clothes. These terms were more typically dictated by local and guild traditions rather than by any statute, although some cities such as Coventry did establish minimum conditions for the apprentices.

Both merchant and craft guilds existed at the interstices of feudal society, with varying levels of acquiescence from the monarch. Both were urban formations, sometimes chartered by the city elders, other times chartered by the Crown. The rise of cities from approximately 1000 CE onward represented a growing challenge to the feudal order: if a serf could escape to the city for a year, he became a free man, and the expression *Stadt Luft macht frei* (City air makes free) is indicative of the possibilities that cities (and guilds) represented for those who were at the bottom of the feudal estates.

The guilds and their precursors in the *collegia* were the beginnings of civil society, a social order independent of the feudal order. Each guild had its own internal order, and relationships among the guilds of any given city were dictated by tradition rather than by rational order. Guilds flourished for more than five hundred years in the Middle Ages, until the rise of royal absolutism suppressed them: Charles V, the Holy Roman emperor, banned all guilds in 1528; likewise, Henry VIII in England shut down both guilds and monasteries in 1536. The medieval guilds, the social building-blocks of the emerging cities, were part of the evolution of cities from a no-man's land of warring factions into a civic commons where presumably all, merchants, artisans, and laborers alike, could enjoy safety and security.

Guilds, and the urban life that was based on them, were outside the feudal order. A society that consisted of three estates—clergy, nobility, peasantry, or those who prayed, fought, and farmed—could accommodate those who traded and created only within interstitial spaces, notably cities. For our purposes, it is important to recognize guilds as exclusive clubs, and the goods and benefits they controlled—apprenticeships, access to markets, craft skills, and mysteries—as club goods. The tools that they used—the stonemason's hammer, the butcher's knife, the carpenter's square—were not just productive instruments: they were also badges of identity that were displayed on parade on feast days. When a young man completed his apprenticeship, he might be given a tool, whether a shoemaker's last or a mason's hammer, to signify his status as a journeyman, a member of the club. Beyond serving as a social charter, guilds also had a technological role, both in conserving and promoting skills and techniques, as well as improving them. Journeymen, traveling from city to city, were instrumental in diffusing technical innovations, creating the broader channels of circulation that are necessary for any technical innovation.

The economic role of the guilds is more contentious. Many see them as dead weight on the economy, imposing rents through their monopoly on craft production. In today's world, survivals of the guilds are found first of all in trade unions and second of all in the liberal professions, including law, medicine, and academia. In law, after two years of law school, a graduate can either go into her or his own practice or secure a position as an associate in a law firm, which, after the former has proven himself or herself, may admit him or her as a partner in the firm. The practice of law is regulated by the state bar, which admits the law school student to journeyman status through the bar exam. Similarly in medicine, after an apprenticeship or residency, if the aspiring doctor passes the board exams, she or he is permitted to practice medicine. Likewise, the academic world presents a graduated hierarchy of apprenticeship (graduate students), journeymen (adjuncts, untenured professors and lecturers), and masters (tenured faculty). All of these hierarchies are regulated by state and regional certification and accreditation bodies, which determine what sort of institution can present itself as a law firm or a hospital or a university, and who is permitted to practice as an attorney or a physician or a professor. The entire apparatus of professionalism in America reflected a nation in the making. Until certification boards were established in centers such as Boston, New York, and Philadelphia, anyone could present himself as a physician, surgeon, professor, or lawyer. In short, while the professions in Europe represented a continuity with earlier guilds, in America they represented a rediscovery of the value of such bodies in maintaining standards. Burton Bledstein in *The Culture of Professionalism* (1978) describes how universities and emerging professional bodies such as the American Bar Association and the American Medical Association in the nineteenth century brought order to America.

The type of goods or values that technology embodies is an important theme for us. Adam Smith, the prophet of liberal economics, saw guilds as monopolizing different productive privileges. The *club goods*—skills, standards, reputations—that the guilds controlled were antithetical to the free circulation of *private goods* that Smith promoted in *The Wealth of Nations* in 1776. At their worst, guilds could be rent-seeking monopolies, protecting their masters from disruptive innovations. At their best, they upheld standards of quality and craftsmanship. This tension between the socialization and privatization of knowledge and skill, between sharing and enclosure, and the privileges these create, has been with us ever since.

In sum, the useful arts and trades, and those who governed them, laid the foundation for urban society. The civic commons that they promoted, ostensibly a public good, had many aspects of a club good, inasmuch as the full benefits were only available to those who could claim to *belong* to the city, whether as tradesmen or nobles. In many medieval cities, who could and could not claim to be a "free man of the city" was carefully regulated, with apprentices considered not free but indentured. How the benefits of citizenship are to be shared has been a debate ever since, most recently challenged on numerous fronts with multiple proposals for privatization of education, municipal services, and other public goods. Whether citizens are entitled to education, healthcare, income security, or even public safety is an actively debated question today.

## Governing the Communes

With the collapse of the Roman Empire came a collapse of civil society, if civil society is understood as non-state institutions that support many of the goods and other values of society. From very roughly the fifth to the tenth centuries, cities in Europe declined, only to make a comeback from 950 onward. In this period, powers were concentrated in the emperor, the Church, and feudal lords. Merchants and artisans, clustered in emerging cities such as Florence and Siena, slowly built alternative institutions—guilds, communes, and networks of commerce—that eventually displaced the feudal social order.

The rise of cities, whether the city-states of Italy or the merchant alliances of the Hanseatic League, created new institutions outside the feudal order that over several centuries became instrumental in the demise of that order. Foremost among these was the very concept of civil society, meaning an acceptance of institutions outside yet in harmony with the state. Most notable of these institutions were the guilds of merchants and artisans that eventually became the foundation of city government. The merchants' guilds especially represented major concentrations of wealth and became increasingly indispensable to kings and emperors as they pursued their wars. Over time, other institutions of city government including police and sanitation evolved in response to the pressures of strangers crammed together in small spaces.

In the early cities of Italy and the Netherlands, multiple groups and institutions competed for preeminence, and civic order was maintained less by central authority and more by a balance of power among competing factions—guilds, primarily, but also noble families. Noblemen in public would be accompanied by retainers, a display of power.

Equally notable is the very definition of civic spaces. Roman cities were imperial administrative centers that were organized around the palace whose architecture projected the emperor's authority. In the Middle Ages, cities were often organized around basilica, presenting the authority of the Church. Early cities were often little more than unplanned aggregations of villages, which were shoved together with narrow passageways and no provision for sanitation. It was only later, with the growing communal authority of the cities, that some of the basics of urban life as we now understand it—adequate streets, constabularies providing order, sanitation, a clean water supply (all of which mostly fell into ruin with the Roman collapse)—became features of urban life. The civic commons has emerged as *the* major resource for economic growth (Jacobs 1984). Jane Jacobs, in *Cities and the Wealth of Nations*, has demonstrated that cities are sources of vitality in nations around the world.

A civic commons is a space for friends, strangers, tradesmen, business partners, and colleagues to meet without concern over their safety. We take this for granted, yet a brief glance at the history of the Middle Ages, or even at some urban aggregations in the developing world today, makes it clear that the civic commons was not an inevitability. A civic commons, contrasted to a tribal village or a feudal manor, combines order and variety, creating a dynamism that is absent in villages or manors. The modern world was born in the civic commons of Florence and Paris and Toledo, and numerous other medieval cities.

Civility—the understanding that we should all get along together—is not an automatic feature of society. Although cities jam thousands of unfamiliar people into small spaces, understanding how to live together in peace does not come spontaneously, and in some early cities, like in some cities today, public order is less a popular commitment among citizens than a balance of power among competing families and factions. City government as understood today—zoning, policing, maintaining infrastructure—was almost completely absent. Urban architecture in the Middle Ages frequently included towers that functioned as fortifications for defense against other families.

Cities, whether in ancient or medieval times, were the foundations for republican virtues, which were understood as mutual respect and the ability to govern oneself and get along with one's neighbors. Republicanism was counterposed to monarchy, the hereditary rule by a king, emperor, or strongman. Numerous republics of the late Middle Ages and early modern era, such as Florence, the Netherlands, and, from 1776 onward, the newly emergent United States, were making a statement: "We can govern ourselves; we do not need an emperor." By contrast, the ideal monarch, whether the Hanovers in Great Britain or the Habsburgs in Italy or the Anscarids in fifteenth-century Spain, were foreigners in the realm that they governed, above the petty quarrels of the people.

In this light, contemporary debates over the privatization of municipal services, most notably education, are the latest form of enclosure, much as the enclosure movement of the eighteenth century engrossed the commons. Neo-feudal institutions with imperial ambitions, notably large corporations, are taking over what was previously a commons.

For example, the ambient commons—the unstructured information that surrounds us in any city and is *the* source of urban vitality (McCullough 2013)—is increasingly enclosed, or at least polluted, with the LED (light-emitting diode) billboard that displays multiple, garish messages: and this is only the latest incursion. Zoning restrictions limit this form of visual pollution, recognizing that the ambient commons is a shared resource. Similarly, media has continued to occupy larger and larger spaces of our consciousness, a situation that is furthered with every technological advance, from radio to television to social media. For another example, the privatization of public goods (in the form of copyright extensions see below Chapter 2) is contemporary enclosure driven by advances in information technology and the corruption of the media. The multiple threats of pollution and enclosure and expropriation, a hazard for every common pool resource, as we will see in subsequent chapters, have intensified with every advance in technology.

In sum, the communes—early medieval cities of Italy, the Netherlands, and later France and England, were also *commons*, inasmuch as they were defined by the shared resources that are fundamental to civilization. Recently, as shared resources such as fisheries and agricultural meadows have come under threat, increased scholarly attention has been paid to the issue of the protection of the commons. This scholarly effort was led by Elinor Ostrom (1990), whose *Governing the Commons* focused on common pool resources. This subject will be the focus of the next chapter. More recently, Charlotte Hess and Elinor Ostrom (2007), in *Understanding Knowledge as a Commons*, developed a distinction among private goods, public goods, common pool resources, and club or toll goods, all of which are essential to civilization.[2] The last few decades have seen multiple assaults on these shared goods, whether in the name of efficiency, privatization, or individual liberty. These assaults have multiple dynamics, not the least of which is the adulation of technology. This adulation, which David Noble (1997) characterizes as the "religion of technology," is a distinctively modern trope.

## Colonization and Conquest

Three historical developments altered the stability of the social order and decisively changed the status of the useful arts in Europe and beyond. The first, and probably the prime mover, was the decline of the feudal system. A stable world order, which for centuries had governed Europe, was by the sixteenth century showing signs of corruption and decay. For those who had chafed under its restraints, whether learned monks who were not permitted to pursue their inquiries, artisans whose cleverness went unrecognized, navigators who dared to explore beyond the known world, or enterprising gentlemen who wished to create new trades, this was the beginning of a new era.

The second development was the opening of the geographic mind. Europe in the Middle Ages, in Leslie Fiedler's phrase, was a "world without a West" (1968: 29), a closed universe. When the early explorers dared to sail through the Pillars of Hercules, today known as the Strait of Gibraltar, they discovered, or perhaps created, the New World. I will not so much delve into long-standing debates about the meanings of "discovery," "invention," and "creation," but will note that each (discovery, invention, creation) involves not just a physical aspect but also a cosmological construction: of course Christopher Columbus did not "discover" the New World ("We were here all along," many Native Americans remind us, although the fact that they are named after Amerigo Vespucci is significant), but rather he led the way for its colonization (which is part of the story here). However, the fact that it was named the New World, rather than the Rest of the World, is, as Fiedler has described, indicative of a changing imaginary of relationships between humanity and the cosmos. The world was far more diverse and complicated than medieval Europeans imagined. European identity, hitherto confined to an appendage of the Eurasian landmass, now bestrode the narrow world. Subsequent colonization of "New Worlds" in Africa and the Americas created a cosmological challenge, with the discovery of peoples who did not share Christian ideals of a God in heaven or the immortality of the individual soul. The stimulus to philosophy resulting from the Age of Exploration has been well documented, and it gave rise to utilitarianism and the liberal economics of Adam Smith.

Civilizations both ancient and modern have been discovering, colonizing, and enslaving other peoples for millennia, whether the Romans in the Mediterranean or the Vikings in Northern Europe. After the Age of Exploration was well underway, and after Spanish and British colonizers began building sugar factories in the Caribbean operated by African slaves, a third historical development, originating in England and then spreading throughout Europe and beyond, decisively changed the character of colonization. This was, of course, the Industrial Revolution, which was marked by James Watt's steam engine, which made it possible to harness and accumulate the labor of the lower orders on a scale previously unimaginable. The useful arts, and the artisans who practiced them, acquired a newly found importance in the constitution of an emerging social order, and a rising class of industrialists began to reshape the political order.

The Industrial Revolution was not so much a technological breakthrough as it was a social upheaval that, like all social revolutions, was enabled by the ossification of the *ancien régime*, whether England in the sixteenth century or France in the seventeenth. Institutional decay and corruption created the opening for technological advance. A consequence of this social revolution was the scaling up of possibilities of colonization and conquest. Conquest, which was formerly limited by adjacent landmasses and the very rare plundering expedition, became in the modern era a normal expectation in relations among states. The empires of Spain, France, Britain, Portugal, and other nations achieved unprecedented reach. Likewise colonization, the occupying of niches in a host (social or natural) environment, a process that has existed for millennia, acquired new energy and new possibilities as technologies such as Google and Facebook colonize the consciousness of contemporary societies (Wu 2016).

It is important to distinguish between these two dynamics of colonization and conquest, as they figure in much of the narrative that follows. Conquest is the forcible domination of one people by another for purposes of plunder, tribute, slaves, or territory. The Roman conquest of Gaul, or of Scythia, was less a high-minded spreading of civilization and more a search for slaves, arable land, and other productive resources. Although conquest in the modern era is often justified by advancing the beliefs and values, variously, of prosperity, Christianity, liberty, communism, democracy, or *une mission civilatrice*, each of these is the project not of a universal humanity but of a particular imperial power, perhaps accompanied by laments about the "burdens of empire." This tension between a universalistic rhetoric and particularistic objectives creates a fundamental instability that has caused several modern empires to fall. Modern empires, in comparison to their precursors in Rome, Mesopotamia, and China, are notably prone to corruption and collapse. The Roman Empire lasted approximately five hundred years, from the Battle of Actium in 31 BCE to the deposition of Romulus Augustus in 476 CE. By contrast, the sun set on the British Empire only three centuries after its first adventures in the New World, the millennial Soviet Empire lasted approximately 70 years, Henry Luce's "American Century" lasted roughly from the end of World War II to 1970, and Germany's Thousand Year Reich was gone after 68 months.

Colonization, by contrast, is the occupying of an ecological niche in a host environment, whether a natural environment or a social environment. The colonizers do not so much subjugate their host as they exploit previously unexploited opportunities, whether for trade or agricultural or settlement or mineral production. In colonization, eradicating the host would be self-defeating. In the New World, the European settlers found it impossible to subdue the Native Americans, so they eradicated them, and exploited the natural resources using imported slaves. In Africa, by contrast, the Europeans found it more profitable to harvest an ongoing supply of human labor for shipment to the New World, rather than to eradicate entire African villages, although at times there was sufficient resistance from indigenous African kingdoms to keep the Europeans at bay. In today's society, the ethnic cleansing of indigenous peoples is no longer acceptable, but the colonization of indigenous cultures is an ongoing project.

The Industrial Revolution is usually associated with the advancement of humanity, for it created new sources of wealth that, when generally distributed, benefited all. If the new sources of wealth only benefit a tiny minority, or create massive dislocations, then it is difficult to justify the social upheavals and mass immiseration that industrial revolutions have demonstrably created. The dark side of the Industrial Revolution was the new possibilities it created for the domination of some peoples by others, ideally with only a dim awareness of that domination, a situation eloquently described both by Charles Dickens and Karl Marx. If exploitation can be hidden inside a machine, or behind a flat-panel display, or inside the connections of a global data network, then the exploitation is more difficult to resist. The intimate association of productive devices and energies on the one hand with the historical facts of imperial domination on the other is the subject to which we now turn.

## Notes

1. At the outset, I should make clear that throughout this book my use of the word "technology" is more consistent with contemporary discourse of technology as comprising sophisticated tools, devices, and instrumentalities, and less consistent with the commonplace archeological usage of "technology" as referring to any assemblage of tools or instrumentalities. Prior to 1612, there is no documented joining of *téchnē*, learned skill, with *logos*, the authority of the written word. To be sure, many of the architects and builders of the ancient and medieval world were learned men who wrote accounts of their works. The rise of "technology" as a named class of objects and instrumentalities is associated with specific historical and po-

litical developments in history, notably the Industrial Revolution. Hence, it is demonstrably ethnocentric, or at least anachronistic, to impose the term "technology" on all human productions and fabrications, unless one (following Adams 1996) accepts that everything man-made can be called "technology." Few, however, have followed his suggestion. By contrast, one notes that in the *Handbook of Science and Technology Studies* (Hackett et al. 2008), there are no chapters on prehistoric toolkits. The gendered language here is intentional.
2. In the next chapter, I will examine these distinctions and demonstrate how they are problematized by technological development. For the moment, I wish to posit a continuity between the public goods, club goods, and common pool resources on the one hand whose governance principles Ostrom describes (including clearly defined boundaries, monitoring, collective choice arrangements, and conflict resolution mechanisms; Ostrom 1990: 88ff.) and on the other hand the institutions of civic life including education, public safety, and boundaries of privacy. Ostrom demonstrates in *Governing the Commons* that it is possible to avoid the "tragedy of the commons," but only by attending to specific institutional arrangements, which will be elaborated in the next chapter.

Chapter 2

# Goods, and the Common Good, in a Liberal Society

As a species, *homo sapiens* is composed of social animals, despite considerable philosophical effort over the last three centuries to prove otherwise. *Individualism*, the idea that a man or woman can live on his or her own without recourse to society, would have been completely fantastic to Plato, the author of *The Republic*, and most moral philosophers since. It is only in the modern era that serious thinkers have imagined that humans can live apart from their fellow beings, culminating, perhaps, in Margaret Thatcher's famous 1987 statement: "There is no such thing as society."

Having reviewed the stable social (if not political) order of the feudal society of the Middle Ages in the previous chapter, I now turn my attention to the disruptions of that order that ultimately resulted in the modern revolution. My objective here is to highlight the decline of the commons, the rise of private property and its justifications, and the emergence of a technological discourse that enabled and provided a legitimation for these developments. The commons, broadly understood not just as common pool resources (forests, meadows) and public spaces, but as shared values and identities, is central to any understanding of the common good (cf. Bollier and Helfrich 2012). Shared values and identities and perspectives, in addition to shared natural resources, are the foundation for any people to feel that they have something in common. In describing the changing character of the commons and the common good, I hope to demonstrate that the Industrial Revolution was less a technological revolution than a rearrangement of a social order that had provided stability to Europeans for more than a millennium. In reclaiming the Industrial Revolution as primarily a social revolution, I hope to rescue its understanding from the technological determinism that pervades much of modern historiography.

The idea that technology drives history goes at least as far back as Karl Marx and Friedrich Engels (2014), who in 1848 wrote in *The*

*Communist Manifesto* that the steam engine gave us capitalism and the factory system. The historical fact that some of the earliest capitalists, such as the Medici in Florence and other medieval merchants, preceded James Watt's invention by at least four centuries, or that sugar factories in the Caribbean came at least a century before the steam engine, suggests that the causal sequence was the other way around: changing relations of production created a technological void, which James Watt ultimately filled. Technological determinism was embodied in the evolutionary anthropology of Leslie White, who wrote (in *The Evolution of Culture*):

> Culture thus becomes primarily a mechanism for harnessing energy and putting it to work in the service of man, and secondarily for channeling and regulating his behavior and not directly concerned with subsistence and offense and defense. Social systems are therefore determined by technological systems, and philosophies and the arts express experience as it is defined by technology and refracted by social systems. (White 1959: 390f.)

By way of contrast, a separate school of thought, sometimes called the "Social Construction of Technology" (SCOT) (Pinch and Bijker 1984), argues that technological artifacts and systems represent the interplay of problems (such as mobility), artifacts (such as the arrangement of cities), and relevant social groups (such as urban dwellers). The bicycle, for example, designed by Leonardo da Vinci in 1493 but not prototyped for several centuries, did not catch on as a serious means of mobility until civic spaces and the rhythms of daily life took on new forms in the late nineteenth century, presenting new challenges of mobility and hence creating new opportunities for the circulation of citizens and services. Although technological determinism is no longer accepted by serious students of the history or social significance of technology, its popular endorsement is evident in the awe that greets every technological breakthrough, be it driverless cars or new social media or wearable computers.

Missing in both of these formulations (SCOT and technological determinism) are the unique formulations with which human populations *make sense* out of their social and material environments. In earlier societies, authority for sensemaking was invested in priests and magicians and cult leaders, who could explain to their followers how human suffering was all part of God's design. In modern society, magic and superstition have (mostly) lost their authority, and science is invested with ultimate authority. In today's society, "technology" is a "key word" (Williams 1983), perhaps a "god term" (Burke 1961) establishing both semantic distinctions (such as natural and artificial, or strong and weak, or useful and useless) and poetic moods (such as inspiration, empowerment, or helplessness). The quixotic search for technological solutions or technofixes to ongoing social problems such as crime or hunger or pandemics itself represents a naïve faith in technology as an ultimate good.

## The Commons, the Common Good, and the Commonwealth

How to think about what members of a society share in common is the central question of the *social* sciences. An early formulation contrasts a republic or a commonwealth, in which the people are equals in their rights and mutual obligations and manage their own affairs, with monarchies, in which a single ruler decides what the people need and should have. Political philosophers since Plato have debated the optimal size and scale of a commonwealth, whether as a city-state (Athens) or larger aggregations (such as the Commonwealth of Pennsylvania), although there is widespread agreement that empires and republics are distinctively different arrangements.

Empires, embracing multiple nationalities, religions, and languages, are substantially different civic spaces from republics. Interest in the common good, as evidenced by discussions in the popular press, culminated in the 1940s, during World War II, when democracy was pitted against imperialism and totalitarianism. Though not a modern invention, totalitarianism, terror-inspired rule by a singular figure— whether Joseph Stalin or Adolf Hitler—grew to threatening proportions in the twentieth century. More recently, perhaps in response to the hyper-individualistic 1980s, there has been a revival in scholarly attention paid to defining the common good, with an increase in numbers of books and articles examining the common good. Foremost among these is Elinor Ostrom's 1990 *Governing the Commons*. The common good rests on shared resources, whether tangible (meadows) or intangible (trust). As will be developed below, the *sharing* of resources inevitably creates social bonds: the rediscovery of the social (Latour 2005), ironically, is one of the challenges of the technological society.

The communitarian Amitai Etzioni (2004), for example, examines this tension and some of the dilemmas of particularistic obligations within a society based on universalistic assumptions and a supposedly libertarian ideology. Universalism is the assumption that all human beings and all human situations have some common characteristics. Word of a child next door going hungry is more likely to mobilize one to action than reports of thousands of starving children halfway around the world, although from a universalistic perspective the latter should outweigh the former. Libertarianism, the *ne plus ultra* of "individualism" (a concept that existed only with the beginning of the modern era), posits that we are all on our own. A truly universalistic perspective, making no distinctions of kin or kind or place, would treat all hungry children the same, making no distinction of race or nationality. Similarly, from a libertarian perspective, I should feel no obligation to care for the hungry child next door, although most people would agree that it would be shameful if I did not. Etzioni makes a forceful argument that the common good is a reality (an assertion that only ideologues would disagree with), and that nourishing the common good requires building communities larger than the family yet smaller than the nation. Cultivating a sense of common, shared values is an ongoing challenge in nations divided by class, race, and region, something most recently noted in Robert Reich's *The Common Good* (2018).

A separate, although potentially convergent line of thinking comes from economists and political scientists who have tried to reconcile a concern with shared resources with the liberal individualism of a market-based society. An early formulation of this was Mancur Olson's 1965 *The Logic of Collective Action*, in which he observed that cooperation, whether in forming a political movement or managing a shared resource, is at best difficult to achieve. "Rational" behavior from this perspective, Olson argued, is to stand aside and let others undertake the effort of building coalitions and communities, and then share in the benefits. This is the so-called "free-rider" problem that is familiar to all social movements, particularly labor unions. Organizing a labor union is difficult and perhaps risky work, but once the union has achieved bargaining rights, all employees, even those who sat on the sidelines, share the benefits. Union organizers understand that on a purely rational, individualistic basis nobody would join a union, leaving everyone just as badly off as before. Instead, many contracts call for a "closed shop," in which one must either join the union or (at least) pay for the expenses of collective bargaining in order to enjoy its benefits. Recent enactment of "right to work" statutes in multiple states endorse free-riding. Free-riding is thus about something more profound than self-absorption: it is perhaps *the* cosmological dilemma of contemporary society, posing the questions of "who are we?" and "what do we have in common?" and "where do we fit into the larger scheme of things?" These questions, of the cosmology of the commonwealth, and their profound implications for the character of society will be discussed in the next section of this chapter.

A popular variation of this conundrum of the tension between liberal individualism and the stewardship of the common good is found in Garrett Hardin's "The Tragedy of the Commons" (1968), in which he observed that in an environment of shared resources ("the commons"), "rational" behavior (maximizing the means–ends calculation) is to take as much as possible, thus exhausting the resource rather than preserving it for future growth. This has been the fate of many common pool resources around the world, be they fisheries, meadows, or forests. From this liberal perspective, selfishness always trumps cooperation.

Free-riding has been the bane of collective efforts for centuries, although it has only been in the last few decades that free-riding was named and recognized as such. In the age of neoliberalism free-riding was endorsed, ironically, by those who disparaged "moochers" in other contexts. Only with the celebration of the individual and the denial of the social with the advent of neoliberalism, a doctrine dating back to the final decades of the twentieth century in which individual freedom was made paramount, was an inflection point reached. Numerous thinkers became concerned with free-riding behaviors such as tax avoidance and zoning restrictions and the neglect of civic spaces. The rise of concern with free-riding seems to be coincident with the decline of labor unions and other collective efforts for the common good: a 1995 essay by Robert Putnam, "Bowling Alone: America's Declining Social Capital," traces the decline of community institutions generally since the 1950s. In today's technological society, the contest between the common good and individual advantage is perhaps more intense than ever before, with numerous examples of individuals and institutions pursuing their own ends, whether in the form of educational advantages or residential zoning, at the expense of the common good.

Elinor Ostrom's *Governing the Commons* (1990) is a response to Garrett Hardin's pessimistic assessment, and earned her the Nobel Prize in Economics in 2009. This careful, thoughtful study and several that have followed (Cornes and Sandler 1986; Bromley 1992; Ostrom et al. 2002; Hess and Ostrom 2007) identify several conditions under which communities have been able to manage shared resources. These conditions include:

- clearly designed boundaries;
- congruence between appropriation and provision rules and local conditions;

- collective choice arrangements;
- monitoring;
- graduated sanctions;
- conflict resolution mechanisms;
- minimal recognition of rights to organize; and
- nested enterprises.

(Ostrom 1990: 90)

It is worth noting that Ostrom's conditions are more easily achieved in small-scale social formations, such as village communities. "Collective choice arrangements," for example, are more easily negotiated on a face-to-face level than on social media or in a legislative or parliamentary body, just as "monitoring" works more easily on a local scale. Participants in face-to-face relationships have a substantial and nuanced palette of sanctions, ranging from a lowered tone of voice to a sharp look to a silent stare to physical intimidation, all of which are unachievable on social media or in larger social arenas. On a larger scale, considerable institution-building ("nested enterprises," Ostrom's eighth criterion) is required for successful management; empires, large-scale by definition and aspiration, seem unable to achieve a sense of the common good.

Several of these conditions deserve elaboration. "Boundaries," for example, are essential for shutting out predators and free-riders; the commons can be governed only to the extent that the community governing the commons can shut out or at least regulate those who use it. "Collective choice arrangements" and "monitoring" concern the institutions that govern the commons, as does "conflict resolution mechanisms." "Minimal recognition of rights to organize" refers to self-government, distinguishing the commons from a prison courtyard, implying capabilities for self-government. Finally, "nested enterprises" are essential for common pool resources larger in scale than a village meadow or lakeshore, where multiple ecologies and communities potentially interact. By delegating authority, based on local conditions (Ostrom's second criterion), a large-scale commons can be successfully governed.

Paul Stern, in "Design Principles for Global Commons: Natural Resources and Emerging Technologies" (2011), describes how some of the principles derived from managing local natural resource commons need to be modified when scaled up to address issues that are of a global scale, such as the atmosphere and the seas. Irreversible technological developments create new forms and levels of risk for these global commons, which then must be managed. Pär Blomkvist and Jesper Larsson, in "An Analytic Framework for Common-Pool Resource Large Technical System (CPR-LTS) Constellations" (2013) add an issue of "sociotechnical alignment" to issues of local alignment (well established in the literature) and contextual alignment (implicit in the requirement of nested systems). Examining summer farms and civic roads (roads that are maintained by the users), they show how these commons were embedded in large-scale technical systems, a unique class of technologies (Hughes 1983) having widespread geographic reach. Large technical systems, by definition, are embedded in or at least impinge on multiple cultural, geographical, linguistic, and institutional contexts, a fact that leads to institutional failures at their peripheries (Mayntz and Hughes 1988; Gras 1997; Batteau 2010). Sociotechnical imaginaries (Jasanoff and Kim 2009), the shared images with which people comprehend their technological systems, accompanied the emergence of these large-scale systems in their uniquely national contexts, and created a new bounding of national technological projects. Large-scale systems enable cultures to *imagine* bestriding the narrow world with dreams of imperial glory, not as a fable but as an imagined fact.

Although Ostrom's analysis is primarily focused on resources—goods that are consumed and enjoyed, even if they are not necessarily depleted—it may be instructive to extend these distinctions to other values. Resources, whether natural (forests, water tables) or artificial (RF spectrum, footpaths) or institutional (libraries, schools) or even cultural (trust), are enjoyed by some or all members of a society, and one vision of the common good might be the adequacy of resources (broadly understood) to support a community: resource failures, whether institutional or ecological, whether ecosystem collapse or betrayals of trust, obviously detract from the common good. Likewise, efforts to sequester public resources, whether through theft or privatization, constitute a latter-day enclosure movement analogous to the eighteenth-century enclosure movement in England, in which the commons was appropriated by the landed gentry. That which was formerly supportive of the common good is now used for private benefit, further weakening the common good. The self-reinforcing dynamic that this sets up—with betrayals of trust being reciprocated in kind—ultimately destroys the commonwealth (Levitsky and Ziblatt 2018).

The common good is about more than just shared resources such as meadows and public spaces; it is also about shared fellow-feeling, shared spaces, shared purposes, and shared institutions. These are basic elements of any society and are not "consumed," although often they are no less valuable than depletable resources. The first of these social

**Table 2.1.** Types of goods by exclusion and subtractability (Hess and Ostrom 2007: 7).

|  |  | Subtractability | |
|---|---|---|---|
|  |  | Low | High |
| Exclusion | Difficult | **Public goods**<br>Useful knowledge<br>Sunsets | **Common-pool resources**<br>Libraries<br>Irrigation systems |
|  | Easy | **Toll or club goods**<br>Journal subscriptions<br>Day-care centers | **Private goods**<br>Personal computers<br>Doughnuts |

goods is most evident in civic spaces, the original version of a republic or a commonwealth. Civic spaces, as we will see in the next section, are about more than simply cramming more people into limited spaces: they are about new functions in society, including trade and industry, and a new cosmology, in which fellow-feeling—a sense of common identity— is extended beyond one's tribe and neighbors to include other races and creeds. The civic commons, the foundation of any republic, might be considered *the* archetypal common pool resource of a civilization. For most of humanity after the rise of cities, the civic commons was a shared resource, a source of vitality and growth. As the civic commons migrates from open-air spaces to social media platforms, defining the new rules of engagement is an ongoing, unresolved challenge.

Ostrom makes an important distinction among private goods, public goods, common pool resources, and toll or club goods. Public goods, for example safe streets, are those that are neither subtractable nor excludable, meaning that everyone shares equally in the benefits. Subtractability is the condition where the use of a resource diminishes its availability; exclusion the ease or difficulty of controlling others' use of the resources. The two dimensions of Ostrom's analysis, subtractability and excludability, set up a fourfold table of different types of resources (Table 2.1).

Each of these types of goods carries basic cosmological assumptions—that is, assumptions regarding the nature of the universe and humanity's place within it. Private goods are related to individual consumption, even as they make assumptions about social institutions:

we assume that doughnuts are safe to eat because the Food and Drug Administration provides assurances (a public good) of their safety, and personal computers would be impossible to imagine without the apparatus of standards (a public good supported by state formations, as described in the next chapter) that make them possible. The other three are inextricably social, supporting shared identities (club goods), shared citizenship (public goods), or a shared fate (common pool resources). Public goods, club goods, and common pool resources provide and are based on connections with neighbors, with society, with our natural surroundings, and with the heavens above.

All goods, even public goods, have both obvious and hidden costs. To Milton Friedman's famous "There is no such thing as a free lunch," implying both that someone had to pay for it and that accepting a "free lunch" creates an obligation, we can add the counterintuitive "There is no such thing as a free sunset." To enjoy a sunset on a summer evening, one has to take time away from other, possibly more important activities, be they housekeeping chores or putting in overtime at work. These are the obvious opportunity costs of a sunset. Yet the hidden costs of a sunset, and landscapes in general, are also significant—even if not obvious: the architectural or transportation systems that permit us to get away, whether via train or car or footpath from the city, and enjoy the sunset. In recent years, these costs have been extended in some cities to include "sunlight rights"—zoning restrictions (a cost) that enable citizens to enjoy the sunset. In many large cities, "air rights" (the maximum height of a skyscraper) and (the above-mentioned) "sunlight rights" (the maximum shadow that a building can cast on a clear day) are actively traded, often as part of the calculus of real estate development.

Part of the cosmology of any commonwealth is a consideration of what costs are recognized, and which ones are not. Unbooked costs, sometimes called "externalities," are no less real simply because we do not tabulate them, and turning a blind eye toward these hidden costs is a first step in dissolving the commonwealth. The challenge of these unbooked costs on Facebook and Twitter will be considered at the end of this chapter.

Once one accepts that all goods have hidden costs, then one is provoked to uncover them, even if they are costs that cannot be quantified. Public goods such as safe streets have the obvious costs of the taxes that citizens pay to support municipal government; they also have the less obvious cost of the civic-mindedness of the population in general. No one likes taxes, and bragging about not paying taxes is shameless; but most accept that taxes, in the famous words of Justice Oliver W.

Holmes, are the "price we pay for a civilized society," and a willingness to voluntarily pay taxes is the difference between free and totalitarian societies. Widespread tax evasion is a first step away from democracy toward autocracy. Community solidarity is a public good, yet solidarity without sacrifice is, in Mary Douglas's (1986: 1–8) words, merely "arm-waving." These sacrifices are accepted by most members of a community as the price of civilization. More pointedly, all public goods rest on a foundation of the careful stewardship provided by governments of common pool resources. Ideological controversies between advocates of "small" and "big" government are controversies not simply over political power but over what sort of goods (public, private, common pool, club) we value, and hence over who we are. The stewardship of the common good requires sacrifice, not free-riding.

The dynamic of sacrifice is an important part of this story. Sacrifice—the voluntary surrender of something of value—confers on both the sacrifice and the sacrificer a sacred value far more profound than monetary calculus. Nations have sacred monuments to those who made the "ultimate sacrifice" in wartime, but nowhere is there a monument to the "unknown file clerk." Nations, in contrast to other political formations, are imbued with this sacred value, a common good shared by all who identify with the nation (Anderson 1983; Gellner 1983). The persistence of memorials to the Lost Cause (the Southern view of America's Civil War) testifies to the endurance of these sacred monuments (see also Hubert and Mauss 1964 [1899] on the dynamics of sacrifice).

Similarly, club or toll goods have the obvious costs of the money one pays for club dues or journal subscriptions, as well as the opportunity costs of foregone subscriptions to other journals. They also have hidden costs in terms of solidarity with other members of the club or the attention demanded to keep up with, review articles for, and perhaps contribute to the journal. A network broadcast is a club or toll good, and in recent years more and more American tribes are defined by their source of news, whether it is the *New York Times*, MSNBC, or Fox News, or, more recently, online clubs such as QAnon (see Chapter 5 on "filter bubbles").

Common pool resources, which in Ostrom's analysis are nonexcludable yet subtractable, provide the test case for this proposition that everything has a cost. A common pool resource, such as a forest in which villagers have usufruct rights and can hunt animals and harvest firewood, has an obvious, ecosystem cost. Nature bears the cost of replenishment, even if that cost is only booked cosmologically. If well governed, the common pool resource also has a hidden cost, in the sacrifice or willingness of villagers to forgo excessive harvesting. Just because costs (and benefits) are not always quantified and monetized does not mean that they are nonexistent. The assumption that something must be counted for it to be of any importance is a cultural and an institutional statement rather than an ontological one.

Of these four types, only private goods are fully marketized. The idea of a market in public goods is completely illogical—how could one possibly privatize a sunset? How can we sell *real* friendships? Despite paradoxes such as these, efforts to convert public goods into toll goods—toll highways, for example, or health, or charter schools—are actively debated. I describe some of these debates in the next three chapters. Similarly, copyright restrictions, putatively applying to expressive productions, can in fact limit the sharing of useful knowledge. Ongoing debates over the privatization of public goods—schools, social security, law enforcement—all of which are too extensive to be reviewed here, indicate that the boundaries among public, private, and toll goods are in play, as in fact they have been for several centuries.

It is important to recognize public goods as state and institutional formations. Education and public safety are obvious examples, and nearly every nation around the world makes an attempt to provide education and some level of civic order. "Failed states," those entities such as Somalia and Syria where civic order has collapsed, are exceptions that affirm the rule. The *failure* of some jurisdictions in the United States to affirm a right to literacy or to maintain their infrastructure suggests that "failed states" can be closer to home. Public goods are expressions of civic values of order and pluralism and commerce, broadly understood not just as trade in goods and services, but also as the sharing and exchange of ideas and ways of life. This is a sense of common purpose that the Romans called *civitas*, an agreement binding together citizens, their rights, and their obligations. Civic values contrast to tribal values of identity and exclusion and opposition, yet, as should be clear, tribal values are never entirely absent, even in supposedly advanced industrial nations. The persistence of tribal "othering" (the emphasis on exclusionary identities) is testimony to this.

But how can a sunset, which Charlotte Hess and Elinor Ostrom identify as exemplary of public goods, be a state project? To be precise, sunsets, or more accurately landscape vistas, acquire cultural value and significance as a function of transportation infrastructures joining city and countryside: for the seventeenth-century Puritans in the Massachusetts Bay Colony, the regions beyond their settlement were a "waste and howling wilderness," where no civilized gentleman or lady would care

**Figure 2.1.** Thomas Cole, *The Oxbow* (1836). Wikimedia Commons, public domain.

to venture. Two centuries later, with the joining of city and countryside through railways, educated ladies and gentlemen ventured into the countryside to appreciate its beauty, now made part of nature, which became a nationalistic icon. Paintings of the Hudson River School, such as Thomas Cole's *The Oxbow* pictured here (Figure 2.1), and poets such as Walt Whitman celebrated the American interior, and with the creation of national parks in 1872—"America's best idea"—wilderness became a state project. In 1862, Henry David Thoreau wrote that "in wildness is the preservation of the world," a sentiment that has been echoed by millions of visitors to national parks and protected wilderness areas ever since. By contrast, a neoliberal ideology of privatization and resource extraction, described below in Chapter 4, threatens not just a shared resource but the very foundation of America's unique identity.

With respect to its status as a public good, can we view "useful knowledge" as a state project or, more accurately, as an institutional project? "Knowledge," as distinct from "information," is focused around an objective, whether it is curing a disease or finding the best route to work or school. Such objectives are functions of community and civic life, moreso than private endeavors. The test case of this point would be craft skills, knowledge that is embedded in the heads and hands of craftsmen, often called "tacit knowledge" because it resists verbal communication or decomposition. Craft skills are club goods, which in the Middle Ages were closely guarded secrets, "mysteries," of craft guilds. Contemporarily, whether through apprenticeships or instruction, productive skills—useful knowledge—are embedded within social relationships, whether between masters and apprentices, teachers and students, or supervisors and employees. Knowledge is a shared resource, sometimes called the "knowledge commons" (Hess and Ostrom 2007), including entirely new industries such as entertainment and social media, which have become engines of innovation and growth.

Club goods, which communities have created throughout history, combine excludability with low subtractability. These goods (a country club membership, for example) are not for sale to the highest bidder, since their central value—social exclusivity—would be irredeemably harmed by opening it up to those other than "our kind of people." A club good can be polluted if it is accessible to the wrong kind. Club goods and toll goods can be subject to market forces—journal publishers adjust subscription rates to what the readership will bear, and country clubs adjust their dues to what their community will bear, but editorial decisions (acceptance or rejection of articles) and admission to the club have a separate dynamic. Exclusive clubs do not auction off memberships to the highest bidders.

Despite their common features of easy exclusion and low subtractability, club goods and toll goods have a distinctively different character, inasmuch as possession of club goods depends on a social identity typically marked by boundary symbols and rites of passage. Examples include the Freemasons, the Rotary Club, and even the Boy Scouts. Although a highway is a public good, permission to operate a motor vehicle on the highway is a club good, available only to those who have earned a driver's license (a rite of passage often associated with coming of age). Selling driver's licenses at any price would be scandalous. Other, historical examples of club goods have included residential real estate (before housing discrimination was outlawed), "insider knowledge" in many fields, and many fundraising mailing lists. Although in financial markets trading on "insider information" such as foreknowledge of a calamitous or beneficial business event is strictly illegal, what we might call "community knowledge," such as a subtle understanding of the dynamics of a market, is essential to success in them. Caitlin Zaloom, in *Out of the Pits* (2006), describes how tacit knowledge of market signals, acquired through experience and participation, is used tactically by stock traders to better their counterparts; Karen Ho (2009) describes how the assumptions of Wall Street (a club) subtly shape market expectations. At the pinnacles of the economy and finance, as Zaloom and Ho demonstrate, some of the most strategically important flows are of club goods.

This social character and ubiquity of club goods and public goods provides an intersection between Ostrom's (1990) analysis of the commons and Etzioni's (2004) understanding of the common good. The architectural and institutional foundations of communities—safe residential streets, tight networks, shared commitments—might be considered club goods, and strong communities have substantial and complex foundations. The craft and merchant guilds discussed in the last chapter were clubs, and trading privileges and networks, like craft skills, were club goods available only to those who had been admitted to the guild. This close association between club goods, identity ("our kind"), and kinship reveals an important dynamic in any conception of the common good, an extension of the homology of "kin" and "kind" that Lewis Henry Morgan first noted. Sentiments supporting the common good extend only to those one feels something in common with. Etzioni's conception of the common good is built on this, making it clear that the common good is, at best, a form of "thin universalism."

In sum, "the commons" and "the common good" and shared goods (including public goods, club goods, and common pool resources) exist in separate although convergent discourses, and part of civilization is achieving a balance among public and private and club goods and common pool resources in the commonwealth. This new analysis of "the commons" is an epicyclic refinement of neoclassical economics that is being led by political scientists to account for the undeniable fact that *most* goods—the things we value in life, including love, friendship, civility, and security—are *not* subject to market forces. "The common good" presents itself as an effort to rescue shared values from the hyper-individualism of the last 40 years. It is an easy demonstration to show that most values, and indeed most human activities, are not marketed or marketable, even as considerable effort is made to privatize public goods and open intimate values up to bidding: Facebook has monetized "friendship,"[1] clean air is marketized through "carbon offsets," copyright extensions fence in cultural reproduction, and the financial industry synthesizes, buys, sells, slices, and dices "trust," invariably creating speculative bubbles that immiserate millions (see Chapter 6, Section 2, on financial technology or "FinTech"). Kleptocratic initiatives toward privatization of education and public safety and even national defense through outsourcing to mercenaries, like the enclosure movement of early modern England, are further assaults on the common good.

A critical yet unexamined dimension of both the privatizing of public goods and the enclosure of the common good has been the pivotal role of technology. The role of technology in altering the common good and blurring the boundaries among different types of goods goes back to the close association between the enclosure movement and the Industrial Revolution. Beginning in the eighteenth century, small peasant holdings and the agricultural commons were increasingly sequestered and enclosed, driving the peasants off the land and into the growing industrial cities of England. More contemporary examples include, with the emergence of the technological society, efforts to enclose as many public goods as possible, including education, income security, clean air, and knowledge. Today, as will be described in the next two chapters, efforts are underway to make a business out of many of these, with varying success. The cosmological costs of the eighteenth-century enclosure movement, including the hollowing out of the domestic commons and the degradation of labor, were described in Peter Laslett's *The World We Have Lost* (1965) and E. P. Thompson's *The Making of the English Working Class* (1963). By contrast, the cosmological consequences of these contemporary enclosures, whether the privatization of education, public safety, national defense, or municipal services, remain unexamined. These cosmological costs include (but are not limited to) the increasing tribalism of contemporary politics and a decline in national attachment, which have received considerable attention in recent years. As more activities can be performed by automated systems, whether surveillance (through facial recognition technologies) or even political mobilization (through social media), the *magic* of technology substitutes for the *engagement* of citizenship.

Part of the dynamic of contemporary enclosures has been the growing role of technology in contemporary society. As the instruments of production and control and even consumption become more technologically intensive, citizens are reduced to serfs watching their commons enclosed whether in the workplace or in neighborly discussions. A contemporary enclosure of the commons, under the banner of "neoliberalism" dating back to about 1980, seeks to devalue any government infringement on individual liberty. In *The Road to Serfdom*, published in the middle of World War II in 1944, Friedrich Hayek argued that socialism, and more generally any overreach in government regulation of ownership, would eventually result in "serfdom." Interest in *The Road to Serfdom* took off in the 1980s, providing a charter for neoliberalism. The glaring error of *The Road to Serfdom*, and much of the rhetoric of neoliberalism, is that it takes almost no cognizance of technology, even as information technology from the 1980s onward was building a new road to unfreedom. Similarly, neoliberalism, while promising to free human energies from government, the commons domination, in fact ushered in new forms of technological domination (see Chapter 5, Section 1, "The Square and the Tower on the Net").

In sum, the different goods that communities value today, whether public goods such as landscapes or private goods such as doughnuts, all have a technological foundation, whether in the architectural arrangements of civic spaces or the communication media of contemporary politics. Technological innovation creates new opportunities for the common good and undermines the old. In today's society the commons is a technological creation.

## The Cosmology of the Commonwealth

Most goods have values and significance that go beyond usefulness. Beauty, affection, sacrality, and family ties can all be encoded within "goods" that are nominally bought and sold, but which are actually *valued* less in terms of their purchase price and more in terms of their *significance*. A family heirloom, for example, may have been purchased decades or centuries ago, but its *value* is reckoned not in terms of what it would bring in a pawnshop, but in the value and values attached to the family. Family photographs are tokens of family solidarity. A large part of these values are statements about *who we are* and where we fit into the larger scheme of things.

Once we recognize that goods can be (and frequently are) tokens of identity, then we are provoked to examine what sorts of identity they encode. Private goods, for an obvious example, encode individualistic identities; private goods, strictly speaking, are not shared. This contrasts to club goods, which by definition are shared and which, in fact, are tokens of club identity. A university degree is *earned* by passing certain qualifications over a period of time, and purchasing university degrees would be scandalous: "diploma mills" test the boundaries of this taboo, and bragging about a degree from "Corinthian University" (a now-defunct diploma mill) or posting its certificate in one's office advertises nothing more than cluelessness, the fact that one is (unwittingly) claiming a false identity. Social class has aspects of club membership and brings with it knowledge of the distinctions between *vrai* and *faux* status, distinctions not always evident to outsiders.

Public goods are tokens of citizenship, and did not exist before the rise of cities, the creation of shared spaces that were more than simply a collection of villages jammed together. Cities, by definition, include public spaces; they also include public services, whether in the form of police protection or running water. Part of being a "good citizen" lies in maintaining public goods, such as clean streets, public order, mutual assistance to neighbors, and voluntarily paying one's taxes. Public goods are nominally provided by government authority, but the difference between a democratic and a totalitarian state is that in the former public order is maintained *without* the constant intervention of the police: drivers obey traffic regulations, and pedestrians do not discard trash on the sidewalks, even when the police are not watching. Public services, such as police, firefighting, safe streets, clean sidewalks, and emergency response, are likewise public goods, entitlements of citizenship. Recent efforts to "privatize" government services, supposedly in the name of efficiency, are actually a form of enclosure: they are placing the civic commons under a regime of private profit. A city and associated civic spaces can be considered a commons: unlike a village, in which the intrusion of outsiders is noticed and possibly sanctioned, a city, at least in its nonresidential quarters, is open to all, open to all to enjoy civil order and the protection of its services. With some poetic license, one might say that *Stadt Luft*, which in the Middle Ages was a token of release from serfdom (*Stadt Luft macht frei*), is today a common pool resource, not only for respiration but also for identity.

Even the archetypal commons of common pool resources, which form the basis for much of the literature on the commons, are tokens of identity, in this case the identity of being in harmony with nature. Most human societies have had an intimate relationship with nature, both in terms of biological subsistence and cosmological self-understanding: the few that abused this relationship, such as Easter Island or early Norse settlements in Greenland, simply disappeared (Diamond 2005). During the Middle Ages, forests were sometimes overcleared, and fields were exhausted by villagers that had not yet discovered the principles of crop rotation, but the possibility of exhausting global resources such as the atmosphere would have to wait until the Industrial Revolution.

Part of living in harmony with nature, for many tribes, has been the formation of *totemic identities*, characterizations about "who we are" in terms of the natural order. For the Ojibwa, the Eagle Clan is as different

**Figure 2.2.** Harley-Davidson Softail Breakout FXSB103. © Lothar Spurzem. https://creativecommons.org/licenses/by-sa/2.0/de/deed.en.

from the Wolf Clan as eagles are different from wolves: the social order is analogical to the natural order. In contemporary society, totemic objects from the natural world have largely (although incompletely) been replaced with tribal attachments from the industrial world, a phenomenon that David Hess (1995) calls "technototemism," whether they are automobiles or airplanes or computers or motorcycles: the Harley-Davidson, a large, iconic American motorcycle, a symbol of muscular masculinity nicknamed the "Hog," as pictured in Figure 2.2 (in contrast to "sissy scooters" favored elsewhere around the world), has its own (corporate-sponsored) tribe, the Harley Owners Group, with tens of thousands of members nationwide, and an annual rally in Sturgis, South Dakota.

In the early days of personal computing, PC and Mac users had distinctive identities, with the former being more no-nonsense business types and the latter being more artistic. Similarly, in contemporary America guns are more a statement of identity than they are tools for self-defense or foraging, and increases in gun sales have coincided with challenges to identity, the sense of *who we are*. "Harmony with nature" may sound like a pre-industrial, nostalgic characteristic of tribes who defined who they were in terms of identification with natural species (such as the above-mentioned Eagle Clan and Wolf Clan). More recently, harmony with nature has been resurrected as industrial societies begin to discover the limits of nature, whether in the capability of oceans and atmospheres to absorb pollution, or the planet to absorb rising temperatures. Negotiating our relationship with our natural surroundings, and what this means for *who we are*, turns out to be an ongoing project even in the most advanced civilizations.

Controversies over global warming are thus not simply controversies over economic efficiency: they are controversies over our identity, which always has a cosmological dimension, a statement of how one fits into the universe. Does our technology enable us to transcend natural limitations, or do we attempt to do so only at our peril? Do our transportation devices permit us to conquer nature, or expose inexorable natural constraints? Do new transportation and communication technologies expose natural constraints previously hidden? In sum, the disposition of shared resources is the strongest possible statement of *who we are*: do we share anything in common, or are we simply a plurality of monadic individuals wandering aimlessly on this planet? When technological systems collapse, whether nuclear power plants or space shuttles or residential towers, it calls into question our basic understanding not just of engineering standards but also of who we are and what we stand for.

## Goods and Identity

Human tribes assemble their sense of "who we are" using several resources. Perhaps the most fundamental are the tribal distinctions between "us" and "them," whether coded in terms of race, class, religion, or social origin. An important part of the identity of the Nuer of southern Sudan, for example, was the fact that they were "not Dinka," and considerable effort has gone into proving or disproving this proposition, thus demonstrating its importance. Similarly, in the states of the American South, a critical part of white identity was "not Black," even though an occasional white family might have a "taint of the tar brush," or a light-skinned African American might be able to "pass" for white. Maintaining these "racial" distinctions was critical for maintaining positions in slavery and racial domination, not only in the era of slavery, but for more than a century since. Other perhaps tribal distinctions between "us" and "them" can include social class, language, nationality, and numerous other tokens of "identity politics," a phenomenon whose recrudescence has been linked to the decline of state formations (Friedman 1994).

A second part of a people's identity has to do with the roles and norms that it encodes. In most societies, women are expected to behave one way, and men another, and to explain these distinctions as "just natural" is no more than a totemic trope. Many human societies explain their social distinctions, whether the "obvious" superiority of the Eagle Clan over the Wolf Clan, or the historic dominance of the "white race," as "just natural," a figure of speech, an analogy that Claude Lévi-Strauss ([1962] 1969) demonstrated to be at the heart of totemism. Naturalizing that which is a cultural production gives it cosmological authority, ramifying far beyond the here and now. Distinctions between white and yellow and Black—or "Caucasian" and "Oriental" and "Negroid"—or among nations, it is argued, are part of the order of the cosmos.

These identities are embedded in networks, whether the networks of residential communities or occupational guilds or Twitter feeds. People listen to and associate with those they feel something in common with, and to say that this is "just natural" simply reinforces the point of the previous paragraph. In order to "pass" for white, a light-skinned African American would not only have to adopt white mannerisms, but he would also have to move to a new community where anonymity would protect his previous identity. Threats to and disruptions of these networks, whether through the breakdown of racially segregated neighborhoods or the desegregation of lunch counters in the twentieth-century South, like the arrival of uninvited guests at a party, disrupt not just the social peace but the individual's sense of "who I am." The arrival of a mixed-race president in 2009, with a white mother and a Black father, for many Americans disrupted not only the political order but the cosmological order. Contemporary American politics is torn not simply by party, but by much larger questions about "who we are."

Finally, identities are expressed and represented with objects and tokens (goods) that are displayed, shared, and circulated, particularly on ceremonial occasions. Universities have largely abandoned the wearing of academic regalia in lecture halls, but at commencement, *the* crowning ceremony of the university, the academic robes are on full display. In many occupations, particularly where substantial control of resources is involved (such as banking), there is an expectation of "proper attire," and one would give no credibility (or credit) to a banker who dressed like a plumber. In numerous occupations, *tools* are not just practical implements but also badges of identity. As noted above, on feast days medieval guilds would parade with the tools of their trades, and even today many occupations make a public display of their tools—a stethoscope draped around the neck, for example, signals a medical specialist.

The importance of these elements—distinctions of identity, norms, networks, and tokens—is that they are the foundation of individuals' sense of "who I am" and "what am I supposed to do?" When these are disrupted—when firefighters in a hazardous situation are ordered to "drop their tools" (Weick 1993) or when diehard racists find themselves subservient to an African American president, or, more recently, when educated citizens confront a carnival huckster in the nation's highest office—it creates what the social psychologist Karl Weick termed a "cosmological crisis" at the very foundation of the culture—a "collapse of sensemaking," in which groups and institutions break down. A shared sense of identity is a club good, and one's deeply held sense of "who I am" encompasses "what am I supposed to do?" as well as "who are my friends (and enemies)?" and "how do I make sense of all this?"

In a society where technological values of performance and concentrations of power eclipse values of stability, authority, and sociability, sensemaking is an ongoing challenge: how does one *make sense* of disruptive innovations (Bower and Christensen 1995)? Disruptive innovations, celebrated by many, in fact disrupt the social order. Social media is perhaps *the* disruptive innovation of the past 20 years, and yet is still a problem for America's political discourse. Even if authoritative voices are assuring us that disruption is a good thing, for most people such innovations can be unsettling, unless they have the social resources to adapt. How does one make sense out of technological failures without calling into question the entire project of the technological society? Technological acceleration has become perhaps the only constant in a technological society. Whether per Moore's Law (see Chapter 5) or Henry Adams's anticipation of it in "The Dynamo and the Virgin" (1961 [1900]), both of which are described below in the Conclusion and both of which stipulate geometric acceleration of technological capabilities, investments in technology *inevitably* stress a society's institutions.

## Factories and Farmhands: Rearranging Productive Spaces

The rhetoric of private goods and privatization is pervasive today, yet with a glance back at history we can remind ourselves that for most of human history private goods were exceptional, rather than foundational.

Throughout most of the Middle Ages, for example, England's rural economy was based on what is called the "open-field system," in which villagers enjoyed customary access to forests and fields for grazing, planting, firewood, and hunting, albeit under the suzerainty of the lord of the manor. Similar arrangements across Europe created shared resources and shared obligations under the overall authority of feudal lords. These rights were "customary," perhaps under the lord, who might collect rents but who could not evict the peasants at whim, as the manor was not his *private* property. While these arrangements hindered economic growth, they provided security and stability throughout society; the trade-off between stability and the disruption, particularly for the lower orders, of a dynamic economy has never been adequately modeled (see Chapter 6, Section 2, "Wealth and Poverty"). The evolution of the modern social order out of the decay of the feudal order combined with the discovery of the New World opened up not only new economic opportunities and geographic spaces, but an entirely new conception of the universe and humanity's place within it, an entirely new cosmology.

Historically, as described above, the most distinctive effort to take a resource out of a shared domain and place it into private hands was the enclosure movement. In the Middle Ages, most agricultural land was commonly held—forests, fields, perhaps marshlands were associated with specific villages, and the villagers shared grazing, planting, and hunting rights in these commons, sometimes dictated by law, sometimes by custom. Beginning in the eighteenth century, more and more parcels of land were taken out of these commons and placed under private ownership, sometimes through an act of Parliament, sometimes through purchase, sometimes through land grabs (the three were not always easily distinguishable). Small farmers who had enjoyed customary rights to the land for centuries were converted to cash tenants or driven off the land and into England's growing cities. The enclosure movement might be seen as a template for efforts that have sought to privatize public goods, club goods, and common pool resources in the centuries since.

Contemporaneous with the acceleration of the enclosure movement was the rise of the factory system, in which productive activities such as the carding and spinning and weaving of wool were moved out of the household and into "factories," central locations where a master could supervise the process, quality, and productivity. Although the factory system in England, beginning with Richard Arkwright at Cromford, is usually dated to the early eighteenth century, we have reports of sugar factories in the Caribbean, manned by unfree labor (either African slaves or Irish indentured servants) in the mid-sixteenth century. Slavery and colonialism were the initial drivers of the factory system. This opened up an opportunity for improved sources of energy, which steam engines invented by Thomas Newcomen (1712) and perfected by James Watt (1775) filled. The factory, in short, gave us the steam engine.

The factory system has three basic components, which when brought together create a durable order. The first of these is the centralization of the workers in one location or "factory." This separation of domesticity and production has been frequently commented on, and all that can be added here is that it represented a change in the meaning of each. Domestic spaces became associated with consumption rather than production, and social aggregations served a purpose other than civic participation.

The second feature of the factory system was process supervision, meaning that a foreman or superintendent instructed workers on how to spin, weave, or work metal. Under the guild system, which I discussed above, these craft skills were personal, or perhaps owned by the guild, and the sharing of and instruction in the skills, whether among journeymen or between masters and apprentices, was one of the privileges of guild membership. In the factory system, as Harry Braverman (1974) described for twentieth-century industry, skills and quality became the property of the masters. Although craftsmen and craft unions jealously guard their skills and standards, within systems of mass production a "de-skilling"—a twentieth-century form of enclosure—reduces craftsmen to proletarians. Likewise, contemporary efforts to automate education with online systems reduce scholars to file clerks.

The third component, which speaks most directly to our concerns with technology, is mechanization, the application of motive force, whether from water wheels or later from steam engines. Under the guild system, the journeyman or master owned his tools, and owned the product including its quality. Under the factory system, the capitalist owned the most important productive instruments, and also owned the quality. Early resistance to the factory system by the "Luddites" as E. P. Thompson (1963) documents, was less a protest against technology than it was a protest against the inferior quality of the cloth that they were forced to weave on the new "frame-weaving" machines. However, the Luddites were protesting not simply the degradation of finished goods but rather the degradation of an entire way of life, in which self-sufficient craftsmen were being turned into proletarians dependent on the factory owner. Industrialization, and the Industrial Revolution, for the self-sufficient craftsmen of the early modern era, amounted to a cosmological crisis, a collapse of the values—craft skills, self-sufficiency, independence—that defined an entire way of life. Investments in technology gave shape and sturdiness to this rearrangement of the social order of the guilds, which had previously been the masters of productive skills, substituting an economic order in which a debased product and a debased quality of life were the norm.

Traditionally, craft production such as spinning, weaving, metalworking, and carpentry was undertaken either as domestic labor that the housewife or artisan undertook on his or her own account or under what came to be called the "putting-out system," under which a merchant supplied the householder with raw materials on credit and sold the finished product. The rise of the "factory system" presented a vast cosmological shift, seldom recognized as such because it most profoundly affected illiterate countrymen. A substantial change in the meanings of time and space irrevocably hollowed out the familial commons, leaving domestic life but a hollow shell of what it used to be. Peter Laslett's *The World We Have Lost* (1965) eloquently describes the hollowing out of the domestic commons.

In short, just as the enclosure movement hollowed out the village commons, the rise of the factory system hollowed out the domestic commons, privatizing social interactions and skilled craft work. Arguably, today's enclosure movements—the effort to privatize public services—are now hollowing out the civic commons, suggesting that there is no possibility of a common good. The privatization of public services includes, but is not limited to, the police and even in extreme cases the military (through the use of mercenary forces such as Blackwater Security, which, under contract to the US Army, provide security in Iraq and Afghanistan). This comes in addition to the privatization of public education; the migration of civic life to social media platforms such as Facebook and Twitter; and the privatization of the trillion-dollar health industry (as described in the next chapter). Technology, whether in the form of water wheels or steam engines or the internet, was not the prime mover of this, but, once added to the new productive arrangements, gave them a force and vigor that made them seem inevitable. The tragedy of the commons first began at home.

## Justifying the Erasure of Society

As colonialism and the enclosure movement accelerated, philosophers such as John Locke, Adam Smith, and Jeremy Bentham labored to demonstrate that this massive rearrangement of the social order was not only beneficial, but also in accord with natural law (although others such as Karl Marx disagreed). As turmoil in the countryside accelerated, turmoil in the court led to the overthrow of James II and his replacement by William of Orange in 1690. In this atmosphere, Locke's *Two Treatises on Civil Government*, perhaps the foundational text for modern society for many centuries since the Industrial Revolution, sought to provide justification for the newly emergent mercantile and colonial order. The *First Treatise* was a polemic against Robert Filmer, arguing that the patriarchal forms of the Middle Ages, including the "divine right of kings," had no logical justification. Locke's *Second Treatise*, which speaks to more contemporary concerns, argued that property is the foundation of government, that property begins with one's ownership of himself, and that through labor a man creates additional property to which he is entitled. Governments are created to protect private property, a premise that has lately become contentious as private property has become more amorphous with ongoing disputes over the "ownership" of social media.

Locke's ideas about private property and civil society fit uneasily with his ideas about slavery. The *Fundamental Constitutions of Carolina*, which Locke had a major hand in drafting in 1669, presents a remarkable document of toleration and religious liberty extended to the "Jews, heathens, and other dissenters from the purity of Christian religion." At the same time, it allowed that "every freeman of Carolina shall have absolute power and authority over his negro slaves, of what opinion or religion soever." This accommodation of tolerance and egalitarianism with colonialism and servitude, and the recognition that slaves were human (inasmuch as they could have religion), has challenged the common good ever since. The only way to achieve a sense of the common good in a colonial regime is to assume that some individuals are worth less than others. Colonialism and the common good are fundamentally incompatible concepts: as technological empires extend their reach (see below on the colonization of conscience on social media), the common good is under greater assault.

Building on Locke's work, Adam Smith's *The Wealth of Nations*, which is more frequently invoked than read as the foundational text of the modern economy, argued that the market is the most natural organization of the economy, and that the "hidden hand" of the market works best if left undisturbed. As is sufficiently well known so as not to require development here, a *laissez-faire* (leave it be) approach to governing, in his view, is best for assuring the general prosperity. Smith's argument depends on separating economics (producing, distributing, consuming) from politics (allocating, adjudicating, resolving), and asserting that the latter should not interfere with the former. For more than two centuries, Adam Smith and the market have been invoked as fundamental to the economy. In recent years, however, an accelerating accumulation of "epicyclic" refinements such as market imperfections, knowledge asymmetries, transaction costs, externalities, and in fact even the identification of nonmarketable club and public goods suggests that the liberal egocentric paradigm may soon collapse under the weight of discrepant data. In the Middle Ages, a Ptolemaic, geocentric cosmology, placed the Earth at the center of the universe, which in its later years required adjustments and fine-tuning (epicycles) to account for improved astronomical observation of discrepant planetary movements. As described by Thomas Kuhn in *The Structure of Scientific Revolutions* (1962), this fine-tuning ultimately resulted in this cosmology's collapse; it was to be replaced by the Copernican (heliocentric) paradigm. Likewise, the egocentric liberal economic paradigm may be on the verge of collapsing as its limitations and imperfections are exposed. In the physical sciences, the Copernican Revolution was the beginning of modern physics; by contrast, the social sciences are on the verge of a paradigm shift.

As an alternative to the egocentric cosmology of Adam Smith, a vector-centric paradigm, suggesting that the fundamental realities of society are not centered on the individual but rather on connections and flows, would better account for the multiple sorts of goods in the economy. In mathematics, a vector is a variable that has both quantity and direction; the vectors of contemporary life are the flows of resources, rather than simply their accumulation. "Friends" on Facebook, for example, are vectors, the accumulation of which is a mark of sociality; similarly, on social media a tweet is a vector, and the accumulation of "followers" is an objective of many users of social media.

For our purposes, this line of thought culminates with Jeremy Bentham's utilitarianism, which argues for a "hedonic calculus" to weigh pleasure and pain. For Bentham, and followers such as John Stuart Mill and many contemporary philosophers, acts are to be judged in terms of the "greatest good for the greatest number," with "good" being equated with "pleasure." Omitted from this calculus are actions such as sacrifice or devotion or trust or commitment that may not directly result in greater pleasure. If it feels good, then it is not really a sacrifice at all. Yet the act of *sacrifice* invests a person or a good or a social arrangement with a sacred power that goes beyond pleasure or usefulness. Although a quantitative judgment of "more" or "less" would be spurious here, it is demonstrable that many people and many peoples devote large parts of their lives to activities, whether devotion to family or sacrifice for the community, that are outside the "hedonic calculus." Contrary to Adam Smith and Jeremy Bentham, sacrifice and its associated sense of connectedness, more so than any accumulation of material wealth, are the primary means by which peoples and nations give meaning to their lives.

In sum, there are many values—sociality, friendship, sacredness, wisdom, patriotism, style, *li*, *halus*—that can only be reduced to "pleasure" or "usefulness" with considerable violence. Some of these are so completely foreign to Westerners that they even resist translation: *li* is a Confucian virtue that can be translated as "ritual" or "respect" or "proper conduct," whereas *halus* is a Balinese good roughly translated as "poise" (Geertz 1973). However, translating these as "poise" or "proper conduct" misses their deep significance within their respective societies. Similarly, friendship is a virtue in Western societies, and we take not only pleasure but also deeper meaning from our friendships. But true friendship is much deeper than simple pleasure, and it would be considered unthinkable to do a monthly cost–benefit tabulation of one's friendships. Only Facebook tabulates friendships. The accumulation of thousands of "friends" on Facebook accomplishes little more than a debasement of the currency of friendship.

The rise of utilitarianism in the seventeenth and eighteenth centuries, from Hume to Bentham to Mill, was coincident with the colonial discoveries of cultural diversity—the fact that there were peoples around the world whose values were totally foreign to those of the European colonialists. "Pleasure," on the other hand, however superficial, is something that everyone can agree upon, and so by reducing all value to pleasure or utility, a least-common-denominator framework was achieved for embracing cultural diversity, albeit at the expense of intellectual rigor.

"In the beginning, all the world was America," Locke wrote in his *Second Treatise*, positing that precolonial America was an archetypal "state of nature," not recognizing that *invariably* the "state of nature" was some other tribe's commons. Aboriginal inhabitants had no rights in the forests and fields, inasmuch as they did not "labor" on them, according to Locke. This line of thought was completely oblivious to other values of a more social character, whether values of sacrality or totemic identification or tribal authority with which indigenous inhabitants invested their "natural" surroundings. It was also ignorant of the fact that foraging—hunting and gathering—can often be hard work, at least for the women of the tribe (who were more typically the gatherers). For Locke, writing in 1669, labor meant either agricultural labor in the fields or factory labor in the colonies, the latter of which was the property of the master. The indentured property of the master in man, and its subversion of the common good, was the foundation of a liberal society.

## Note

1. Or, more accurately, Facebook has decomposed social life into network connections and data on the demographic characteristics and network positionalities and preferences ("likes") of its subscribers, data sufficiently valuable to marketers to give Facebook a market valuation in excess of $200 billion.

Chapter 3

# Technology and the Commons

In the previous chapter, we established that the emergence of "technology" as a named class of artifacts and practices was coincident and coterminous with the shifting character of goods and the common good in the seventeenth and eighteenth centuries. We can now inquire as to the distinctive character of modern technology, in contrast to the simpler tools that existed prior to the Industrial Revolution, and how that created a challenge to how we understand the common good and common goods. Technology is characterized by such characteristics as scalability and portability, new channels of circulation and representation, a godlike, futuristic imaginary, and even the creation of new resources for exploration, whether of the depths of the oceans or the empty spaces of the skies. These have created the systems, landscapes, and technoscapes that now bestride the narrow world.

All human societies, even the most advanced industrial societies, live within social and natural constraints; only science fiction imagines slipping these surly bonds. The goods and resources that citizens or subjects extract from their natural and institutional environments are foundational to the character of their civilization. Some societies have collapsed because they overexploited their natural environment (Diamond 2005); more complex societies have collapsed when social harmony was disrupted by overexploitation of the institutional environment (Skocpol 1994; Levitsky and Ziblatt 2018). *In theory*, democratic societies maintain harmony by a diffusion of power among citizens, as contrasted to monarchies or oligarchies where an autocrat or a small clique dictate the terms of institutional order. As information technologies enable the scaling up of systems of surveillance and control, even as they decentralize production, and the centralization of systems of distribution create new industrial empires such as Amazon, this democratic character and the common good it supported are called into question. The technological society, particularly with the beginnings of the internet at the close of the twentieth century, has now slipped the constraints of time and place.

As documented in the previous chapter, the principles of maintaining harmony with the natural environment are now well understood, even if in certain institutional environments, notably extreme inequality or the domination of predatory elites, these principles of reciprocity and sharing are ignored or flat-out denied. We turn our attention now to an array of goods, both public and private, in the institutional environment of industrial societies, in order to examine shared goods as problems of collective action. After reviewing what we have learned from maintaining the natural order, where a wealth of research has described the requirements for maintaining the commons of natural resources, we look at selected systems essential to maintaining the commons of civic order: cities, transportation, education, and healthcare. Although one is tempted to suggest that the observations proffered here are both superficial and blindingly obvious, as a matter of fact they are increasingly problematic in a neoliberal society: for millennia, providing water has been recognized as essential to urban settlements, yet the difficulties of Flint, Michigan, Jackson, Mississippi, and numerous municipalities in California in providing a safe water supply are symptomatic of a deteriorating institutional environment. Similarly, a swelling chorus of "anti-vaxxers," questioning the benefits of immunization, and free-riding on the herd immunity of the remainder of the community, suggests that settled questions of public health have become unsettled in the internet age.

A pervasive irony in all of this is that one of the world's most technologically advanced societies simultaneously displays some of the most blatant ignorance in its public discourse. This ignorance takes the form of denial of the established facts of anthropogenic climate change and the facts of evolution and the value of civic order. Or more broadly, how does it happen that a democratic civilization, whether in Europe, Latin America, or the United States, self-destructs?

Perhaps this ignorance is not so much a consequence of not paying attention, or not trying hard enough to solve a puzzle, as it is, like knowledge, a *social construction*. A social construction is a willful, stable configuration of institutions and artifacts and pervasive problems, congruent with a community's cosmological outlook, that affords it at least short-term adaptability. For example, so-called "creation science," which has multiple adherents, research institutes, a museum in Kentucky, and classes at Bob Jones University, was practically nonexistent for a hundred years after Darwin published *The Origin of Species* in

1859, yet took off in the late 1970s at a time when fundamentalist religious institutions felt under assault in an increasingly secular society, a cosmological crisis that has never been fully appreciated. Like "fundamentalism," a religious movement that traces back not to biblical times but rather to the 1920s, creationism was a less a rediscovery of ancient truths than a reaction to contemporary trends.

Collective sensemaking is perhaps *the* overriding common good, and the fragility of sensemaking may well be one of the major hazards of the technological society. When people's basic assumptions about the natural and social order are challenged, as described in the previous chapter, they experience a cosmological crisis, a collapse of sensemaking (Weick 1993, 1995). Another example of the social construction of ignorance was evident in 2008, when millions of Eurocentric Americans found themselves in a country with an African American as its foremost figure, which they could only rationalize by claiming he was an imposter born in Kenya. Eight years later, when educated citizens discovered that their country with its proud traditions going back to the Enlightenment would soon be headed by a semiliterate carnival huckster, a development that many are still trying to comprehend, conspiracy theories abounded.

Sensemaking, in other words, is more than simply puzzle-solving; it is the assembling of a worldview that can embrace the past and the present, the facts on the ground and the order in the heavens, and our place in both. Just as Galileo and Copernicus presented a challenge to the cosmological assumptions of the Middle Ages (the Ptolemaic or geocentric universe) as noted in the previous chapter, so too today artificial intelligence and computational systems present a challenge to egocentric sensemaking, particularly in the absence of a sociocentric paradigm. A sociocentric or vector-centric paradigm would recognize that the primary facts of human existence are *social*—that is, connections with fellow members of one's society—and not the individual desires of the liberal, egocentric paradigm.

The argument of this chapter pivots on the paradox that in a neoliberal society an increasing wealth in *private* goods for consumption is *inevitably* accompanied by the devaluation of *public* goods and common pool resources, whether the mutual discourse of a republic or the shared natural resources of the environment, and hence of the common good. An entire institutional and philosophical apparatus is deployed to reassure citizens that this is both beneficial and inevitable, even as millions find their lives immiserated. The paradox of the "affluent society," of public squalor in the midst of private affluence, which John

Kenneth Galbraith first noted in 1958, at the height of postwar prosperity, becomes less paradoxical once one understands that affluence in terms of private goods for consumption is purchased at the expense of the common good. As discussed further in Chapter 6, private goods come *invariably* at the expense of the common good, both in their accumulation and in their appreciation.

"Common sense," a common good, is a social construction. The institutions of a democratic society are more fragile than is often imagined. Just as collective action is required to maintain commons such as forests and water tables and public squares, so too collective action is required to maintain the common institutional foundations of society.

## The Character of Technology

Contemporary discourse, as I noted on the first page of Chapter 1, identifies technology with sophisticated tools and instrumentalities, and not the entire range of useful devices. If utility was a prerequisite for assuming something to be technological, then some of the software on my computer would certainly not be considered technology. Usefulness, of course, depends on the context and the problem at hand, and "technology" is notably independent of both.

In contrast to such an instrumental understanding of technology, focusing simply on its utility, I would like to focus on five additional characteristics of modern technology:

- Independence of locality
- Translation and compression of energy and information
- Scalability
- Autonomous representation
- Modernism

Unlike the tools of less complex societies, technologies do not represent local adaptations: they are context-independent, or more accurately they can be effectual in a variety of cultural, geographic, and industrial contexts. They may be *adapted* to different linguistic and cultural communities, a process known as "recontextualization," but the basic protocols of the internet are the same in the Northern and Southern Hemispheres. Vertical water wheels, for instance, which Vitruvius described more than two thousand years ago, depend on being located near a fault line, where the stream level drops sufficiently to power the device. By contrast, the steam engine can be located anywhere, thus freeing powered factories from the tyranny of location. They depend, of course, on a supply of fuel, but their versatility permits many different fuels, although most typically carbon-based and often transported halfway around the world. Similar observations could be made for nearly every technology; although many, such as transportation devices, require infrastructure, a public good, the public goods of roads and airports can be built almost anywhere.

Definitive of technological devices is their translation and compression of energy and information. In contrast to the mechanical linkages of earlier devices, which were typically powered by animals, technologies can harness millions of foot-pounds per second of horsepower, and translate it over long distances. Turbines in Europe can be powered by dynamos in Asia. Similarly, in contrast to earlier tabulating devices such as the abacus, today's computer can perform stupendous calculations instantaneously and send the results not only around the world but also into outer space.

Closely related to this relationship to energy and information is the extreme scalability of many technological devices. Although a horse and buggy has obvious limitations of scale, horseless carriages (automobiles) clearly are less constrained, and have been both scaled up and scaled down to fit different circumstances. One of the great technological inventions of the twentieth century, the transistor, could be both scaled down on printed circuit boards and scaled up to gargantuan devices.

Part of what makes this possible is a fourth defining feature of technology, autonomous representation, the independence of representations from the actual object. A key difference between traditional tools and modern technologies is that in traditional techniques the design and rules for use are (most typically) embedded in the hands and customs and guild mysteries of the craftsmen. In modern technologies, they are frequently subject to renegotiation and are embedded in representations including design standards and descriptions and operating manuals. The Roman architect and civil engineer Vitruvius, whose idealization of the human form described in Chapter 1 can be considered a set of design standards, was the basis for Renaissance artists a millennium later. Several centuries later, the airplane, for another example, flew around the world in 1912, not as an actual, physical aircraft, but in the pages of *Le Monde* in an article celebrating the Wright brothers' flight at Hanaudriere. The consequence of this is that technologies slip the surly bonds of locality, planting themselves anywhere around the world, even as they take on substantially different meanings in different cultural contexts.

**Figure 3.1.** The airplane flies around the world, *Le Monde Illustre* (1912). *Chronicle* / Alamy Stock Photo. Used with permission.

A final defining characteristic of technology is its association with magic (Gell 1988), which is reinforced by the aesthetics of technology and their association with modernism. The design of airplanes is closely based on the laws of aerodynamics, but beyond these we have an idea of how an airplane *ought* to look: smooth surfaces with components concealed, so that the actual mechanism is not evident. One might observe that modernist aesthetics and the technological society grew together, and in fact the emphasis within modernism and modernist aesthetics on a break with the past is part of the allure of technology (Berman 1982). *Magic*, as any magician can explain, is a sleight of hand, hiding cause and effect; so too the translation of matter and energy and information is invisible to the contemporary eye, simply magic.

Part of the magic of technology is what Bryan Pfaffenberger (1992a) calls "technological drama." The initial achievement of any technology, whether the first airplane taking to the sky or the first man landing on the moon, is a dramatic event, sometimes witnessed by millions. After time, these events become routine, but at first they are dramatic. Part of the drama is the agon of whether or not it will work, and by and for whom—the technologies' role in contemporary life. Will flying only serve the military, or will it eventually result in flying cars in every driveway? Will computers be primarily for laboratory research and business productivity, or will they become entertainment devices? Will they sit on our desks or be carried around in our pockets? New technologies are exciting. After a while, they become routine, but at the time there is a sense that all is changing, changing utterly.

Each of these characteristics means that technologies potentially pose challenges to the commons that simpler instrumentalities do not. The independence of technology from locality means that monitoring can take place anywhere around the world. Scalability poses challenges for local conditions and hence appropriation rules, and the association of technology with magic (and religion) can lead to feelings of helplessness. The awe and wonder of modernist aesthetics suggest an awesome power and inevitability. Each of these challenges will be elaborated in the remainder of this chapter.

In sum, technology poses a challenge to collective understandings and the common good in a way that simpler tools could not. These challenges include (but are not limited to) *sensemaking* ("what does this all mean?"), *staging* ("where is this being acted out?" and "on what sort of national or international stage?"), and *cause and effect* ("isn't this just magical?"). The *character* of technology at times defies achieving a sense of the common good.

## Natural Resources and the Common Good

The most obvious foundation for the common good is those common pool resources from which members of a society cannot be excluded, but which, through overexploitation, can be depleted or polluted. Air and water are obvious examples of such resources, with which human societies lived in harmony for millennia. Although in some remote corners of the world ecosystems have collapsed, whether those of the Norse in Greenland or the Anasazi of Central America, it was only with the Industrial Revolution that exhausting the entire planet's natural resources became a possibility.

As we saw in Chapter 2, in *Governing the Commons* Elinor Ostrom identifies four different types of goods, based on subtractability and excludability: private goods, public goods, club or toll goods, and common pool resources, as shown in Table 2.1 ("Types of Goods by Exclusion and Subtractability") in the previous chapter. Private goods, which are depletable but also excludable, have been the focus of liberal economics for nearly three centuries, with the result that their accumulation has become a singular objective of policy at the expense of other forms of wealth. Natural resources—air, water, forests, meadows—are the prime examples of common pool resources, which are depletable yet not excludable, and human societies have at times exploited these to extinction. These can be enclosed or privatized, as in the example of "air rights" or "sunlight rights" noted in the previous chapter. Public goods, such as safe streets and primary education, are neither subtractable nor excludable, and a measure of civilization, as contrasted to tribal formations, is in its provision of public goods. Primary schooling, at least since the nineteenth century, has been widely recognized as a public good, although contemporary efforts to privatize it in the form of "charter schools," seen here as a latter-day enclosure movement, raise the question of just how advanced modern societies truly are. Club goods or toll goods, whether libraries or journal subscriptions, on the other hand, are not depletable yet are excludable, and hence require different institutional arrangements.[1]

The entire character of a society's institutions can be analyzed in terms of which combination of goods—public, private, common pool, or club goods—they optimize. In the medieval village, the "commons," a common pool resource, took precedence, yet with the advent of the liberal economy private goods became ascendant. In a class-based society, club goods and family heritage are most important, and tokens of family, whether names or heirlooms, occupy a more prominent location. Adam Smith's *The Wealth of Nations*, arguing for the primacy of the free market in the provision of (private) goods, is the foundational text for the liberal order.

As outlined in the previous chapter, Ostrom identified eight conditions under which communities have preserved their commons. These include

- clearly designed boundaries;
- congruence between appropriation and provision rules and local conditions;
- collective choice arrangements;
- monitoring;

- graduated sanctions;
- conflict resolution mechanisms;
- minimal recognition of rights to organize; and
- nested enterprises.

These institutional and technological conditions enable societies to govern their commons and maintain the common good.

Some conditions such as "minimal recognition of rights to organize" are clearly institutional, but others, such as "monitoring" or "clearly designed boundaries," have a technological dimension. Most of the eight conditions are dependent on informal connections among local or regional actors. "Monitoring," for example, or "graduated sanctions" are more easily achieved in village-level societies, where a sharp look can be sufficient to discourage inappropriate behavior. With the exception of large-scale systems, which Ostrom demonstrates require "nested enterprises" to manage, every one of these governing requirements exists within a context of collective thought and action.

Most of these are enabled or constrained by the tools and technologies that are available. "Monitoring," for example, takes on a different aspect with the availability of facial recognition technologies that, with sufficient resources, could be deployed on an industrial scale (and indeed have been in China's "social credit system"; see Chapter 4, Note 3). Likewise "local conditions" are affected by the bounding of the "local"; with a hillside meadow, this is fairly obvious, but a deep sea fishery with new harvesting technologies is more problematic, and with Facebook this is even more so. The networks that Facebook explores and exploits have virtually no boundaries, or at least none that we have discovered yet. *Attention*—an ambient good, desired by political leaders, becomes a new resource with business models that rest on harvesting eyeballs, as described in Tim Wu's *The Attention Merchants* (2016). Facebook, the new public square, gives away its services to billions of users, and collects and aggregates terabytes of data on the users' preferences ("likes"), network connections ("friends"), and personal characteristics. "Friendship" is thus cultivated and harvested within this new commons, and such data is invaluable to Facebook's primary customers, advertisers. "Click bait" is a new good, nonexistent before the appearance of the internet. Facebook, Google, and other social media companies have innovated with business models based on these new enclosures.

The rapid acceleration of technological capabilities is indicative of a more general race between education and technology (Katz and Goldin 2008). "Nested enterprises," of course, the final condition in the list above, can be glossed as "institutions," and in contemporary society an immense institutional apparatus, from the United States Environmental Protection Agency to the National Oceanic and Atmospheric Agency to agencies in every state and many municipalities, exists to maintain the common pool of clean air, water, and uncontaminated soil on which our society depends. For many of these institutions, there is a race between the agencies' capabilities and newer sources of environmental degradation, whether in the form of new chemical pollution or new forms of energy extraction, with a strong chorus of denial that a problem even exists.[2] Technological breakthroughs, whether hydraulic fracturing or offshore oil rigs, are applauded, with environmental impact statements being only a *pro forma* afterthought. For an example of this frivolity, the "environmental impact statement" for the offshore oil rig Deepwater Horizon, which exploded in the Gulf of Mexico in 2010, included the potential threat to seals, a species rarely found at temperate latitudes. It would be simplistic to assert that energy companies such as ExxonMobil are indifferent to their activities' environmental consequences, yet the competitive nature of their industry and the positive accent given to new technologies create a pressure for adopting new technological advances. Technology puts this competition on steroids, creating a self-reinforcing cycle between advances in environmental degradation and competitive success.

Perhaps the most alarming technological threat to shared natural resources is found in concerns over global warming, in which clashes between technological acceleration and institutional failure are on display in the halls of Congress. When Senator James Inhofe (a Republican from Oklahoma, a major oil-producing state) brought a snowball onto the Senate floor on 26 February 2015 to prove that global warming was a myth, it was widely mocked as an ignorant stunt. Yet millions fail to understand the distinction between climate (long-term atmospheric trends) and weather (conditions at the moment). Time horizons are an important part of any culture, and Americans' focus on the here and now blots out any comprehension both of history and of future states. The horizons of time and space are fundamental to the cosmological assumptions of any culture, assumptions about "who are we?" and "where do we fit into the universe?" Even more fail to understand how this sort of ignorance (described in the final section of this chapter) can seem "just natural," that is, embedded in cultural axioms including horizons of space and time. Such public failures to understand may be one of the greatest hazards of a technological society. The "race between education and technology," for example, is symptomatic not simply of an institutional failure to keep up with technological acceleration. It also represents a degradation of education from a rite of passage opening doors to civic life into preparation for standardized tests.

## Technologies and Institutions of Nation-Building

One of the major innovations of the Industrial Revolution, not always recognized as such, is the emergence of the nation-state as the dominant locus of civic identification (Anderson 1983). In contrast to the tribes and kingdoms and dynasties and villages through which most people derived their collective identity for nearly all of recorded history, the nation-state, based on the republican form of government it encapsulates, is a very recent invention in human history, and is closely associated with the Industrial Revolution (Gellner 1983). Although nations are built around mythologies that extend into the mists of a distant past, it has only been in the last three centuries that the nation-state has come to be recognized as a preferred civil unit.

The Industrial Revolution brought together several social forms that all existed prior to the seventeenth century. The first of these was the factory system, in which production and process supervision exist in a central location. Tasks such as spinning and weaving, which were previously domestic tasks, were assembled into factories. Sugar factories in the Caribbean, using unfree labor, were probably the first appearance of the factory system and, as described in the previous chapter, predated James Watt's steam engine by several centuries.

The second social form brought in by the Industrial Revolution was external power. Although water wheels had provided power for productive tasks such as milling and grinding for millennia, James Watt's invention of the steam engine gave this new force, and no less importantly freed production from the geographical tyranny of location.

The third social form, which was truly the innovation of industrialization, was the scaling up of production. What was previously a local affair confined to village and household is now deployed on an intercontinental scale, with supply chains moving raw materials, intermediate components, and finished goods around the globe. This creates a movement of people and information, overcoming local distinctions with the emergence of national identification. This independence of scale, which technology uniquely achieves as noted above, creates the potential that the good produced by technological means is not *common*, but rather sequestered within corporate empires.

The idea of the "common good" pivots on both a shared concept of the good and also on "common-ness," a shared fellow-feeling that "we are all in this together." The *common* good is distinct from the *collective good*—it is possible for an entire population to enjoy abundant material wealth, yet not share in any sense that they have anything in common beyond a statistical abstraction. This lack of felt commonality is often the fate of "class" in America. In contrast to many European nations that still retain strong class traditions, for the most part in America "class" has been reduced to "socioeconomic status," a sociological invention that no one is strongly attached to. How can members of the "lower middle class" feel that they have anything in common? By contrast, in several European nations retaining traces of estate traditions, identities such as *ouvrier et bourgeoisie* or *Arbeiter und Bürger* are loci of strong attachment.

Throughout human history, different peoples at different times have constructed and invested in different collectivities to express a common identity from the earliest foraging bands, to tribes and chiefdoms, and with the development of agriculture, states, dynasties, and empires. Contemporary society contains a plethora of collectives whose *members* would assert that they have something in common, whether cities, churches, or neighborhoods. Many, perhaps most of these imply degrees of "unfreedom"—that is, social bonds—which for most of human history has been part of the human condition. It was only with the rise of the nation-state as a political unit that people could imagine that they shared something in common with their fellow citizens, and only in the nineteenth and twentieth centuries that "nation-building" became a new away of constructing the common good.

Although "nations" are constructed around narratives that extend back into the mists of a distant past, "nationalism"—the idea that a nation of shared ancestry was the appropriate political subdivision of human society—is a more recent invention, dating back only to the Congress of Vienna, which helped settle the European order after the Napoleonic Wars. Benedict Anderson in *Imagined Communities* (1983) charts the growth of nationalism in the eighteenth and nineteenth centuries, and identifies multiple intersecting trends: the decline of dynastic realms, increased geographic mobility, and the growth of print capitalism, through which readers of newspapers could imagine on a daily basis that they were sharing a conversation with compatriots hundreds of miles away. Furthermore, a nation is distinct from all other collectivities, in that it is sanctified by the deaths of those who have made the "ultimate sacrifice."

Nations are distinct from other human aggregations, whether empires or villages, in terms of their coordinates in time, space, and cosmology. Three characteristics of the nation and nationalism, as described by Benedict Anderson and Ernest Gellner, bear on our conceptions of the *common* good. At the top of the list is what Gellner calls "interior universalism"—the idea that all members of the nation have something in common. He contrasts this with "global universalism," the assumption that all of humanity has something in common. Nationalism embodies a form of tribalism, yet one larger than "tribes" in the traditional sense: some nations embrace hundreds of millions of citizens, whereas others have only a few hundred thousand. Each of these embraces a shared idea that "we are special."

The time horizon of the nation extends backward, as noted above, but also forward, imagining perpetual growth. Gellner notes that it was only with the Industrial Revolution and the advent of nationalism that societies could imagine a future of perpetual growth, and create a metric, Gross National Product, to measure it. As discussed further in Chapter 6, although societies have been counting heads since time immemorial, it is only with the rise of the nation-state that they counted economic output. Similarly, it is only with the eighteenth-century "idea of progress" (Bury 1932) that perpetual growth could be imagined.

Perhaps most important is the cosmological horizon of the nation, embracing a unique sense of "who we are" and "what makes us special." For China, the "Middle Kingdom" at the center of the universe, it is the source of harmony between heaven and earth. For France, particularly Paris, the "city of light," it is the apex of human learning that is enshrined in the French language and the heritage of the Enlightenment. For America, it is the perpetual frontier nation, advancing civilization into regions of savagery. Despite the Bureau of the Census declaring the frontier closed in 1889, Americans have always imagined themselves on the frontier or created "new frontiers," most recently the "electronic frontier" of the internet. In America, from the very beginning, the frontier has been a commons.

Each of these has profound implications for how nations, as contrasted to other collectivities, define and perceive the common good, both in terms of what *good* they pursue, and what they might have in *common* in pursuing it: is the common good material or immaterial, broadly or narrowly shared, limited or unlimited, sacred or profane? In

France, still basking in the heritage of the Enlightenment, reason and the Cartesian method are not simply academic exercises; they define the nation. In China, by contrast, harmony on earth and in heaven and in between is an idealization of the cosmic order. In sum, the Industrial Revolution and the consequent rise in nationalism both opened up new possibilities for the common good, but they also created new challenges.

After World War II, a cataclysm that rivalled the Napoleonic Wars in territorial scope and ended with the foundation of the United Nations, "new nations" began emerging around the world. The United Nations was founded in 1945 with 51 members; 70 years later, it had 193 members, with "new nations" such as Tuvalu and Tonga creating a "new nations movement" that reorganized the world. The archetype for these was the United States of America, the "first new nation" (Lipset 1963) to emerge in the eighteenth century out of a monarchial past. "Nation-building" was a collective project around the world, constructing new nations out of the ashes of World War II and colonial ventures.

In the nineteenth century, the United States of America—the "first new nation"—set out on an experiment in nation-building that was celebrated in many distinguished works, including Alexis de Tocqueville's *Democracy in America* (1835/1840), Walt Whitman's *Leaves of Grass* (1855), and James Bryce's *The American Commonwealth* (1888). De Tocqueville, a French aristocrat, visited the United States in 1831, at the emergence of Jacksonian democracy, and found the American attitudes toward their community so strange that he had to coin a new term for this attitude: "individualism." Two generations later, James Bryce, a British Minister of Parliament, visited the United States at the height of the Gilded Age and published his reflections in *The American Commonwealth*, in which he offered guarded hope for a nation at the forefront of the world's technological development. In between, Walt Whitman, perhaps the most original American poet, celebrated American uniqueness and exuberance in *Leaves of Grass*. The landscape that Whitman supplied, of exuberant freedom and exploration, has also been definitive of America.

The American archetype for nation-building had several components that have been replicated around the world. These components include settlement of the wilderness (typically displacing indigenous peoples); they also include transportation systems uniting different localities and landscapes. Further, education and other civil institutions and community-building are central to nation-building.

Occupation of territory is the first step, whether in Gaul, the Americas, China, or Russia. Typically, this results in the displacement of indigenous peoples, giving *every* new nation a brush with colonialism. To occupy territory, nations must build settlements, roads, and other infrastructure. Infrastructure is the foundation of civilization, and it is usually not recognized as such because "infrastructure" is such a colorless term. Without systems to promote movement, overcome geographic separations such as rivers, supply clean water, and dispose of waste, cities, such as many third-world aggregations even today, are little more than pestilential slums that are avoided by those wealthy enough to retreat to their country estates, a dilemma that has persisted even into the current century. It was only with the rise of industry, and the consequent need to aggregate large numbers of working men, that governments began to take an interest in urban infrastructure. Although ancient imperial cities such as Rome and Beijing were architectural monuments, beyond them urban order was at best haphazard. The earliest cities, as Lewis Mumford (1961) asserts, were about projecting power, whether that of priests or warlords. Marcus Vitruvius Pollio, in the first century BCE with his *The Ten Books of Architecture*, gave these projections of power a nobility that has defined urbanity for thousands of years since (see Chapter 1).

Industrial scale infrastructure is dependent on standards, which as noted above are *the* defining characteristic of technology and are closely associated with nation-state regimes: the difference between metric and imperial weights and measures is adequate testimony to this. Standards for the width of highways, railway track gauges, and the voltage of electrical current and even such mundane details as the pitch of screw threads are required to stitch together local affairs into large-scale assemblages. Standards are a form of collective action, a public good, and the "standards wars" that accompany the introduction of *any* new technology create momentary winners and losers, yet all agree that a settled standard is preferable to an array of nonstandardized components. Perhaps the earliest "standards war" was the competition between alternating and direct current and voltages for electric power transmission, a competition that was settled differently on different continents. Standards are a form of public good, and ultimately require the sanction of state-level standard-setting.

"Infrastructure" has recently become a political football, with most proposals falling far short of the $4.6 trillion that is needed for upgrading America's infrastructure.[3] This is in large part because, while most citizens appreciate paved roads, fewer are willing to support the taxes needed to maintain them. Roads, and infrastructure generally, are archetypal public goods, and the failure of the public to support them is nothing less than free-riding on a continental scale, living off the efforts of a previous generation.

The earliest roads, whether Roman roads or the military roads of the Qin Dynasty, initially served the interests of centralized states, projecting their power into the provinces. Transportation systems reflect the nation's self-conception, whether a collectivity of small settlements, a confederation of republics, or a continental empire. Prior to independence, there was no transportation system uniting the 13 Colonies. Beginning in 1775 with Daniel Boone's Wilderness Road, which linked the eastern seaboard with the interior through the Cumberland Gap, the United States began to build an integrated nation. In 1789, the Constitutional Convention authorized the creation of Post Roads to facilitate commerce, and in 1811 construction started on the National Road, whose name, like Dwight D. Eisenhower's National System of Interstate and Defense Highways in the next century, made clear that it had far greater resonance than simply "infrastructure." Transportation systems generally reflect a nation's self-conception, and in the United States, a federation of 50 states, most transportation systems devolve into state-organized systems. Only when transportation technologies *inevitably* leap over state boundaries, as is the case with air transport, does the federal government take a lead role.

The most recent achievement in transportation, the Interstate Highway System, modeled after the German Autobahn that Eisenhower observed in World War II, is a project of nation-building. The most recent frontier of surface transport, high-speed rail, which has been implemented in Europe, China, Japan, Taiwan, and other countries, has stalled in the United States. Outside of the northeast corridor, where the Acela runs from downtown New York City to Washington, DC, in 3.5 hours, thus rivaling air transport, efforts to get high-speed rail implemented have been stalled by a lack of imagination about the future and by a lack of imagination on the part of the nation. Unlike many other countries such as Japan, France, China, and even Taiwan, implementation of high-speed rail has foundered in the United States.

With the Louisiana Purchase in 1803, the United States acquired an immense tract of interior land, and the National Road, from Baltimore, Maryland, to Wheeling, West Virginia, completed in 1837, united the eastern seaboard with the Ohio Valley. Two decades later, the Transcontinental Railway united the continent, although building this would have to wait until the slave states had withdrawn from the Union. The

**Figure 3.2.** A. J. Russell driving the Golden Spike, Promontory Point, Utah (1869). Wikimedia Commons, public domain.

United States government had acquired tracts of land, which it awarded to the land-grant universities, the railways, and homesteaders. The earliest railways connected mine mouths with waterways on which coal and ores could be transported, but with the acquisition of the continental interior there was an urgent need for uniting the nation, which was finally achieved with the Transcontinental Railway. An iconic image from 1869, the driving of the "Golden Spike" at Promontory Point in Utah (Figure 3.2), celebrated the unification of the two coasts. Rail transport and associated technologies (most notably the steam engine) have been central to the definition of the American nation.

Although the United States of America achieved national independence in 1776, building an American *nation* has been an ongoing project, one that became possible only when the lingering remnants of colonialism, chattel slavery in the Southern states, was removed from the Union. A nation that was founded on the rejection of a colonial, imperial power could only realize its destiny when the lingering remnants of colonialism were expunged. From 1861 onward, the United States undertook a massive exercise in nation-building, The Homestead Act, passed in 1862, granted 160 acres to any family that would settle or "homestead" on the land; in 1866, it was clarified to include "Negroes," and in many circles was seen as a counterweight to the tendency (in the Southern states) to amass immense plantations with unfree labor. Overall, more than 1.6 million homesteads were created on the western lands. In 1865, newly emancipated slaves were promised "40 acres and a mule," which soon began a list of broken promises to America's colonial subjects.[4]

In similar fashion, the Morrill Act of 1862 reserved one section in every township for the creation of what became known as land-grant universities, such as Purdue University, Texas A&M, and Cornell University; these were dedicated to the "agricultural and mechanical classes," an unprecedented democratization of higher education that contributed much to the nation's prosperity. Land-grant universities, and the rural and agricultural innovations that they supported, made American agricultural activities some of the most productive in the world, and made rural communities into a throbbing engine of American prosperity in the early years of the twentieth century. An offshoot of the land-grant universities, the Agricultural Extension Service, brought improved farming and homemaking techniques to rural farmers, and was in large part responsible for the fact that by the end of the century American agriculture was the most productive in the world.

The land-grant universities were a logical extension of the common school movement, identified with Horace Mann, the Secretary of Education in Massachusetts from 1837 to 1848. The earliest public schools in what is now the United States were established in the Massachusetts Bay Colony in 1635, and for many decades afterward Massachusetts took the lead in the spread of public education. In 1837, Horace Mann was appointed Secretary of the Massachusetts Board of Education, and he spent the next 11 years promoting what soon became known as the "common schools," taxpayer-supported public schools open to all. For the remainder of the century, the common schools, which today we would call public schools, spread all over the country, albeit with massive resistance in states with large African American populations. Even well into the twentieth century, to identify a young man or woman as having attended the "common schools," was a mark of class inferiority. The entire jurisprudence of racial equality in education, from Plessy v. Ferguson in 1896 to Brown v. Board of Education in 1954 can be understood as an extended exercise in American self-definition.

Even today, the character of education remains an unsettled question: is it a public good (from which all benefit), a club good admitting a select few, a toll good available to those who can pay, a private good, or a common pool resource? Cogent arguments can be made for each of these positions, in large part because in modern society "education" is a "key word" (Williams 1983), metaphorically embracing goods of all character. As a private good, vocational education trains young men and women for specific job skills, which they can then use for gainful employment. As a club good, higher education admits aspiring young men and women to the select company of professionals, while "prep schools" educate the children of the elite in preparation for admission to institutions such as Harvard or Yale; this preparation extends far beyond "reading, writing, and arithmetic" to include both knowledge of social traditions and social graces that are tokens of exclusive membership. Yet as a public good, primary and secondary education elevate the character of citizenship, so that in a democracy citizens can make informed decisions about their government. There is a general public benefit from a community's level of educational attainment in multiple ways, including general prosperity, social stability, and democratic participation. Nations with higher rates of educational attainment are more stable and prosperous than others, and education is unfailingly *the* industry of nation-building. By contrast, the contemporary emphasis on science, technology, engineering, and mathematics (the so-called "STEM" disciplines), at the expense of history, the humanities, and the social sciences, views education as primarily for creating interchangeable parts for the industrial machine.

Current controversies over public education illustrate these tensions: movements for "school choice" and "charter schools" diminish the public character of education, using public resources (tax revenues) to underwrite *private* advantages. These movements occupy a range of possibilities, from "charter schools" privately managed yet funded with taxpayer dollars presented as an alternative to "failing" public schools, to "school choice" proposals giving parents a choice as to which primary and secondary schools their children can attend, to for-profit proprietary academies.

The privatization of public education, even when it is not motivated by the rent-seeking of proprietary academies, is a neoliberal enclosure movement. In this enclosure, cultural spaces are fenced off from democratic participation. In a postindustrial society, the cultural resources, fundamental to civic participation become an exclusive preserve of those whose wealth, education, and social capital enable them to make strategic and informed decisions regarding their children's education. This twenty-first-century enclosure, making public goods into a private investment, is similar in character to the enclosing of agricultural resources in the original enclosure movement.

In 1983, the National Commission on Excellence in Education, appointed by President Ronald Reagan, published a report, *A Nation at Risk*. This report found that a marked decline in test scores, verbal and quantitative capabilities, and 19 academic tests of American students indicated that educational standards were declining. Americans were never first or second and, in comparison with other industrialized nations, were last seven times (National Commission on Excellence in Education 1983). Although subsequent studies failed to confirm the dire warnings (Ansary 2007, for example), the rhetoric of *A Nation at Risk*, coinciding with the neoliberal turn in national and international politics, touched off the "school wars." For several decades, controversies over the character of education have dominated American educational discourse. Before the 1980s, America had generally accepted a two- (or three-)tier educational system, in which (often segregated) public schools served a majority of the population and a thin, upper crust of private schools served the elite. Racial minorities were consigned to a backwater of underfunded and undersupervised schools. Coincident with the rise of globalization, in which global competitive forces battered the American economy, *A Nation at Risk* stated forcefully that America's standing in the world depended on upgrading the quality of education. Numerous proposals for standards, tracking, "school choice," charter schools, and privatization began to emerge.

Coincident with the common school movement headed by Horace Mann has been the rise of standardized tests, a technology whose proliferation (in terms of machine scoring) in the 1970s onward marked the beginning of the "school wars" that still rage. Prior to the 1830s, standardized, multiple-choice examinations were practically unknown, and when students had to be evaluated it could be on the basis of written essays or oral recitations. Multiple choice exams, when they existed, were graded by hand. But with a flood of children of illiterate agriculturists and mechanicals coming into the schools, a new, scalable mechanism for sorting and classifying the charges and for deciding who could advance and who should withdraw was needed.

A standardized test is a technology: it is the software of academic sorting and grading. It is an instrument that can be scaled up to test literally millions of students. It is a separate but closely related matter to the computerized scoring that is now pervasive. The Scholastic Aptitude Test (SAT), first introduced in 1926, was scaled up with machine scoring after World War II. It is based on written standards, and converts a raw material (students) into a finished product (classified students). The entire apparatus of standardizing reduces the product of education to that which is machine-scorable. Other grading mechanisms, whether oral recitations or written essays, are pushed aside in favor of that which can be processed on a massive scale. Most recently, the College Board has added to the verbal and mathematical segments of the SAT an "adversity index" to quantify the advantages or disadvantages that college-bound students have or must overcome. Standardized tests are a technology of nation-building: the classifying and disciplining of an entire population before they reach adulthood into winners (graduates) and losers (dropouts). In a competitive economy, diplomas are seen as the surest ticket to success, and those who fail are consigned to the margins of society.

Education is closely related to citizenship, both in its foundation and in its purpose. In the Middle Ages, the king's *subjects* outside the nobility neither needed nor were entitled to an education; only those entering the priesthood needed to be able to read and write. Noble families hired tutors, and merchant families made their own arrangements. In America, it was only in the Jacksonian era and with the birth of the common school movement, ostensibly providing a publicly supported primary education, that the idea of education as a public good began to gain traction. Yet for the past nearly two hundred years, the combination of education (literacy, preparation for citizenship), training (in a specific skill), and discipline (both mental and emotional),[5] as well as issues such as tracking (separate educational tracks for students of different abilities), integration, and most recently school choice and charter schools have muddied the waters. Behind all of these is the question of the character of a society—whether it should be one where aristocratic traditions survive in an educational system that determines a young man's or woman's life chances from an early age, or a democratic society with opportunities open to all. In England, universal schooling was introduced in the nineteenth century, with a distinction among grammar schools and secondary schools; in France, universal education dates back to the Revolution. In a democratic society, education is a public good, and education's failures are less an institutional failure than a failure of democracy.

Perhaps the biggest challenge to the character of public education, in part because it is presented by forces that seem efficient with an aura of inevitability, is the use of computer technology in education.

Although the use of media goes back at least to the 1950s with instructional television, and today is ubiquitous in PowerPoint presentations and "smart" classrooms, proposals to replace in-person instruction with Massive Online Open Classrooms (MOOCs) have seduced public officials and institutions of all sorts, from for-profit universities to Harvard. The massive fraud of MOOCs is, of course, that while they may be effective for teaching a static and highly structured body of knowledge, such as mathematics or Latin, they are completely pointless in teaching the interpersonal or conceptual skills or social graces critical for most managerial or professional occupations, let alone civic life. Imagination, critical thinking, judgment, creativity, and other mental faculties can only be taught in an interpersonal, dialectic context. Nobody would want a surgeon who had learned his skills sitting at a computer terminal, or a lawyer whose only experience in advocacy was interacting with a MOOC. These technologies are completely useless for teaching creativity or critical thinking except in a structured (i.e., predictable) format, an irony that often escapes their advocates. The counterpart of MOOCs in the classroom is the use of robots in the workplace, which has been a subject of speculation and nerdy fascination for more than a century. By robotizing all of education, except education for the most privileged, MOOCs mechanize all of cultural and civic production, freezing invention and evolution at a fixed point in time.

Education holds up a mirror to a nation's soul, and schemes for tracking and school choice and charter schools and robotizing signal that the nation has given up any notion of the common good. For the few whose only understanding of the good is confined to private goods, this may be acceptable, but for the vast majority of citizens it represents an abdication. Educational technology is hardly the cause of these trends, but once invested and implemented it gives them a shape and sturdiness that is difficult to undo.

In sum, the "nation" should be understood as a "commons," and transportation technologies, communication technologies, and educational technologies all were central to nation-building in the nineteenth and twentieth centuries. This was successful for most of these two centuries because there was a national *vision*, a feeling of shared fate. More recently, as neoliberalism has undermined the sense that "we're all in this together," these same technologies are now prying the nation apart. The enclosure movement of neoliberalism, like the enclosure movement of the early Industrial Revolution, is a frontal assault on the common good.

## Health as a Public Good

Common goods, whether public goods, club goods, or common pool resources, in contrast to collective goods, are shared: they define a commonality among the members of a society, a bonding that implies mutual obligations. Human societies have at times approached natural abundance like pigs at a trough, consuming as much as possible with little concern for the others. This phenomenon is evident in what is sometimes called the "resource curse," also known as the "paradox of plenty," the fact that societies such as Saudi Arabia, Venezuela, and Angola, blessed with an abundance of natural resources, often do not feel compelled to develop the institutions of civil society, retaining an absolute monarchy, with an ample treasury, at a time when monarchies around the world are on the decline. In contrast, countries such as Japan or Switzerland, which are relatively resource-poor, have developed strong institutions including both government and civil society institutions. Although closer inspection has shown that other variables such as dependence on exports and history of development play a part, the general pattern of poverty in the midst of plenty is a paradox not confined to undeveloped nations.

A major debate in the current century is over the nature of health and healthcare as goods, whether public or private. It was decided at the beginning of the twentieth century in a rapidly urbanizing society that "public health"—sanitation, hygiene, safe drinking water, pure food—is a public good. This resulted in the passage of the Pure Food and Drug Act of 1906, and in similar measures in nearly every city and nearly every industrialized country. In the current century, deciding whether an individual's health is a matter of social concern or "personal responsibility" is fiercely debated, with many arguing against vaccines and other public health measures. On the one hand, advocates of Medicare for All insist that the government has a responsibility to underwrite individuals' health, pointing to similar schemes in Canada and Europe. The Canadian healthcare system, or more accurately Canada's 13 provincial and territorial systems, supports doctors' visits and hospitalization through taxes on incomes above $20,000. On the other hand, strong political interests point out that unhealthy behaviors such as excessive drinking and overeating and drug use are matters that are up to the individual—matters in which the government should not intervene. Behind this argument, of course, is the insurance industry and the pharmaceutical industry, both of which have monetized health and illness, with the result that the United States spends more per capita on health than any other industrialized country yet has some of the poorest results. Also underlying this argument is what one might call "lifestyle industries" promoting drinking, sugar-rich foods, saturated fats, and (at least until the late twentieth century) smoking. Among the OECD countries, the United States ranks dead last, spending more than $10,000 per capita on healthcare (compared, for example, with Great Britain, which spends approximately $4,000 per capita), yet having some of the highest mortality and morbidity rates for many diseases. This actually is no paradox at all once one recognizes that American society optimizes private goods not simply at the neglect but also at the expense of public goods, a dynamic that has yet to be confronted. Health is a public good, with many of the same characteristics (low subtractability and difficult exclusion) that Hess and Ostrom (2007) identified for other public goods.

The *act* of sharing a common good, whether a public good or a club good, is an enactment of kinship, an affirmative statement that we have something in common. Efforts to privatize or monetize public goods, whether education or health, are a statement that "we have nothing in common."

Communicable diseases might be considered a "public hazard": they are not subtractable, nor are individuals easily excluded. At times of major plagues, one could avoid them only by withdrawing from society altogether, as sometimes was necessary during the Middle Ages. "Hazards," of course, are the obverse of "goods," and can be similarly classified; further, we can examine and classify private hazards (unsafe behavior), public hazards (communicable diseases, reckless driving), common pool hazards (pollution), and club or lifestyle hazards, which are excludable but not depletable. That is, one's participation in an unhealthy lifestyle does not diminish the hazard for others, but rather one can *choose* to undertake an unhealthy lifestyle. Similarly, in the absence of government regulation, unsafe food can only be avoided by returning to a rural lifestyle and growing all that one consumes. Lifestyle hazards, by contrast—obesity, alcoholism, drug addiction, unprotected sex—are clearly matters where individual volition plays a major part, although each of these has a dimension of *belonging*—drinking, drug use, and eating start out as expressions of sociability, although subsequent overindulgence makes them hazardous.

Belonging and sociability deserve more attention as impulses toward consumption. These impulses were first tapped into with the growth of advertising and media in the twentieth century, and now with social media they have acquired additional appeal. As described in Section 3 of the next chapter on "The Landscape of Desire," they have become a major driver in the economy, and Tim Wu's (2016) "attention merchants" have monetized belonging.

In the twentieth century, a multi-trillion-dollar advertising industry seeks to harness individual volition toward corporate ends, and certain lifestyle hazards such as alcoholism and obesity, might be considered club hazards, inasmuch as the root of such behaviors is frequently a wish to belong. Max Weber developed the concept of *Lebensführung*, which is typically translated as "lifestyle," as an attribute of status groups: "In content, status honor is normally expressed by the fact that above all else a specific *style of life* can be expected from all those who wish to belong to the circle" (Weber 1946: 187). This concept is often misappropriated to refer to any pattern of behavior. For Weber, *Lebensführung* was associated with a social status: membership in a status group. In modern, non-estate societies such as the United States, with far weaker class traditions, status groups as bounded entities have largely been replaced by statistical abstractions such as social strata. By contrast, "lifestyles" are clearly tokens of identity and belonging. Brands, for example, are far more than trademarks; they are sources of identity, club goods, and "brand equity" is one of the major factors in a postindustrial economy.

Between private and public hazards are numerous ambiguous situations where parsing the line between the individual and the social is impossibly complex: are cancers caused by lifestyles, heredity, environmental conditions, or some combination of all of these? Is the decision to smoke tobacco a matter of individual volition or social pressure? The same question could be asked about many or perhaps most illnesses. In the face of answering (and litigating) such hopelessly complex issues, most industrial nations have opted to make, at least to some limited degree, healthcare a public good supported by taxes, and have done so with strong public support.

The solution in the United States, by contrast, particularly following World War II, a time when wage and price controls limited salary increases, was for many employers to offer their workers health insurance, thus creating what is today a trillion-dollar industry that was practically nonexistent two decades earlier. Insurance, which might be considered a toll good, was in its early years considered "socialism;" an accurate description, but in the United States carrying overtones of xenophobia. Insurance in many forms is now an accepted and profitable business. "Social insurance," first started in Germany in 1883, and adopted in the United States in the form of Social Security in 1933 (which itself was denounced in its early years as "socialism"), is now strongly defended across the political spectrum. In 1965, the Social Security system was extended to provide health insurance (Medicare) to those over 65; controversial at the time, and denounced by Ronald Reagan as a precursor to socialism, it is now also strongly defended. "Keep your big government hands off my Medicare" was the slogan of thousands in 2010 whose difficulty with the Obama administration was not simply ideological but cosmological. An ideological difference can be settled by discussion and compromise, whereas a cosmological difference, a challenge to "who I am," cannot. Hurling the label "socialism" at anyone who wants to retreat from the privatization of nearly any good taps into deep-seated concerns about "who we are."

A strict definition of socialism is the making of goods and hazards a social rather than an individual responsibility. Liability insurance for automobile drivers, for example, which is required by law in most states, results in a common pool hazard of risk. (By "pooling" risk, insurance schemes turn individual hazard into a common pool hazard.) An *ideological* definition, by contrast, is any infringement on the profit-making potential of any good or any hazard, whether healthcare or old age, and proposals to privatize social security early in the current century ran up against a brick wall of impossibility. As befits the world's most individualistic nation, any matter that infringes on the individual can be painted as an alien imposition. If benefits are shared with "those people" (typically racial or ethnic minorities), it becomes an assault on one's identity. More bluntly, one of the greatest threats to ideas of the common good is the (tribal) denial that citizens have anything in common.

This back-and-forth history points to an abiding issue in the construction of the common good. In countries such as Denmark, with little ethnic diversity, social welfare schemes are broadly accepted, whereas in diverse countries they are less so. In the United States, with the lingering effects of a heritage of slavery, resistance to social welfare schemes is colored by racist suspicions. Construing the common good among people who feel that they have little in common is, at best, an arduous task. With the advance of medical science and technology, offering remedies for multiple infirmities at a cost, the stakes have gone up on healthcare, making the provision of healthcare one of the hottest political issues today. A public health crisis such as the pandemic of 2020 accentuates these stakes.

More generally, some goods are inherently private goods, whereas others are inherently shared. The *value* of an heirloom is in the family history that it is a token of, not in the *price* it would fetch at a pawn shop. Similarly, a meal can be a club good: insofar as it is *shared*, it can become a token of kinship. Contrapositively, useful skills, whether in auto repair or carpentry, are private goods: they are the exclusive property of the person who has acquired them, although in guild systems these should be considered club goods. The value of goods, in other words, is as much in their institutional context as in their intrinsic character *per se*. When one surveys the entire expanse of goods over the course of history, it is difficult to find very many that are exclusively private. *Knowledge*, which Ostrom identified as a typical public good, can be widely shared, yet the lack of knowledge, ignorance, like communicable diseases, is a public hazard, all too common in a technological society.

## The Constitution of Ignorance

In the social sciences, "social constructionism" is a widely accepted perspective recognizing that technology, knowledge, and even reality are all socially constructed: they represent not a "natural" evolution from discovery or invention, or even the "natural" order, so much as a willful focus on specific (socially negotiated) problems by diverse groups attempting to solve diverse problems and the material environment. The concept of "social construction" was first introduced by Peter Berger and Thomas Luckmann in 1966 in a monograph titled *The Social Construction of Reality*. In technology studies, the "social construction of technology" is widely accepted (Pinch and Bijker 1984), stipulating that technological objects evolve in response to social pressures and interests. The bicycle, as noted above, was first designed by Leonardo da Vinci, yet it would have to wait until the end of the nineteenth century, with the growth of cities and new transport challenges, before it would become a serious transportation alternative. Similarly, even nature is socially constructed, with numerous tribal societies defining their totemic clans in terms of kinship with the "natural" order. The French anthropologist Claude Lévi-Strauss, in *La Pensée Sauvage* (translated as *The Savage Mind*, although perhaps more accurately as *Thought in the Wild*; see Lévi-Strauss [1966] 1969) identified the classification of natural species and human tribes as analogical constructions; the Eagle Clan was to the Wolf Clan as eagles were to wolves: not in terms of biological descent, but rather in analogical resemblance. John Locke's (1968) "state of nature," as noted at the end of the previous chapter, was, in fact, less a discovery and more a conceptual assemblage created to solve the moral and cosmological problems of European expansion, contrasting the "state of nature" with civilization and making clear the superiority of the latter.

In today's technological environment, we are confronted with the fact that technology facilitates ignorance and discord as well as knowledge and enlightenment. Any comparison of "more" or "less" would be spurious here, but it is undeniable that conspiracy theories and xenophobia thrive on the internet. In this final section, I would like to suggest that this is a feature, not a bug—it is an inevitable consequence of the technology, not an accidental by-product of it. Knowledge- and reality-defying movements thrive on the internet, a state of affairs unknown before the end of the twentieth century.

An optimistic view favors the forward march of enlightenment, as science pierces the veil of nature, revealing truth, which, when applied, leads to the improvement of society. The idea that history bends toward improvement, however, only was discovered in the eighteenth-century French Enlightenment, when the decadence of the feudal order, as represented by the Bourbon monarchs, contrasted with the exciting possibilities of the New World. Events of the twentieth century—whether warfare on a scale previously unimaginable, or totalitarianism that led to millions of deaths, industry altering the planet's climate, or surveillance on a gargantuan scale, all abetted by technology—have called this optimistic view into question. Although all of these are contentious issues, the fact that significant parties, factions, and interests promote climate change or mass killing or invasions of privacy or racial hostility on a global scale, often in the name of "progress," and the fact that such promotion is typically accelerated on the internet, suggests a more sinister process. Although the advancement of knowledge is undeniable, the advancement of wisdom—knowledge coupled with judgment—is more dubious.

Although the brilliant light of knowledge dispels the shadows of ignorance, the willful avoidance of knowledge—ignorance—is not only an ongoing issue, but an abiding paradox in a technological society. Just as useful knowledge is a public good (Ostrom and Hess 2007), so too organized ignorance is a public hazard: this is an inevitable dynamic in a technological society. More pointedly, technological advances, whether large-scale industry in the twentieth century or large-scale information technology into the twenty-first, has been accompanied by a rise in knowledge-denying social movements, such as "fundamentalism," in the twentieth century, and internet trolls in the current century, who have been orchestrated on an industrial scale by Russia's Internet Research Agency. Once one recognizes that, in today's world, ignorance can be both intentional and weaponized by technology, then one is provoked to uncover numerous examples of this, whether anti-vaccination crusades, propaganda masquerading as journalism over the internet, or financial instruments whose opacity and complexity nearly wrecked the world economy in 2008 (Ho 2009; Tett 2009; Batteau 2012a). "Fintech," as elaborated in Chapter 7, uses the magic of technology to persuade millions that they can achieve wealth without effort or risk.

The resolution of this paradox is that any given technological object is focused on augmenting a *limited* range of human capabilities, whether spreading messages, building dwellings, aggregating liquidity, or killing other humans, crowding out much of the full spectrum of human interest. Thus, text messaging, for but one of many examples, speeds alphabetic messages around the globe at the expense of the many subtleties—facial expression, body language, tone of voice—of face-to-face discourse. Nuance—perhaps *the* critical attribute of any successful negotiation—is discarded in favor of "emojis," whose cartoonish character mocks genuine human feelings. Communication thus becomes a race to the bottom, in which the key to a message "going viral" is to go vile, and public discourse is cheapened.

The ignorance that is created has three elements: the first is a strong sense of almost tribal identity, meaning a sense of self that cuts off connections with other who are not members of one's tribe. "Racial" identities are an obvious example, but cult memberships or some political affiliations can equally be tribal. "Tribalism" is the basis of "othering," the denial that some other groups have anything in common with us. It is the opposite of openness.

The second element of the constitution of ignorance is a cosmology, a sense of the order of the universe, which gives divine sanction both to perceptions and fabrications. As described above, if one's sense of order is based on biblical narratives, then the *facts* of evolution must be rejected. Many other examples of cosmologically driven ignorance would include denial of climate change, or affirmation of the "natural" superiority of the white race. The fact that millions subscribe to these ideas is evidence of the durability of the constitution of ignorance.

The final element of the constitution of ignorance is a conviction that one's "knowledge" is privileged, along with that of other members of one's tribe, and the rest of the world does not know what they are talking about and need not be listened to. A closed discussion is inevitable. The constitution of ignorance, as presented here, is the opposite of the "constitution of knowledge" as celebrated by Jonathan Rauch

(2021) and other members of the "reality-based community" that Rauch embraces. Truth is thus private, not public, and professionalism and institutionalism are discounted. In the race between technology and education, described earlier in this chapter, the triumph of ignorance is inevitable.

The capability of social media to promote outlandish conspiracy theories, such as "pizzagate" (the allegation that Hillary Clinton was running a pedophile racket) or "birtherism" (the allegation that Barack Obama was born in Africa) is obvious. In a barroom argument, we have many signals to help us determine whether someone shouting is just a raving drunk or truly to be taken seriously: not just the smell of his breath, but his posture, body language, physical appearance, and tone of voice, all of which are mostly unavailable through social media. Further, in the bar, he might be a recognizable character and accordingly credited or discounted. By contrast, the only basis for crediting or discrediting an anonymous post is whether or not it conforms to our earlier prejudices. The triumph of ignorance is inevitable.

In the currency of communication, Gresham's Law (bad money drives out good) applies as well, and brief, impoverished messages over the internet drive out rich and subtle expressions. Bad tweets drive out good. This trade-off between reach and richness of any information system is a well-understood story in the history of communication technology (Evans and Wurster 2000), yet is applicable with certain adjustments to any technology: the steam engine, for example, increased human productivity in many sectors, yet led to an impoverishment of domestic life as production shifted from the household to the factory; similarly, search engines on the internet vastly amplify the array of *facts* at anyone's fingertips, yet *narratives*—the stories that unite us and give facts meaning—are frequently lost in a fog of facts. In the absence of unifying narratives, nations dissolve into competing tribes (Friedman 1994), and sensemaking collapses, to be replaced by algorithms. More pointedly, as nations dissolve into competing tribalisms, whether of ancestry or ideology, any hope of achieving a common good disappears. The role of technology in facilitating this dissolution of the nation-state, to be eclipsed by technological empires, is a major theme discussed in my final chapter.

More broadly, knowledge is accepted *only* if it makes sense, that is, if it fits into one's cosmological outlook. If one's cosmological outlook is based on biblical narratives, then the *facts* of evolution not only can but *must* be rejected. If one's cosmological outlook is that "those people" are not "real Americans," then the ascension of one of "them" to the highest office in the land results in a cosmological crisis, a collapse of sensemaking. Conversely, if one's sensemaking is based on facts—a state of affairs associated (derisively) by a presidential official as belonging to the "reality-based community"—then one's arguments can be dismissed as nonsensical.

Thus ignorance—the methodical avoidance of facts and knowledge—is commercialized, weaponized, and deployed on an industrial scale, a state of affairs unimaginable without modern technology. The denial of facts perhaps reached an apex when Donald Trump's press secretary offered the assembled reporters in a press conference "alternative facts," but had as its harbinger a remark made by an aide to President George W. Bush to *New York Times* reporter Ronald Suskind at the height of the Iraq War:

> The aide said that guys like me were "in what we call the reality-based community," which he defined as people who "believe that solutions emerge from your judicious study of discernible reality." [...] "That's not the way the world really works anymore," he continued. "We're an empire now, and when we act, we create our own reality. And while you're studying that reality—judiciously, as you will—we'll act again, creating other new realities, which you can study too, and that's how things will sort out. We're history's actors [...] and you, all of you, will be left to just study what we do." (Suskind 2004)

From the perspective of a decade later, one must ask how these "new realities" of imperial domination worked out. Both these responses, "reality-based community" and "alternative facts," represent a mindset in which a failed imperial power manufactures narratives to fit its worldview. As technologies create additional possibilities for aggregations of power, whether on the ground or in the media or in cyberspace, facts hang in the balance.

"Things are in the saddle, and ride mankind," Ralph W. Emerson wrote in 1847, in his Ode inscribed to W. H. Channing, at the *beginning* of what we now understand as the technological era. A hundred years later, Daniel Bell (1947) described the problem of "adjusting men to machines" as one of adapting humans to the "basic institution of industrial society, the factory," suggesting that if there was any contest between humanity and technology, the contest was over and technology had won. Today, opaque computational machines called "algorithms" subtly manipulate our desires and our attention, and social media dominates our waking moments. The technologies, whether of nation-building or of education or healthcare, which at their outset seemed to offer abundant promises of benefits for all, are now tearing the commons apart.

After examining in Chapter 4 the technological foundations of some newer commons, including airspace, brands, and landscapes, and social media, in Chapter 5 I will examine how some specific communities have deployed the cultural resources to tame the technology that rides mankind.

## Notes

1. Libraries, as I will develop below, are an interesting case. Hess and Ostrom (2007) identify libraries as common pool resources, yet before the advent of free public libraries in the nineteenth century libraries were club goods.
2. A technological breakthrough, hydraulic fracturing, or "fracking" has boosted petroleum and natural gas production substantially, with the consequence that the United States is one of the top exporters of oil. At the same time, fracking produces waste products that can contaminate drinking water supplies. The fact that these controversies are unresolved is indicative of an institutional failure.
3. See https://www.infrastructurereportcard.org.
4. The fact that African Americans, and often other racial minorities, did not achieve the full rights of citizenship, including the right to vote and the right to use public accommodations for more than a century after the Civil War, is indicative that building the "first new nation" remains a work in progress.
5. The close relationship between education and punishment, particularly in nations with stark racial divisions, bears commenting here. The notorious "school to prison pipeline" makes clear that in the United States, more so than in any other industrialized nation, a third, uncelebrated, function of public schools is the disciplining of subaltern populations, most notably racial minorities (Foucault 1975, 1977).

Chapter 4

# Beyond the Traditional Commons

Having established both a historical perspective of the common good in terms of the turn toward a liberal society, a conceptual foundation in terms of shared goods (public goods, club goods, toll goods, and common pool resources), and an understanding of "technology" as a unique class of instrumentalities combining portability, autonomous representation, and translation and transformation of energy and information, we now turn our attention to unique resources and their interplay in a technological society and in an age of mechanical reproduction. These unique resources include airspace, attention, and desire, none of which could be assembled in a pretechnological age. The technological orchestration of identity and desire created new resources for enclosure, most notably in an elevated place for the arts in a postindustrial society. Governing these newer commons is an ongoing challenge.

The Industrial Revolution changed the sense of community from villages, valleys, dynasties, and urban communes into larger aggregations of nations and multinational empires, with a diversity of cultures, styles of life, languages, and greater mobility among all. Similarly, the rise of technology from the seventeenth century onward altered the character of goods and the good, making it possible to produce private goods on an industrial scale. Mechanical reproduction, whether of art or artifices, has altered the character of culture and its production, creating new senses of community and new senses of identity. In Walter Benjamin's 1936 work *Das Kunstwerk im Zeitalter seiner technischen Reproduzierbarkeit* (The Work of Art in the Age of Mechanical Reproduction), the "work of art" can be understood both as the *object* and the *act* of producing cultural objects ("art") (Benjamin [1936] 2015). By creating an understanding of engineering as one of the useful arts (in contrast to the fine arts), it expands our understanding of the dignity of technology.

In a dynamic economy, technology is continually both expanding and overrunning the frontiers of the commons. New public goods, new common pool resources, and new club goods are created, and the boundaries of the old are under assault. Institutions are then established to maintain the new commons, and the institutions that defended the old crumble or are corrupted.

To introduce this perspective, we first examine three commons whose very existence is entirely dependent on technology: airspace, radio frequency (RF) spectrum, and brands. "Commons," as I will emphasize throughout this book, is a metaphor, a synecdoche, for shared resources (public goods, club goods, common pool resources) that enable a community to feel that "we have something in common." Although the sky above has existed since the beginning of time, and the first humans to penetrate it were the Montgolfiers in 1783, it did not become "airspace" until the 1920s, when the passage of the Air Commerce Act regulated entry into an increasingly overcrowded sky. Subtractability in the space of two decades since the Wright Brothers' first flight had become an issue. Similarly, electromagnetic radiation is as old as time, yet only with Guglielmo Marconi's 1895 invention of the "wireless telegraph" became a resource for exploitation. And *desire*, while it has always been a part of humanity, did not become a *commons* open to exploration, exploitation, and enclosure until the disciplines and technologies of branding, marketing, and merchandising defined its boundaries, and fenced off iconic images, which then became objects of identity and desire.

These three commons, not one of which existed before the modern era, now are all essential parts of the civil order as well as the economy and social life, and put new stresses on governing the commons. The "tragedy of the commons," Garrett Hardin's (1968) evocative view of the inevitable fate of common pool resources, takes on added complexity in a civilization where creativity and invention are now central to the production, distribution, and consumption of public and private goods and services, and where expanding the frontiers of the commons is a central dynamic of the economy. Likewise, "governing the commons," which Elinor Ostrom (1990) demonstrated to be possible, confronts new institutional challenges in the context of the *technological commons*.

The pioneers in pushing forward the frontiers of the commons are artists, poets, inventors, and musicians experimenting with new creative forms and opening up new landscapes and dreamscapes, be they the noble scenes of the Hudson River School or the imaginations of science fiction. Software developers also join these ranks as the twentieth century's contribution to artistic production. Like many pioneering efforts, these are motivated more by the thrill of exploration and discovery than by any immediate monetary gain. Like the Romans in Gaul two millennia ago, the Vikings in Europe, or the settlers of the nineteenth-century American Wild West, they are discovering, or more accurately creating, a Wild West in which institutional authority and the rule of law are a work in progress. Technology alters how we think about the commons and shared resources, and how we govern them.

In this chapter, we turn to an examination of specific, technological commons and their meaning in society. These commons include not only spaces like airspace, but also new institutional arrangements such as branding. The net result is a transformation of the character of the commonwealth, in which discovering what the members of a community have in common is not given but negotiated.

## Technological Commons

Just as the magnetic compass enabled fifteenth-century explorers to expand the boundaries of the world they knew, opening up immense territories for exploration and exploitation, so today the internet and air travel expand the boundaries of mobility, communication, and even identity, reshaping the commonwealth and the common good. I am calling these newer spaces "technological commons," inasmuch as their very existence is dependent on technology. How these new spaces and resources are bounded and explored is the subject to which we now turn.

When we talk about "technologies," whether steam engines or airplanes, we are talking about instrumentalities whose meaning extends far beyond their utilitarian or productive value: technologies create new connections, and they also enable the scaling up of activities that were previously confined to localities. Furthermore, as we have seen, technology has a close association with magic and magical expectations: although pilots and engineers can explain the dynamics of flight, for most people these are *hidden* features, making them seem like magic or at least stirring the imagination.

Technology, whether that of the printing press, the railway, or statistical analysis, has a potency that earlier tools and tabulations lacked. The tools of the Industrial Revolution were scalable, meaning that production would no longer be confined to the household. Production could be scaled up on a national, continental, or global level, as indeed it was in the twentieth century.

Technology also creates connections, whether the obvious ones of transportation and communication devices or the less-obvious ones of shared identities. Branding is built on an immense technological foundation, including mechanical reproduction, statistical analysis, and modernist aesthetics, to become a major foundation for the contemporary economy.

Airspace is central in today's society, a commons that did not exist two hundred years ago. Although the sky above has been a common pool resource that has existed since the beginning of time, it became "airspace" only as human flight began to overcrowd the commons. Air travel and air commerce knit together the globe, something that was unthinkable before the Wright Brothers took to the sky in 1903. Similarly, the RF spectrum, which was not discovered until the nineteenth century, occupies a central place in social life all over the world, not only in broadcast radio and TV but also in text messaging and social networking. "Screen time" with cellular telephones depends on this commons. Likewise, brands, the images and reputations of firms and their products, became a major force in the twentieth-century economy, and "brand equity" became a major force in finance only with the neoliberal turn of the 1980s.

Prior to the Montgolfiers' first ascent in 1783, the heavens above were the domain of gods and angels and thunder and lightning, not a place of human habitation or exploitation. As flying devices improved, exploitation of this wilderness increasingly became an issue, and the Air Commerce Act of 1926 provided the initial step in its governance. Today, there is an immense national and international apparatus for governing airspace, which is centered on the International Civil Aviation Organization. This governance is increasingly challenged by technological developments such as unmanned aerial vehicles (drones) and flight management systems, computers that fly the airplane.

Entry into this domain is highly restricted. Passengers on airliners, in contrast to flight crews, are just tourists passing through, unaware of when they cross the boundary between airspaces. Using accidents and fatalities as indicators of successful governance, the governance of airspace is one of the great success stories in the management of a commons, a high-performance commons where all the nations of the world have agreed on basic principles of its management. In proportion to passenger-miles traveled, airspace is safer than the comparable public good of modern highways.

The standard classifications of airspace were first established by the International Civil Aviation Organization in 1944, and in most of the world there are published maps identifying the boundaries of different classes of airspace and the flight rules within each. In North America, for example, there are seven classes of airspace (Alpha, Bravo, Charlie, Delta, Echo, Foxtrot, and Golf), and labeling them with the so-called "phonetic alphabet" is a linguistic marker used to identify members of the club, that is, airmen. Each of these has precise boundaries: Class Delta airspace, for example, used for smaller, towered airports, typically has a radius of a few miles and extends upward from the surface to a height of 2,500 feet, although this is usually tailored to local conditions including population centers and neighboring airspaces. Within Class Delta, the pilot must advise the tower that he is entering the airspace, although permission to enter is not required. By contrast, in Class Bravo airspace (typically around the busiest airports), permission is required to enter and the pilot must remain in contact with Air Traffic Control (ATC) throughout the flight. In Class Alpha airspace, from 18,000 feet to "flight level 600" (60,000 feet) pilots must fly by Instrument Flight Rules (IFR) following airways, highways in the sky, that are marked by radar beacons. Only in Class Golf airspace (from the ground up to 700 feet above ground level in unpopulated areas, although in some western states up to 14,500 feet above ground level) is the pilot even approximately "free as a bird"; elsewhere, his movement and communication are highly regulated.

In short, the borders of this commons are not just physical lines on a map, but cultural, linguistic, and technological demarcations that assure that airspace can be shared by high-performance devices transporting millions of passengers. It works in large part because airspace is a club good, meaning that free-riders can be excluded, but the resource has low subtractability (see Table 2.1 in Chapter 2). Members of the club are those who have been admitted to this space, on the basis of possessing an airman's certificate, the earning of which is a rite of passage, signifying not simply a new set of skills but a new cultural identity. This identity is highly ritualized, with the primary rite of passage being the first solo flight, which in many flight schools is accompanied by a ritual of humiliation: a pair of scissors is produced, and the back of the initiate's shirt is cut off "to make room for his tail feathers." This ritualization makes it clear that we are talking not just about a new skill set based on intensive training, but a new identity in a new commons. More generally, we might note that significant identities, whether of educational attainment, employment, citizenship, or even friendship, are linked to club goods, whose creation and disruption stems from technological threats.

Only a few years earlier than the Wright Brothers' first flight, Marconi's "wireless telegraph" took to the air, enabling information to circulate instantaneously across national boundaries and ultimately around the world. The radio frequency (RF) spectrum is a common pool resource that is high in subtractability yet low in excludability. Two stations cannot broadcast on the same frequency (or harmonics thereof) without degrading the quality of both transmissions, and in recognition of this fact in 1925 the International Broadcasting Union was founded, initially encompassing ten European nations, but eventually extending to the entire world. Today, the entire RF spectrum is highly regulated, and embraces numerous activities that are now considered essential to contemporary life: not only broadcast radio, but also two-way radio transmission, television, mobile telephones, and numerous new ways of connecting including video-sharing, text messaging, and using GPS (global positioning system) data. More than ever before, social life is in the ether, embracing billions around the world. Although it is an open question currently debated at the highest levels about whether or not Twitter has contributed to the common good, the technological conquest and governance of the ether is now fundamental to the texture of contemporary life. In today's society, the common good and the sense of community that it rests on is a technological creation. Today, electronic communications have created an immense number of club and toll goods, whether for movie-streaming services or chat rooms. The boundaries of the radio frequency (RF) spectrum, for example, while well known to specialists (Figure 4.1), are invisible to everyone else, yet learning these is essential for everyone in these spaces other than the end users. Those chatting on their cell phones are unaware that they are confined to a limited segment of the spectrum, yet the designers of cellular networks understand this.

In similar fashion, the "local conditions" of the new commons gives a new meaning to "local," where "locality" is less a matter of physical propinquity and more a matter of technological impact: most automobiles have catalytic converters, although it required the Clean Air Act of 1966 to recognize that the air we breathe is a common pool resource. Similarly, RF harmonics give new meaning to "locality."

Advances in transportation and communication technologies go hand in hand, whether railways and the telegraph, air travel and radio, or automobiles and telephones. Each is dependent on a shared resource, whether on the ground or in the sky. Today, the urban commons is being reshaped by ride-sharing and bike-sharing, practices that would have been unimaginable before the internet and mobile telephone apps.

100 • Technology and the Common Good

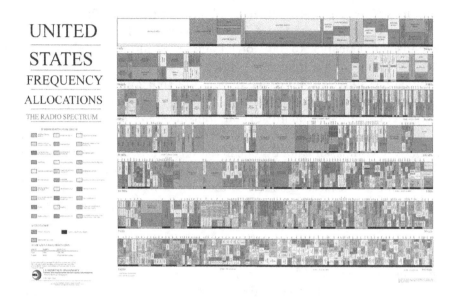

**Figure 4.1.** The RF spectrum. US Department of Transportation. https://www.transportations.gov/pnt/what-radio-spectrum.

In short, these two classes of technologies reinforce and are reinforced by each other, with the consequence that economic life is firmly wedded to the commons.

Perhaps the newest technological commons is what some have termed the "Wiki-Commons" (George 2008), which includes the online encyclopedia Wikipedia plus others that scarcely existed before the current century. Wikis are online, collaborative editing spaces in which users voluntarily contribute their efforts. Wikipedia is a commons that is subject to the same hazards as other commons, notably free-riding and pollution. It maintains its integrity almost completely through the dedication of tens of thousands of volunteers and the strong sense of community embodied in the open source movement. The entire open source movement is an embodiment of a "hacker culture," an ongoing rebellion of highly skilled "techies" against the corporate domination of Microsoft and other software giants who exploit their market dominance to sell inferior products. This, of course, is a unique instantiation of what Charlotte Hess and Elinor Ostrom (2007) term the "knowledge commons," the migration of more knowledge resources to open source platforms. Knowledge, for Hess and Ostrom, is a complex ecosystem, subject to the same dilemmas as natural ecosystems, including overharvesting and pollution. The creation of institutions to manage the knowledge commons, such as the creative commons movement (see the section in this chapter called "The Creative Commons and the Work of Art"), is at the leading edge of reclaiming the commons.

## Landscapes of Identity

Like airspace and the RF spectrum, *identity* has today become a commons; it is available for exploration, exploitation, and enclosure in a technological society. Landscapes in this account are not simply mountains and meadows, but any shared perspective with which a community feels "we have something in common." I am coining the phrase "landscapes of identity" to mean those goods that are shared and also deeply indicative of the sharers' identity. These are similar to club goods, in that they have low subtractability yet easy exclusion, and in an industrial society these are technological products—their composition and their boundaries, as well as their deeper meanings, are functions of technology. As I noted in Chapter 2, landscapes are a prime example of this type of good, which is not subtractable but nevertheless excludes those who lack the conveyances to enjoy them. Mountains and valleys have always existed, but they did not become "landscapes," objects of aesthetic appreciation and ultimately national veneration, until railways enabled educated ladies and gentlemen to venture for an afternoon into the hinterland. Ostrom (1990) identifies landscapes as an emblematic public good, but in terms of the *meaning* of a landscape it has aspects of a club good, insofar as people use it to construct their identity (Marx 1964; Novak 1980). The "machine in the garden," in Leo Marx's phrasing, is a uniquely American construct.

The close association of landscape, railways, and national definition, whether in the paintings of the Hudson River School or in the creation in 1872 of the National Park System, points to a critical issue: the role of technology not only in reshaping our environment, but also in giving new meaning to the commonwealth. The hinterland became nature, an icon of American identity, something that proudly set the New World apart from the Old. Although forests and fields have existed for billions of years, this cultural appropriation and subjugation of nature is a modern invention that is associated in America with the settlement of the continental interior and the emergence of a distinctively *American* nationalism. American nationalism since the nineteenth century has had a strong technological component, whether in the appreciation of the American landscape enabled by railways, or in the "final frontier" of the conquest of space (Miller 1956; Novak 1980). *Domination* of nature, rather than living in harmony with nature, is uniquely American.

This nationalistic appreciation of nature culminated with the creation of the first National Parks in 1872, and increasing reverence for natural areas, primarily in the West but also remote areas of the East (Acadia), the South (the Everglades), and beneath the surface (Carlsbad Caverns). All of these are carefully bounded and protected, a trope that was further extended with the Wilderness Act of 1964, which protected more than 9 million acres of federal land, and "wilderness management" became an increasing concern. More recently, with an increasing awareness of the externalities of automotive transport including pollution and urban sprawl, renewed attention to rail transport has started to subtly reshape the American landscape (Stilgoe 2007).

Landscape is an example of a public good that is both created and threatened by technology. Although the physical features of the terrain existed for millennia, as an object of human appreciation and appropriation in Western traditions landscape is an architectural and technological creation. Chinese and Japanese appreciations of landscape, originating in animist cosmologies, are a completely separate vernacular. As distinguished from the physical terrain, landscape typically refers to the aesthetic experience of a meadow or a mountain or a sunset: an experience that acquired meaning only as reflected in the multiple discourses of landscape painting, architecture, pastoral poetry, and intimate conversations. As contrasted to a private garden, a landscape is a public good, which is both created and threatened by technology. One can note that the rise of interest in the American landscape was coincident with the development of railways, which created a dialogue between nature and culture (Marx 1964; Novak 1980), and for decades the American landscape (Grand Canyon, the Rockies, the Arizona desert) was used to promote rail travel, with indigenous, "children of nature" figures assimilated into the landscape. The *sacrifice* of nature, turning the wilderness into nature, with all the ironies that this implies (destruction, veneration), is a uniquely American construct.

What is noticed, sometimes dramatically, is the intrusion of technological developments into the landscape. Landscape, almost by definition, should be unspoiled, even though American landscape painting from the Hudson River School onward, in contrast to European genres, frequently included an intrusion of civilization, a "machine in the garden" (Marx 1964). Thomas Cole's *The Oxbow* (1836), pictured in Chapter 2 (Figure 2.1), for example, presents a panoramic view of the Connecticut River near Northampton, Massachusetts, with forests and agricultural fields, idling ladies and gentlemen on a bluff overlooking the river, and plumes of smoke emanating from factories in the valley. In his "Essay on American Scenery" published in the same year, after reviewing the wildness, the mountains, lakes, rivers, waterfalls, forests, and skies, Cole ends on an elegiac comment:

> The beauty of such landscapes are quickly passing away—the ravages of the axe are daily increasing—the most noble scenes are made desolate, and oftentimes with a wantonness and barbarism scarcely credible in a civilized nation. The wayside is becoming shadeless, and another generation will behold spots, now rife with beauty, desecrated by what is called improvement. (Cole 1836: 12)

"Improvement" in Jacksonian America meant the building of canals, turnpikes, railways, and factories. Fast forward to the twenty-first century with broadly shared concerns over carbon footprints and renewable energy supplies and the development of wind turbines, and controversies rage over the placement of wind farms in New England, California, and the Great Lakes states. These controversies pit a public good, landscape vistas, with a private good, energy supply. Seemingly, this would be no contest, except for the fact that these technological developments stress the boundaries of both: is the vista from my lakeshore cottage a public good or a private good? Is my assertion that a distant wind farm impairs my property value a form of enclosure? Is adequacy of energy in today's society a public concern? A bookshelf of studies and an entire term of court decisions would be required to resolve these issues. More generally, technological developments introduce new opportunities to deplete or spoil (pollute) both public goods and club goods, so that what were once stable agreements on governance must be renegotiated.

Landscapes are actually a club good, a symbol of identity. They share in common with other club goods the properties of nondepletability and excludability, with the mechanisms of exclusion being either the ownership of adjacent property (often subject to zoning restrictions) or the transportation devices that convey one from the city into the countryside. Landscape painting and photography reproduce these goods, and the reproduction of these assures that millions have seen and appreciated Yosemite (Figure 4.2), despite having never traveled west.

**Figure 4.2.** Yosemite Valley. Wikimedia Commons, public domain.

## The Landscape of Desire

My fourth technological commons, after airspace, the RF spectrum, and landscape, is branding, the enclosure and exploitation of identity and desire. I am characterizing this as a "landscape," inasmuch as it creates a shared perspective that is supposedly outside ourselves but in fact is a technological creation. Branding is a commercial project that took off in the twentieth century (Ewen 1976). Although trademarks are private goods, subject to intellectual property restrictions, brands acquire market valuation ("brand equity") only insofar as broad segments of the public identify with them—that is, share and valorize them. The Disney *brand*, for example, and its iconic figure, began with the happy accident of a young corporation discovering "Steamboat Willie," in the 1920s, who quickly evolved into Mickey Mouse. Two hundred movies later, Mickey Mouse is *the* most emblematic representation of "the smile factory" of Disneyland and the entire Disney enterprise (Van Maanen 1991; the industrial production metaphor here is worth noting). Disney Enterprises maintains intellectual property restrictions (a form of enclosure) on Steamboat Willie, despite the fact that the normal expiration of copyright protection is less than a hundred years. The Disney *brand*, a set of images, moods, and attachments, like that of every other consumer-oriented corporation, is worth several multiples of the book value of the Disney *corporation*, a set of assets and liabilities.

Going back more than a century to Sigmund Freud's discovery of the dynamics of the human psyche, the moods, motivations, and impulses of individuals and groups have now become yet another "final frontier" for commercial exploration. This is obviously a commons of a different order, no longer providing the necessities of life such as food and water, but rather luxuries, or at least decencies. Sharing a high-end brand such as that of the Louis Vuitton handbag, retailing for more than $1,000, is obviously a luxury, but for the socially insecure it may be experienced as a necessity. Identification with a "brand," which "reformers" may sneer at, for millions of others such as "aspirers" is a daily part of their lives.[1] Brands have become tokens of identity for millions, and branded images form the frontiers of the consumer economy, with extensive legal resources devoted to protecting brands against pirated (blatantly copied) and "knockoff" (closely imitated) versions.

Brands, and the constellations of identity and desire that they represent, are major tokens in today's economy. The terrain of human desire is no less a commons than a mountain meadow, embracing numerous tokens of values that can be shared, sequestered, subdivided, or circulated depending less on its natural character and more on the institutional and technological apparatus and intentions directed toward it. Just as the "waste and howling wilderness" of the seventeenth-century Puritans became the "noble scenes" of the nineteenth-century Hudson River School (Novak 1980), so, too, the unruly passions of sixteenth-century poets became the sublime raptures of nineteenth-century Romantics and lifestyle market segments for twentieth-century "captains of consciousness" (Ewen 1976).

Although clothing has for centuries been indicative of status, both national and class, the sequestration and enclosure of desire through branding is inconceivable without modern technology. Brands have become, in the words, of Celia Lury's *Brands: The Logos of the Global Economy* (2004), a "social currency," with which people bring meaning to different exchanges. Clothing, automobiles, and even household furniture are tokens of status that are to be displayed as part of personal assertion. These meanings are negotiated between those who identify with the brand and the actual object of branding. In other words, a brand is a club good, unlike trademarks and logos, which are private goods.

Does it seem frivolous to join an investigation of artificial commons of human desire and affect with more tangible and endangered resources such as water tables and forests, on which billions depend for their daily livelihoods? The segmentation and sequestration of consumer affect and desire are major (if artificial) resources in a neoliberal economy. The *trillions* of dollars at stake in brand exploration and exploitation suggest that something serious is going on.

The landscape of identity and desire is fundamentally different in an age of mechanical reproduction, psychometric insight, and commercial exploitation. Mechanical reproduction alters the nature of expressive productions, whether for purposes of entertainment or commercial exploitation. Although ownership of expressive productions has been widely discussed in terms of intellectual property (IP) (and IP legislation determining IP's boundaries), it is less interrogated in terms of the cultural significance of such productions. Works of art, for example, in the Middle Ages were private or club goods, objects of cult-like devotion (Benjamin [1936] 2015). Once they could be industrially reproduced, they became objects of public admiration and consumption. Exhibition value (*Ausstellungswert*), a public good, replaced cult value (*Kultwert*), a club good, and museums are the new temples of this public good.

Today, merchandising and adjudicating the use of trademarked terms and shapes and images is a major enterprise, with numerous consultancies and other cultural entrepreneurs exploring product possibilities. One the one hand, a brand such as Polo (Ralph Lauren), originally associated with men's clothing, creates such a strong identification that it can be extended to numerous other objects beyond its original home: pickup trucks, for example, or household furniture come in Ralph Lauren Polo brands. The entire discipline of merchandising consists of the exploration and potential exploitation of new opportunities for existing brands and products. Merchandising suggests that consumers have an identification, sometimes strong, sometimes weak, with the brand available for commercial exploitation. Such identification suggests some element of sharedness with the brand, meaning that the Ralph Lauren Corporation does not fully own the brand. Although they own the name, the logo, and the trademark, they do not own the brand. Rather, the brand has some aspects of a club good, as it is shared with and among the consumers, and considerable strategic thinking goes into determining acceptable uses and extensions of the brand.

The entire discipline of market research uses psychometric and ethnographic tools and technologies to map out, cross-tabulate, and evaluate desires within a terrain of demographic (age, sex, education, zip code) and lifestyle categories. This, too, is an enclosure. The explosive growth in brand valuations over the last half-century suggests that these unique goods may well overshadow the more utilitarian aspect of nearly everything that circulates in the consumer economy: "brand equity" (an accounting adjustment) overshadows physical assets in the market valuations of the largest corporations. To take one of many examples, in 2014 the consumer products company Procter & Gamble (P&G) had a book value of $69 billion (net assets minus net liabilities), and a market valuation of $317 billion (total shares times share price). The difference between these two valuations, $248 billion, is typically booked as "goodwill" or P&G's "brand equity." Generalizing from this, we might venture that the valuation of brands, including the corporate brand, is one of the largest, if not *the* largest, resource in a neoliberal economy. A most recent extension of this concept is found in "nation-branding," the deliberate effort by state and civic leaders to cultivate a national "brand" in hopes of attracting investment, tourists, and respect. Macedonia, for example, has invented and invested in a substantial narrative, going back to Alexander the Great, of the ancient and imperial splendor of this 25-year old Balkan republic (Aronczyk 2008; Graan 2013). Although trademarks and logos are nominally considered a form of private intellectual property (a subject that has received extensive attention in the literature of the commons [Strathern 2004; Hess and Ostrom 2007; or Nonini 2007, for example]), when they coalesce into a "brand" they become a club good, meaning that they are potentially objects that consumers identify with.

Navigating the terrain of consumer desire often represents the difference between commercial success and failure, and the entire management discipline of marketing represents an effort to bound, sequester, and manage different segments of human desire. The concept of "lifestyle" (*Lebensführung*), as referenced in the section "Health as a Public Good" in Chapter 3, has been adopted by the marketing industry in a multi-trillion-dollar project to stake out and sequester the entire terrain of consumer desire. Although within the sociological or anthropological literature there is no standard model of different "lifestyles," dominant firms in the marketing industry have developed their own models: for example, Young & Rubicam, one of the pioneers of the advertising industry, has created the "cross-cultural consumer characterization model," tabulating seven different kinds of consumers, including "reformers," "mainstreamers," "aspirers," "succeeders," "explorers," "strugglers," and the "resigned." Reformers, in this schema, take the following attitude:

"Don't tell me what to do or what to think" says the Reformer, valuing their own independent judgement. Reformers are the most anti-materialistic of the seven groups, and are often perceived as intellectual. They are socially aware, and pride themselves on tolerance. Reformers seek out the authentic and the harmonious, and are often at the leading edge of society.

The "reformers" contrast with "aspirers," who are

> materialistic, acquisitive people, who are driven by others' perceptions of them rather than by their own values. As a result, they respond to what others perceive as being superficial: image, appearance, persona, charisma and fashion. An attractive pack is as important to them as its contents. Their core need in life is for status.[2]

Cross-tabulated with publicly available data (such as zip code the model of car) and used for targeted marketing, this navigation is itself a form of enclosure (of mass attention) and a central part of modern business. In a neoliberal society where patrimonial restraints have all but disappeared, enclosure can go beyond physical control and appropriation of natural resources to include the segmentation and sequestration of the terrain of desire.

Brands are a lifestyle commons, a club good, and those inside the club can recognize the difference between *vrai* and *faux* members, a distinction often not evident to those outside the circle. An iconic American brand, the Harley-Davidson motorcycle associated with masculinity and described in Chapter 2, is not simply a transportation device: it is a token of club membership, and *real* men would sneer at any aesthete who posed with a hog. *Brands* are also dependent on mechanical reproduction for their circulation. More generally, the enclosure and commodification of identity and desire is today a major dynamic in the industrial economy.

There are many other commons whose existence is a function of technological development. Social networks, for example are now staked out and exploited by Facebook, and personal attention is mined by Google and similar platforms (Wu 2016). Shoshana Zuboff, in *The Age of Surveillance Capitalism* (2019), describes a contemporary world in which algorithms have replaced shop-floor supervisors as enforcers of industrial discipline. The industrial discipline so enforced is less that of physical production than that of *attention*, the eyeballs, mouse clicks, and "likes" that are harvested in a world of digital globalism. Jeremy Bentham's "panopticon," a prison where mirrors had replaced guards and thereby enabled total surveillance, is now at hand with Facebook, with algorithms replacing mirrors as devices for focusing attention. In many respects, Facebook has become the new public square, with more than two billion users worldwide (out of a global population of nearly eight billion), although drawing the line between living, breathing *homo sapiens* users and algorithm-generated artificial identities is not at all straightforward. A recent study found that in the German 2017 election the far-right party Alternative für Deutschland (AfD) amassed sufficient votes to seat members in Parliament, and splinter groups such as Reconquista Germania succeeded in enlarging the "Overton Window," a new name for a commons of acceptable discourse (Overton 2013). These successes came about in part by online trolls and bots that sowed discord among the more traditional parties. "Customer loyalty" is tracked by Amazon and numerous retailers who maintain extensive databases on their customers' shopping habits. The ambient commons (McCullough 2013) of unstructured information is increasingly enclosed or at least polluted by garish advertising billboards and closed-circuit TV cameras, and it is increasingly a resource for commercial exploitation. In the Middle Ages, "the commons" was a fairly static entity, whose boundaries were recognized by all villagers with their watchful eyes. With the inherently expansive nature of a capitalist economy, new commons and their dynamics are out there, waiting to be discovered or invented and then enclosed.

## The Creative Commons and the Work of Art

Branding, and artistic production in general, is based on what might be termed "the creative commons," the spaces and ecosystems in which artistic production flourishes. Perhaps the most dynamic industry in today's society is the commons of expressive productions, whether works of art, writing, design, cinema, or any other creative production. The creative commons consists of those spaces, both institutional and legal, in which creativity flourishes, and efforts to enclose the creative commons are efforts to stifle artistic production.

The first copyright laws were passed in 1710, more than two centuries after Johannes Gutenberg's invention of printing with movable type. Copyright laws fence in the creative commons; they do not enclose ideas, but rather enclose expressions for a limited period of time, but defining the boundary between an idea and its expression is a source of substantial litigation. Similarly, the culture industry pushes for extensions of the term of copyrights, as expressive productions migrate to new platforms such as DVDs and web pages. The original copyright legislation made clear that its purpose was to encourage, not discourage, creative production by granting the originator a *limited* monopoly on their product. With pressure to extend copyrights in perpetuity, a twentieth-century form of enclosure, this purpose could be lost.

Today, the question of "who owns culture?" is a question of shared resources, which is complicated by the disruptive innovations of mechanical reproduction. Although cultural *authority* has been contested for millennia, cultural *sequestration* and *appropriation* in this age of mechanical reproduction and IP litigation is more problematic than ever, as described by James Boyle in "Fencing Off Ideas" (2002). For example, childlike innocence and simplicity is an important trope in American culture and at least a source of amusement in many others. The genius of Walt Disney in 1928 gave us a representation of this value in the character and visual image of Mickey Mouse; in 1998, the extension of copyright laws, beyond the normal 75 years (through the Sonny Bono Act) at the behest of Disney and the culture industry, has maintained what would otherwise by now be a common patrimony as a marketable commodity.[3]

Or, to extend this thought, knowledge, which once was a patrimony, the heritage of a family or guild, today with advances in information technology is examined as a commons, and increasingly sequestered as a commodity. A patrimony is the shared heritage of a group and by definition cannot be privatized, commodified, or depleted, although with misuse it can become polluted or corrupted. For example, the concept of culture, anthropology's "signature concept," a commons in which anthropologists (conceptually) wandered, was discovered in the 1980s by management theorists who quickly developed it into a concept of "corporate culture" that in many respects was ethnocentric (Hofstede 1997; Batteau 2012b), yet a useful *tool* for management in a globalizing economy.

A "commons," as in shared public spaces, contrasts with common pool resources; common pool resources can be depleted through overuse. A common pool resource may be self-regenerating if not overused; if overused, it may collapse. They are similar but not the same as a "public good" such as education, civic order, or public sanitation, which are goods that can neither be subdivided (as common pool resources can) nor depleted, but which must be maintained lest they be degraded or corrupted: if lawbreakers go unpunished, then after a certain point confidence in public order collapses, and social life becomes a *bellum omnium contra omnes*. If higher education becomes dominated by for-profit universities, then the civic value of education collapses.

The *abuse* of public goods such as civic order and knowledge is no less destructive than the *overuse* of common pool resources, and requires similar institutional measures for prevention. Patrimonies, commons, and public goods are by definition shared and not for sale, yet this is under assault as our instrumentalities of sequestration continue to improve. What is the price of "friendship" on social media?

Charlotte Hess and Elinor Ostrom (2007) note that since 1995, when the internet burst into public attention and with that an understanding that the internet was a shared (and finite) resource, issues of commons management have begun to crop up in discussions about the internet: overcrowding and congestion, free-riding, overuse, and pollution have suddenly become problems within the infosphere. The "new shared territory of globally distributed information" (Hess and Ostrom 2007: 4) was in play, and Hess and Ostrom demonstrate that many of the same issues for governing other commons (noted above) might also apply to the internet. The techniques and instruments of creation, storage, retrieval, manipulation, and dissemination apply to information, data, and knowledge, and in many ways we are becoming more efficient at turning information into manipulable data and marketable knowledge. All of this is enabled, though not necessarily driven, by advances in information and communication technologies. The larger context of these developments include a changing character of authority and sociality, in which patrimonial forms of authority—including family, tribe, and the nation-state—recede into the background, eclipsed by technocratic authority, embodied in faceless bureaucrats and anonymous algorithms.

A movement to reclaim the creative commons, started by Lawrence Lessig in 2001, was a nonprofit organization that issues open licenses for creative and scholarly work with a standardized permission-granting format (see Lessig 2004). Creative commons tools include search tools, certificates that attest that the holder understands openly licensed work, and a global network community that works to increase the volume, breadth, and quality of publicly available knowledge. In this, the creative commons can be seen as an effort to reclaim the knowledge commons from its ongoing enclosure.

## Governing the Commons in a Technological Society

In the modern world, the eight criteria that Elinor Ostrom (1990) established for successful governance of public goods and common pool resources all have technological foundations. More pointedly, such matters as "monitoring" and "graduated sanctions" (Ostrom's fourth and fifth criteria) take on a different character in an industrial society, where surveillance technologies and a widening palette of sanctions are available. One need not go to the dystopian extremes of George Orwell's *1984* (1949) to imagine a society where the norms of surveillance and sanctions acquire additional force through technologies. With closed-circuit TV cameras on many corners, facial recognition technologies, location-tracking cell phones in many pockets, and immense government databases of personal data including facial images, and now China's "social credit system,"[4] it is already here.

In a democratic society, some basic norms of good citizenship, even if not codified into statutes, guard against such totalitarian extremes. As technologies of facial recognition and GPS tracking open up chinks in this democratic consensus, these norms begin to break down. Facebook, for example, has created a new commons in which the common pool resource, attention, has virtually no limits on its exploitation, beyond the good intentions of Facebook's management and a growing assemblage of anti–social-network types. Efforts to break up Facebook using existing anti-monopoly statutes are limited by those statutes' focus on private goods: when a company like Facebook, or Microsoft in the 1980s, gives away its most identifiable product, it is difficult to articulate the harm done to *consumers*, although the harm done to competitors, to citizens, to public spaces, and to the common good is obvious. Similarly, when YouTube or WeChat enable *anyone* with an internet connection to pollute the public square with pernicious narratives, with the hope that these will "go viral," it is not so much *consumers* as it is the community that is damaged. The focus of antitrust legislation on private goods and harm to consumers has limited efforts to break up monopolies such as Facebook and Google.

Pernicious narratives reached a climax in the aftermath of the 2020 presidential election, in which *millions* were convinced, based on what they had read on social media, that the election had been stolen. We have already noted the capability of social media to create "filter bubbles" in which disinformation thrives; today, we see these expanding to *filter clouds*, embracing millions of followers on social media, who are reached by information that lives "in the cloud."

Microsoft's business model was to bundle its operating system with hardware purchases, and thus lock in consumers to purchases of its applications, with the resulting network externalities eventually giving it a near monopoly on personal computing. Similarly, Facebook gives away its platform to consumers, yet harvests in fine-grained detail their attention and "likes" (preferences) and friendships (i.e., networks) for sale to advertisers. In both of these cases, they have deployed creative business models, relying on toll goods to lock in a resource, whether consumers' attention or software architecture, to harvest billions of dollars. This may be the final area where the focus of the neoliberal paradigm on private goods and consumption breaks down. Facebook and Windows are platforms, a commons that permits their creators to harvest billions of dollars from users worldwide.

More generally, a recognition is needed that there are many roles that members of a community play in addition to "consumers," and the excessive focus of antitrust legislation on consumption comes at the expense of most forms of the common good. Citizens, family members, parishioners, employees, managers, shareholders, union brothers and sisters, and neighbors are all important roles in contemporary society, all dependent on some measure of shared goods, even if those shared goods are neither tangible nor fungible. Any sense of the "common good" is far more dependent on these roles than on one's status as a "consumer," which typically refers to the enjoyment of private goods, perhaps shared within a household. Yet as regulators struggle with the question of how to restrict Facebook's power, they lack the intellectual tools to assess more broadly the antidemocratic character of technological giants. Stated simply, Facebook, Google, and the rest are monopolistic, imperial powers, not so much controlling our lives as consumers as colonizing the *conscience* of entire communities.

The common good is diametrically opposed to privilege, whether that of kings, priests, emperors, or elites. Whether privilege is earned or an entitlement, just or unjust, is beside the point; in either case, it detracts from a fellow feeling that is or should be the mark of a republic. Democracy, as events of the past few decades have shown, is much more a rare and fragile flower than previously imagined. Technology, not just information technology but more generally devices that amplify the capabilities of an elite at the expense of the general populace, in the absence of institutional guardrails becomes a threat to democracy. In the absence of a discourse of technology's threat—both in spirit and in fact—we are condemned to become slaves to our devices.

## The Character of the Commonwealth

Having established that technology-dependent commons are a core feature of contemporary life, giving meaning and a sense of community to people all over the globe, we can conclude with how technology in its various forms defines and redefines the commonwealth. Just as the

Industrial Revolution is closely associated with the rise of nationalism (Gellner 1983), so too more recent social upheavals, such as the emergence of social media and the "sharing" economy characterized by firms such as Uber, Lyft, AirBnB, and WeWork, in which the boundaries of private property are adjusted (sometimes called "commons-based peer production" [Benkler 2006]), facilitated (although not dictated) by newer technologies, have created new forms of social participation and new structures of authority that are shaking the world. Like any other social revolution, whether the French Revolution or the Russian Revolution, this is creating winners and losers, and the ultimate outcome could end either in a general uplift of humanity or a new Reign of Terror. These newer structures have less to do with the production of goods and services and are more a matter of creating value by aggregating data and building connections, whether of shared domesticity or work opportunities.

In the Middle Ages, "the commons" was understood as an agricultural commons in which villagers could plant their crops and graze their livestock. More recently, economists have extended this to many other sorts of shared goods. As described earlier in this chapter, these definitions have been extended to include artificial resources (the RF spectrum), the creative commons, and club goods such as brands and identities. The social character of common goods, including common pool resources, is in the form of the *attachment* that members of the community have, whether the attachment is in terms of (possibly totemic) identification or *Lebensraum*.

The difference between *common* goods and *collective* goods is that the former are in some respect possessed by a self-conscious social group, a *community* whose members feel that they have something in *common*. Otherwise, any assemblage of objects in the universe could be considered a commons, and any improvement in per capita income, no matter how unevenly distributed, could be considered a common good. Creating the common good is more than simply accumulation of private goods. As social life increasingly goes online, with the limitations of online interaction previously noted (including loss of nuance, and asymmetry of information), digital technology challenges us to self-consciously create *communities* possessed with an aspiration toward the common good.

In antiquity, self-conscious social groups included foraging bands, tribes, villages, urban settlements, kingdoms, religious communities, and dynasties. The interplay among these is the stuff of history. In the modern era, the nation-state has emerged as the leading candidate for fellow-feeling, although how nation-states are defined and assembled is an ongoing discussion. For Benedict Anderson (1983), nation-states are "imagined communities." Anderson notes that some of the earliest nationalisms were among creole peoples of the Americas, who despite sharing a common language and culture with their colonial masters nevertheless created a national self-consciousness to throw off the colonial yoke. The word "creole" comes from the Spanish *criollo*, meaning a person of European descent who was born in the New World. Creole consciousness developed among Spanish and Portuguese colonies in the New World, although the British in the Thirteen Colonies of North America were also creoles, and in throwing off their colonial masters created the first new nation.

For Ernest Gellner in *Nations and Nationalism* (1983), nationalism emerged out of the Industrial Revolution, and the emergence of entropic identities out of the traditional order. The elevation of certain local cultures and sects to "high culture," with the prestige of state authority, and the creation of national languages out of pluralities of local patois, created the nation-state, supplying interchangeable parts (laborers, consumers) for the industrial machine.

Eric Hobsbawm, in *Nations and Nationalism since 1780* (1990), examines the interplay of political subdivision (states), language, and ethnicity. A central part of nationalism and building the nation-state is making education available beyond the class of priests and scribes to the population generally. This was necessary to promote a common language, as contrasted to an array of local dialects and patois that was typical before the rise of the nation-state. It is very difficult to imagine having something in common if we cannot communicate. Indeed, in the eighteenth century, proper French was spoken only in the region surrounding the Île-de-France (Paris and its environs); everyone else only spoke a local "patois." The grand project of French unification, beginning in 1789 and continuing throughout the nineteenth century, focused in part on the standardization of the French language by the Académie Française.

Harris Mylonas, in *The Politics of Nation-Building* (2012), describes how core and peripheral groups, with and without ethnic self-identification, have reshaped national configurations all over the world. Nations and national movements, including deliberate efforts at nation-building and historical accidents such as refugee movements and ethnic cleansing, have reshaped national self-identification. Nations, in other words, are less primordial clusterings and more deliberate policy creations, in which various groups, elites and non-elites alike, manipulate the tokens of nationalism, including language, ancestry, locality, and religion.

*Sotto voce*, if not missing in all of these accounts, is the role of technology in shaping national collectivities, less in their boundaries and more in their felt meaning. Although Gellner points to the Industrial Revolution as a prime mover, that was less a technological revolution than it was a social revolution, which was built on but going beyond a new organization of production. The ensuing movements of nationalism's "blood and soil" embraced a broad variety of kindreds, neighborhoods, valleys, and villages united by more than simple physical propinquity.

By seeing the Industrial Revolution as primarily social, rather than technological, we acquire resources for imagining alternatives other than the scaling up of production and distribution that industrialization has created over the past two hundred years. The genius of Amazon and other contemporary business empires was to use the imaginary of industrialization to scale up distribution, starting with books, but eventually moving into the "everything store," to the benefit of consumers but arguably to the detriment of small producers, warehouse workers, and delivery drivers, who are subject to the same scientific management and industrial discipline that Frederick Taylor first introduced to the Ford assembly line. Amazon's fulfillment centers are a twenty-first-century version of William Blake's "Dark Satanic Mills," albeit with improved lighting and air conditioning.[5]

One feature of the social side of the Industrial Revolution was its close association with imperial domination. Eric Hobsbawm, in *Industry and Empire* (1969), describes the interplay of the growth of the British Empire and the rise of industry, first in the English Midlands and then extending all over England, Europe, and then eventually the world. Colonial possessions created markets and labor supplies for the scaling up of production that industrialism offered. By scaling up not just production but the entire economy of private goods, the Industrial Revolution created empires that now bestride the narrow world. The British Navy was just as much a driver of the Industrial Revolution as was the steam engine, and with the development of steamships in the 1820s the British Empire could dominate colonial possessions not only in terms of territory but also in terms of industrial possibilities.

Understanding the role of technology in shaping communities is more critical than ever: given how the internet, social media, and industrialized entertainment (only the final of which even existed when Anderson and Gellner were writing) are subverting national loyalties and nation-states, in the current environment the meanings and the institutions of communities must be confronted. Or, more accurately, just as Mylonas (2012) describes the assemblages of hosts, immigrants, ethnicities, borders, and political stratagems such as alliance formation and intelligence in building nations, such constellations are now prying nations apart, whether in Italy, Spain, or Mexico. Secessionist movements, whether in Italy (Lega Nord) or Spain, (Catalonia) or Mexico (Monterrey and Ciudad Nezahualcóyotl), undermine the nation (Fisher et al. 2018). In today's society, these constellations and stratagems of local identification acquire new force and vigor, in part (ironically) from finding sympathizers around the world.[6]

In sum, it is not only the character of goods—whether public spaces, or tokens of identity, or cultural patrimony—but also the very concept of "commons" that technology alters, sometimes beyond all recognition. The commons in a technological society, in contrast to the open fields of the Middle Ages, is enclosed and harvested by those who design and build technologies, not by those who use (or are used by) the technologies. The idolization of technology is roughly analogous to the divine right of kings that provided legitimation to earlier social formation, only now far more scalable than any medieval monarch could possibly imagine.

## Notes

1. "Aspirers" are characterized as "materialistic, acquisitive people," whereas "reformers" value their own independent judgment. These terms are taken from Young & Rubicam's "cross-cultural consumer characterization model."
2. http://www.4cs.yr.com/global.
3. There is a substantial literature on the evolution of copyrights over the past three hundred years, far too extensive to be reviewed here, except to note that advances in mechanical reproduction, beginning with the printing press and going today through electronic media, have probed the boundaries of this commons.
4. The "social credit system" in China is an elaborate, big data system for monitoring individual and group behavior and tabulating conformity with written and implicit norms. See Hoffman 2018.
5. For the poem "Jerusalem" by William Blake, see https://www.poetryfoundation.org/poems/54684/jerusalem-and-did-those-feet-in-ancient-time (retrieved 1 September 2021).
6. Benjamin Barber, in *Jihad vs. McWorld* (1995) makes a similar point.

Chapter 5

# Public Goods and Institutions in Cyberspace

In today's economy, *attention* and *desire* have become resources to be enclosed, cultivated, and harvested as part of the information economy. In the nineteenth and early twentieth centuries, the industrial economy was built on a foundation of improved productivity in the agricultural economy; formerly, 90 percent of the workforce produced food, whereas today fewer than 5 percent produce sufficient food to feed entire populations. Likewise, the postindustrial or information economy is built on a foundation of productivity in the manufacturing economy, so that today more than 50 percent of the labor force works in information industries. The unrelenting logic of a capitalist economy, in the absence of institutional restraints, is to search out new commons, whether in the open fields of preindustrial England, in the rubber trees of the Amazon (Grandin 2009), or in the idle musings of the mind (Wu 2016), to create new resources for harvesting. The latest commons for exploration and exploitation are those of the internet.

In *Modernity at Large*, Arjun Appadurai (1996) identifies "diasporic public spheres" as the basic building blocks of our contemporary world. These crucibles of a postnational order, building on ethnoscapes, mediascapes, technoscapes, and other –scapes, mobilize the efforts of refugees, activists, and others to create a plurality of "imagined worlds." In Appadurai's words, the primordia of blood and soil have, ironically, "become globalized," a state of affairs unimaginable before the age of digital globalization. The new commons of these imagined worlds for clever entrepreneurs represent new business models on which to discover new resources and build new fortunes.

### The Square and the Tower on the Net

The spaces within which social life is exercised have changed radically in the course of human history, from villages and valleys to cities and nations, and thence to multinational empires and global networks. Each of these rests on a foundation of tools, the built environment, instrumentalities, and technologies that guide the shape of social participation, whether primitive hunting tools that constrain the range of hunting bands or the transportation technologies that range over entire continents, or the information technologies that now span the globe. Understandings of the common good have evolved from simple shelter and nutritional adequacy, into a full life for all citizens, perhaps *the* crowning glory of a democratic society.

The civic spaces in which citizenship is exercised have also changed over the years. In the Middle Ages, two architectural features of cities—squares and basilicas—defined the coordinates of civic participation: subordination to the monarch (or hierarchy) and the free exchange of ideas in the square (networks). These have been warped in the contemporary environment of information technology. The World Wide Web, originally envisioned as a globe-spanning network potentially linking everyone on the planet and making the world smaller, has been colonized by Facebook, Instagram (now owned by Facebook), Twitter, and other social media platforms, which use sophisticated algorithms to manipulate users' attention, creating a new business model in which mouse clicks are the tokens of value. While in the Middle Ages the edifice of a cathedral inspired city dwellers with the awe and majesty of the Church, and orators could hold forth in the public square with ringing declarations, today these have been replaced by Twitter and Facebook pages, and a Gresham's Law of social media currency prevails: bad tweets drive out the good.

This glib phrase, "making the world smaller," obscures the changing character of the social order in the modern world. Unlike village-level societies, where one's circle encompassed at most a few hundred villagers, in the modern world one typically has at least passing connection with millions of consociates. This is hardly an original observation, but it has profound implications for the meaning of citizenship. Philosophers for thousands of years have debated the optimal size of a republic, which was understood as a self-governing entity and contrasted with an empire. Today, technology has enabled a new species of empire, one that resembles traditional cults, although on a much larger scale, that is enforced with algorithms rather than armies, and that is populated by *users* rather than *subjects*, the implications of which we are just beginning to understand. Allow me to explain.

Although empires in the traditional sense of multiple nationalities under a supreme Caesar, Czar, or *Führer* have largely faded, they have been eclipsed by corporate empires made possible by modern technology. "Corporate empire" is less a metaphor than an apt, literal description of regimes that embrace the working, consuming, and civic lives of millions around the globe, dictating and influencing where and how they work, what and why they consume, in some cases where they live, and their political preferences. These corporate empires in many situations overshadow national governments, rendering one's status as a citizen or subject subordinate to one's status as an employee or a consumer. How else can one explain the low rates of civic participation in America? The United States is near the bottom of all OECD countries in terms of voting in general elections. Americans focus more on their obligations as consumers than as citizens, and the common good is eclipsed by private consumption.

And further: as our homes and our civic spaces become populated with "smart" devices, whether speakers or appliances or devices that use voice recognition and artificial intelligence to understand and anticipate our needs, they colonize the *conscience* of our collective lives. I use *conscience* in the French sense of embracing both conscience and consciousness, in much the way that the French sociologist Émile Durkheim (2013) constructed the idea of *conscience collective*, which is roughly translated as "collective conscience" or "collective culture." To say that technology colonizes our *conscience* is to say that it turns *conscience* into a resource available for exploitation. While this is hardly an original observation, a couple of critical perspectives on technology may give it an additional bite.

The two basic structures of civic life, the square and the tower, in Niall Ferguson's view (2018), or networks and hierarchies, become warped in the ecology of social media. What was once promised to be a worldwide spanning of social connection—the new public square—has instead evolved into a massive architecture of surveillance and enclosure, the new tower. Unlike the tower of earlier times, which could edify the citizens and subjects, the new tower is hidden behind flat panel screens, making it more alienating than earlier forms of domination. Earlier tyrants had a face and a voice, and one could imagine them as heroes or villains; today's tyrants are disembodied computations. Further, the new tower has a global reach, so that one's conversations, one's "likes," and even one's intimate secrets can be monitored from anywhere. This is the true face of digital globalism.

Digital globalism is the aggregation of value less in material terms (piles of cash, truckloads of private goods, or acres of real estate) and more in the accumulation of relationships (eyeballs, mouse clicks, "friend"-ships). In contrast to print capitalism; it is an instrumentality of actual alienation rather than imagined communities, giving rise to a new political form, the internet empire. Just as print capitalism gave rise to nationalism (Anderson 1983), so too digital globalism creates new territories in cyberspace available for enclosure and colonization.

Three features of the technology of digital globalism drive enclosure and colonization. The first is scale: In contrast to earlier communication technologies, including the printing press, radio, and television, the global reach of internet-based devices is built in, so that a photo taken with one's iPhone can be transmitted anywhere around the world. This applies to many other large-scale technologies as well, including air transport and broadcast communication (Gras 1997; Mayntz 2008). One consequence of this new scale is that "collective choice arrangements" (Ostrom's [1990] third criterion) are challenged: are we able to scale up our institutions of governance to match the global scale of the technology? As I examine in Chapter 7, in some cases—such as regional development, air transport, or the high seas—we have been able to; but in many other disruptive technologies, we have not. Social media is at the top of the list of disruptive technologies, as it created new public squares that lack the customary apparatus of law and order found on most city corners. As a consequence, both disturbers of the peace (trolls) and thieves (internet scams) flourish. Or to take technological systems, such as facial recognition systems and identity databases, for example, they encode racial understandings of the institutions, making them more opaque and difficult to confront. Ruha Benjamin, in her book *Race after Technology* (subtitled *Abolitionist Tools for the New Jim Code*; 2019), describes and documents how racist assumptions, including (but not limited to) names, zip codes, and bodily characteristics are hardwired into employment and judicial systems, thus solidifying racist assumptions regarding family background and residence. These assumptions, even a half-century after the civil rights legislation of the 1960s, seem to be more impervious to change than mere statutes.

The second feature of the global reach of technology is its portability: the printing press is a factory-based technology, entailing the different elements of factory production including centralization and process supervision, which was noted above. Although the actual press might not be portable, the fact that printing presses could be installed almost anywhere is an indicator of portability. This lends it a reach that earlier methods of publication, whether scribes sitting at their desks copying manuscripts, or scholars in their libraries, clearly lacked. Mechanical reproduction of both art and literature gives these expressions new meaning. Walter Benjamin's (1936) *The Work of Art in an Age of*

*Mechanical Reproduction* can easily be extended to the poetics of sociability in an age of digital reproduction. Literature became available to all in the fifteenth century, and only a few centuries later literacy would become universally available, although the *right* to literacy is still contested in some quarters. In the twenty-first century, the art of the tweet, pithy thoughts compressed into 280 characters, has become a dominant form of collective expression, and the boundaries of the commons have gone global.

The third feature of the global reach of technology is its standardization. As a technology, printing, for example, depends on standards, whether of page sizes or typefaces, but in the paper world there is an exuberant florescence of visual styles, allowing many different messages to be conveyed in the typeface. By contrast, on the internet expressive opportunities such as these are strictly limited, less by the underlying technology and more by the global topology. The familiar trade-off between reach and richness (Evans and Wurster 2000) applies on a global scale. A rich, expressive production, whether a Leo Tolstoy novel or a Renaissance painting, has limited circulation, while superficial expressions, such as tweets or graffiti, bounce around the world. The global village has much of the sameness as the medieval village, only on a much larger scale, with cranks and loud voices commanding a disproportionate share of attention. The new commons of the global village is now the attention that global villagers invest in their iPhones, computers, and televisions. A myriad of languages, religions, and styles of life are flattened out on Facebook. This is not so much a consequence of the technology as of the topology and its global reach, the structure of connections that it creates and enables both with other actors and with other technologies.

Standards are a form of autonomous representation, which as we have seen is *the* defining characteristic of technology, in contrast to earlier toolkits. Autonomous representation creates multiple degrees of freedom, in both physical and social spaces, for technology that earlier tools lacked. Scale, portability, and standardization both create new commons and undermine the old. Negotiating the governance of this new commons is an ongoing effort.

Technologies, both information and otherwise, have two other features that challenge the common good, broadly understood. One feature its ability to translate and transform, with the consequence that boundaries become more subtle, if not invisible. "Web-surfing" explores new territories, and the boundaries of different discussion groups are marked by subtle signals, which are known primarily to insiders. Who participates in the collective choice arrangements (Ostrom's [1990] third criterion for governing the commons) in an internet chat room? Similarly, facial recognition technology, with its Orwellian implications, has the potential to erase the line between the public square and a prison courtyard, marking the birth of a new prison (cf. Foucault 1975 on the "birth of the prison"). Technology puts incarceration on steroids, with devices such as ankle monitors as the latest forefront. It is probably no accident that some of the world's most technologically advanced societies simultaneously have the largest prison populations, not so much because they have more wrongdoers, but rather because of the augmented powers invested in the state. Although there are many other variables at play here, not the least of which is the national culture, the contribution of surveillance technology to the common good is a pressing question. Legislation is trying to catch up with these technological developments,[1] but Moore's Law (Gordon Moore's observation of technological acceleration; see Chapter 6) suggests that it is a losing battle.

Also relevant to the commons is the aesthetic of "high tech," and the manner in which it dominates the technoscape. "High tech" is a promotional concept rather than an element of engineering analysis. In their daily, sleeves-rolled-up work, engineers never use the phrase "high tech," unless they are attempting to promote the virtues of a new gadget or algorithm. The aesthetic of "high tech"—smooth surfaces and clean lines, rather than a messy tangle of wires—draws on modernism in design, which presents a dramatic, vivid break from classical and baroque design aesthetics, making a statement that the future is here, *now!*

Hiding functionality, high tech promotes the association of technology and magic (Berman 1982; Gell 1988). The futuristic aspect of technology, which is actually more an aesthetic than a temporal statement, emphasizes disruption: "All that is solid melts into air, all that is holy is profaned, and man is at last compelled to face with sober senses his real conditions of life, and his relations with his kind" (Marx and Engels 2014). Illusions of permanence and solidarity fade away before the churn of class exploitation. The aesthetics of "high tech" have the consequence that gatekeeping, defining the boundaries of the commons (Ostrom's [1990] first criterion), is less about physical constraint and more about shock and awe.

In sum, the distinctive features of technology, in contrast to earlier instrumentalities, as described above in Chapter 3, are portability, translation and transformation, scale, the aesthetic of modernism, and the defining feature, autonomous representation. These bear on several of Ostrom's principles for governing the commons: several of these attributes, including recognition of the right to organize, and conflict resolution mechanisms, are primarily normative or institutional; others, such as boundaries and gatekeeping, have a practical aspect. Table 5.1 summarizes the impact of technology on the eight criteria:

With regard to the first item, for example, the boundaries of newer, technological commons, whether airspace, the RF spectrum, brands and brand-related identities, or entire industries, are marked less by lines on a map or by familiar landmarks, and more by the shared understanding of insiders or identities. "Local conditions" (item 2) completely fall apart when "local" is less a physical space and more a social definition. "Monitoring" (item 4) has become a dynamic business in an age of "surveillance capitalism" (Zuboff 2019), as digital globalism and attention merchants (Wu 2016) traffic in new forms of value. Technology has the potential not only to create new commons (see above, Chapter 4), but also to scramble the settled arrangement of existing commons, meaning that the commons must be renegotiated. A society's capability for renegotiating its commons, and for renegotiating its identity, becomes an urgent question.

## Attention and Desire as Common Pool Resources

In the age of the internet, attention ("eyeballs") and desire ("mouse clicks") have become the latest resources to be enclosed, cultivated, and harvested. Malcolm McCullough (2013) defined the "ambient commons" as the unstructured information that pervades everyday life. However, for information to be meaningful, someone needs to be paying attention: if a tree falls in the forest, and no sentient being is around, does it make a sound? If a Facebook page has no followers, does it exist? More seriously, the "-scape"—to use Appadurai's term—of the ambient commons is the attention, focused or unfocused, waiting to be enclosed and harvested.

Stuart Ewen, in *Captains of Consciousness* (1976), describes the twentieth-century rise of the advertising *industry*, in which the nineteenth-century captains of industry were replaced by twentieth-century captains of consciousness, who created new forms of wealth. The metaphors of command and scale are appropriate here, inasmuch as prior to the twentieth century commercial promotion was mostly a craft affair, consisting of announcements of new arrivals of new products, unencumbered by marketing surveys, sophisticated graphical design, or

**Table 5.1.** Technological impact on governing the commons. Table created by the author.

| Ostrom's criteria | Technological impact | Contemporary example |
|---|---|---|
| 1. Clearly designed boundaries | Boundaries are no longer just geodetic, but can be intangible | RF spectrum, filter bubbles |
| 2. Congruence between appropriation and provision rules and local conditions | "Local" conditions can range over the entire world | "Attention merchants" harvesting eyeballs around the world |
| 3. Collective choice agreements | Collectivity is unstable | Variety of privacy laws around the world |
| 4. Monitoring | Numerous possibilities including facial recognition and GPS tracking | Smartphones' monitoring of movement |
| 5. Graduated sanctions | New forms of coercion | Online harassment |
| 6. Conflict resolution mechanisms | Flattening of messages as it extends their reach | Loss of nuance in filter bubbles |
| 7. Minimal recognition of rights to organize | Organization can be promoted or inhibited by technology | Facebook pages |
| 8. Nested enterprises | New opportunities for corporate hierarchies | Supply chains |

clever slogans. Only in the twentieth century did advertising execute a turn toward persuasion, an episode marked by Vance Packard in *The Hidden Persuaders* (1957).

Attention has the two key attributes of other common pool resources: it is difficult to fence off, yet it is high in subtractability—it is a finite resource. Although we have not probed the exact boundaries, it seems obvious that few people can engage with more than two or three television screens or iPhones simultaneously. One might "follow" several thousand Facebook pages, but the seriousness with which they engage these pages is a nontrivial question. Facebook limits users to five thousand "friends," oblivious to the irony it has created. The result is that "harvesting attention" has now become a major business, in fact *the* core business of platforms such as Facebook, Instagram, and Google. Tim Wu, in *The Attention Merchants* (2016), describes how these platforms exploit their monopoly position and unique business model to become some of the largest businesses in the world. Even Amazon, which started out as a bookseller, scaled up to sell *everything*, venturing into new fields including movie production and meal delivery, where its massive data on consumer preferences and algorithms can effectively predict commercial success. For Amazon, the marketplace is more like a factory, where scientific management of demand and supply have created astounding commercial success. The "common good" thus pivots around consumption. Other large-scale activities that long brought people together—civic participation in the town hall, appreciation of fine art in a museum or concert hall, or reverential worship in a cathedral, a temple, or a mosque—are subordinated to the role of the consumer sitting at home.

Desire is also a common pool resource. Philosophers have debated whether human desires are bounded or infinite. Bodily desires including food and sex are clearly finite, and exceptions to this are clearly pathological. But desires for fame, wealth, or immortality seemingly have no bounds. Although material resources and mortality are finite, illusions of these now drive the economy. Today's version of magic, advertising, offers illusions of health, physical attractiveness, and even immortality, which is all just one mouse click away. Although *magic* has largely lost its appeal in modern society, there are two important exceptions. The first is in the realm of advertising, which proposes to millions of gullible consumers that physical attractiveness or lifelong happiness can be purchased in a bottle. As discussed in the previous chapter, the construction of a brand is modern alchemy, "a way in which people bring meaning to different exchanges" (Lury 2004: 10).

The second area of modern life where magic remains relevant is in technology. As we have seen, engineers have a matter-of-fact attitude toward the devices that they design, build, and operate, explaining how an airplane flies or a computer calculates, whereas for the general public all of this is just magic (cf. Hubert and Mauss 1964; Gell 1988). Technology has several features classically associated with magic. First of all, for the average citizen, "how it works" is beyond comprehension. If one lists the technologies that have defined the twentieth and twenty-first centuries—television, flight, the computer, the internet—very few people other than specialists could explain how they work: their transformations of space and time are mysterious, magical. Second, many technologies do have awesome capabilities, whether planting a man on the moon or sending an image around the globe.

Although more and more of the public and scholars have begun questioning technology (Feenberg 1999), there has been no serious substantial discussion in either government or business of alternatives to technology. Scholars question whether technology is an autonomous force or a dependent variable in an industrial assemblage. "Low tech" is more a countercultural riposte than a serious design alternative. More precisely, an array of problems, whether refugees crossing the border, traffic safety, or crime, trigger a search for technological solutions, which often include surveillance cameras, virtual fences, border walls, driverless cars, or tracking devices. Institutional reform—assistance to struggling economies, better education for drivers, improved education for all citizens—is, at best, an afterthought.[2]

## The Changing Character of Culture

"Culture," anthropology's signature concept at least since Franz Boas's *Race, Language, and Culture* (1940), has been a contested term for several hundred years. Matthew Arnold, in *Culture and Anarchy* (1869), defined culture as "the best that has been thought and known in the world current everywhere; to make all men live in an atmosphere of sweetness and light." Culture, in Arnold's view, depended on cultivation, and was an elite possession, a club good. At about the same time the pioneering anthropologist Lewis Henry Morgan (1877) identified even "savage" tribes as having a culture. The standard anthropological definition, "a learned system of shared understandings," gave dignity to the numerous indigenous peoples in the colonial encounter. Yet in an age of mechanical reproduction, culture takes on yet a different aspect, perhaps disappearing altogether.

Arjun Appadurai has observed that in recent years anthropologists are more comfortable discussing the "cultural aspect" of different institutions and behaviors, rather than culture *per se*. This comes from a recognition that in a globalizing world different groups have a stake in multiple cultural assemblages, and that the pristine past, in which indigenous tribes and villages could cultivate their own culture, is long lost. Culture, for better or for worse, is increasingly *organized*, that is, subject to a global regime of instrumental rationality.

To introduce this new perspective on culture in the contemporary world, we need to consider three new dynamics:

1. the changing patterns of communication enabled by digital technology;
2. the dominance of regimes of instrumental rationality and the eclipse of traditional, patrimonial forms; and
3. the changing topology of the networked society.

In the first regard, patterns of communication have undergone multiple technological revolutions over the past five centuries, beginning with the Gutenberg press, which ushered in what Benedict Anderson (1983) calls "print capitalism," through the emergence of electronic media to now with the internet, creating an information ecosystem of digital globalism. One's consociates can now be found all over the world, and the accumulation of "friends" is a new currency.

In the second regard, Max Weber's distinction among traditional (or patrimonial), rational, and charismatic authority takes on a new coloration in the network society. As traditional forms such as family and church are eclipsed by charismatics, whether Donald Trump or Viktor Orbán, the "iron cage" of imperative coordination (Weber 1930) fills the breach in the social order, only now it is enforced with algorithms rather than armies or desk-bound bureaucrats.

In the network society (Castells 1996), connections have replaced communities as repositories of value, with bragging on social media about how many "likes" one has. The world system has evolved from locally isolated communities to imperial domination to the modern world system of core and periphery to a vast, all-encompassing network where members are tied together by their "likes" and "friends," who are just a mouse click away.

*Organized* culture—that is, that which is implicated in regimes of instrumental rationality—is the new iron cage. Culture is organized on multiple levels. State religions, which grew out of the Reformation and the Peace of Augsburg in 1555, made religion an appendage of the state (*cuius regio eius religio*). Similarly, language policy became an instrumentality of the state, with national school systems seeking to replace a plurality of patois with a uniform national language. In the twentieth century, movements of "multiculturalism" have pushed back against the cultural hegemony of imperial states, arguing for respect for indigenous languages and customs in public institutions.

All of this is accelerated in a networked society. Just as print capitalism gave birth to nationalism (Anderson 1983), so too digital globalism has given rise to scale-free networks embracing millions if not billions around the globe. Connectivity vectors—friendships, reputations, brands—are arguably more central to the dynamics of contemporary society than accumulative material resources. Economic resources, including land, capital, and intellectual and real property, were the central dynamic, the primary source of value in industrial societies. Today *social capital*—the value one places in one's relationships and connections—is the currency of the networked age, and attention to social capital, as evidenced by the use of the phrase, is isomorphic with the growth of the internet.

The evidence of this new currency stares us right in the face: even remote Pacific islands engage in trade and commerce. Mobile telephones, perhaps the ultimate global networking technology, have penetrated into every corner of the globe, including the interior of Africa, even those countries where governments try to restrict them. One of the most recognized figures around the world, Ronald, the emblematic clown figure of McDonald's, has become a global icon.

Regimes of instrumental rationality embrace multiple cultures. Culture is no longer (if it ever was) a system of shared understandings, but is now eclipsed by a series of peace treaties among multiple interests: a culture of command and corruption, a culture of accommodation and resistance, and a culture of inclusion and alienation. Cultures of command can (and often do) embrace cultures of corruption ("which of the rules is it acceptable to break?"). Corruption is, obviously, the opposite of the common good. Cultures of resistance are the flip side of cultures of accommodation ("how are we going to get along with those more powerful than us? how far can we push them?"). And cultures of inclusion and alienation include shared understandings ("who below us can we exploit?" "how can we get along with those more powerful than ourselves without losing our dignity?"). These cultures of resistance and accommodation are evident inside any large, well-established organization, whether General Motors or the US Army. Numerous examples of corporate and organizational cultures are found in every large organization that is more than a few years old. In the airline industry, after deregulation, pilots, pushing back against management, perfected a strategy of the "sweet sixteen," delaying a landing by 16 minutes to register in government statistics as a late arrival (Petzinger 1995: 415). In manufacturing after the advent of Frederick Taylor's "scientific management," workers carefully calibrated how *exactly* to comply with management directives, often as an expression of resistance (Zuboff 1988). Unions struck back against Tayloristic ("scientific") management with a strategy of "work to rule," following work instructions *exactly*. In many workplaces, both factory and office, workers display personal artifacts, whether coffee mugs or family photos, in an effort to assert individuality in an environment that reduces them to "the hands," appendages of the machine.[3]

A key aspect of these cultures of organization is that, like any peace treaty, once negotiated, the worst crime is to go back on one's commitments. A breach of faith can lead to a sense of betrayal and to violent reactions, and many terrorist incidents of the twenty and twenty-first centuries have been inspired, not by any innate malevolence of Buddhism or Islam or Christianity, but by a sense of betrayal and threatened identity. Whites reacted to what they saw as a betrayal in the growing assertiveness of African Americans in the late nineteenth century, leading to Jim Crow laws and the rise of America's first terrorist movement, the Ku Klux Klan. Another example is the defiling of Islam's sacred sites in the First Gulf War (1991), which led to a rise in terrorism. The rise in global terrorism, which began before 11 September 2001, is roughly coterminous with the increasing use of computerized information technology, and took off at the close of the twentieth century as the internet burst onto the scene.[4]

In short, in a networked world, culture—the human desire for shared understandings with consociates—has become a source of instability. The internet, which at the close of the twentieth century was supposed to bring the world together, instead is splintering it apart, with consequences yet to be even imagined. The "global village" is now subject to the same feuds and tribal rivalries of villages of earlier times, only now with a broader array of more powerful weapons and a greater geographical reach. Marshall McLuhan's bucolic metaphor of the "global village" (1989), with its imagery of harmony on the village green, obscures the fact that family feuds and tribal rivalries have scaled up in reach and intensity.

At the dawn of the modern era, print capitalism, in Benedict Anderson's phrasing, gave rise to nationalism and ultimately the nation-state. Men and women who were hundreds or even thousands of miles apart, reading the same newspaper, could *imagine* themselves part of a national community. By the twenty-first century, newspapers have become a dying breed, for reasons many have examined, and print capitalism is rapidly being replaced by digital globalism, creating scale-free networks, a topology of communication that now circles the globe with a superficiality that the nation lacked. Just as print is replaced by digital images, so too capitalism is replaced by networks lacking any topological constraints on their growth, and stable social forms—the nation-state and the corporation and the workplace—are replaced by shifting alliances, Facebook pages, and the gig economy. In the nineteenth century, a job was a lifetime commitment, and "job-hopping" was not openly discussed; in the gig economy, with platforms such as WeWork, Uber, Lyft, DoorDash, and Etsy, the stability of employment is no longer taken for granted. Exchanging "likes" may feel akin to building a community, but with a superficial and purely secular investment.

A scale-free network is analogous to capitalism as an economic formation, in that it is a topology for the creation, distribution, and accumulation of value. In this new economic paradigm, what is accumulated is connections, sometimes called "social capital," and a similar dynamic (the rich get richer) also prevails. On Facebook, one can have thousands of "friends," although obviously the meaning of friendship has been debased. Friendship, which once meant a diffuse personal commitment, attention, and solidarity, can now be created and captured in a split second with a mouse click.

This new economy of connections and "likes" has not replaced the old economy of goods and services and financial investment so much as it has eclipsed it. In the Middle Ages, the economy consisted of a mass of peasants, with a few merchants and craftsmen clustered in cities. With the Industrial Revolution, agriculture did not so much disappear, but owing to increased productivity agriculturalists no longer had a prominent role in politics outside the rural states. With the information revolution, manufacturing has receded in importance to be replaced by what we might call "cultural production"—mechanical reproduction (Benjamin 1968) has changed the character of culture. "Cultural production" includes not only the fine arts but also the media and even much of the content of the internet; Hollywood is a new cultural center in the media age, and "reality" TV has become a new political platform. Similarly, *social production*—the creation of social networks ("social capital")—is the new dynamic of accumulation, and many curate their social capital through the followers they get on Facebook.

Matthew Arnold's (1869) classical definition of culture was eclipsed in the twentieth century by the anthropological conception of a learned system of shared understandings, thus giving dignity to indigenous peoples all over the globe. In the twenty-first century, as Appadurai (1996) anticipated, culture has become fragmented—it is no longer a system, but rather an array of fleeting images. The core element of culture, the symbol, has been replaced by the meme, and the "memescape" is now the global conversation.

Obviously, children sitting on their mothers' laps are not inculcated with memes, a form which requires digital literacy. The pursuit of "screen time" even by youngsters, however, does suggest that competition between cultural forms begins at an early age, a fact that leaves traditionalists aghast. "Screen time," a phrase that did not exist before 1920, reached an inflection point near the end of the twentieth century, and is almost isomorphic with the expression "smartphone." Something new is being shared.

This increasing superficiality and evanescence of culture is obvious. What is less clear is what it says about the common good. How can we feel that we have anything beneficial in common if all we share is an array of evanescent memes and mouse clicks? Clearly, memes have value; otherwise, they would not be shared. Describing that value, and its consequences for the common good, is the challenge before us: memes are tokens of connectedness, the currency of digital globalism.

Memes offer us stimulation, intellectual arousal, much like a clever street-corner conversation or carnival barker. We watch obvious grifters with guilty pleasure, but when they move up to major political offices, it is an entirely new game. If the grifter is one of us, we smile at the reactions of the rubes, because he is doing it for us. If we like a meme, we want to share it, put it into circulation. Street-corner conversations, however, cannot go viral. Memes have a superficiality that other large-scale cultural formations, whether Jesus on the cross or the Tomb of the Unknown Soldier, clearly lack. The consequence, as noted above, is a debasement of cultural currency.

Appadurai identified global flows as an array of "-scapes," including technoscapes, ethnoscapes, mediascapes, ideoscapes, and financescapes. Technoscapes are the arrays of technologies available to a people, just as ethnoscapes are the array of self-conscious peoples. These eclipse the landscapes that in the nineteenth and twentieth centuries were central to national aspirations. I will discuss these and what they tell us about the common good in today's society in the next chapter; for the moment, I wish to note that these have eclipsed *culture* as a common binding of a community. Just as culture is that which is cultivated by a community, what we might call the "memescape" is now a significant cultural production, and the *imagined worlds* (Appadurai 1996: 3) of internet chat rooms, filter bubbles, and Facebook "friendships" exponentially pulverize the common good into billions of evanescent commons.

## The New Enclosures

*Facebook is watching:* the rise of social media, a space that was practically nonexistent 25 years ago, is perhaps the most subversive fact today for ideas of citizenship. With the emergence of the internet out of its origins in laboratories and universities, and into democratic spaces, dozens of experiments to colonize that space—Facebook, Twitter, Snapchat, Instagram—burst forth. These corporate social platforms quickly discovered that their most valuable asset was their users or, more accurately, data on their users—not simply demographics, which dominated market research in the twentieth century, but user relationships and preferences—"friends" and "likes" in Facebook terms. Facebook has built an immense edifice of billions of users and a market valuation of nearly a half-trillion dollars based on its ability to capture and manipulate the attention of its users, making Facebook the new *agora* (the open square of the Athenians), although now with surveillance cameras. Unlike the Big Brother of *1984*, where the purpose of this surveillance was to spot subversive behavior and warnings that "Big Brother is watching" were a quotidian reality (Orwell 1949), on Facebook the purpose of surveillance is to manipulate user behavior, beginning with the user's attention. Today, the citizens of Oceania (Orwell's fictitious country) all carry around in their pockets monitoring devices (smartphones), which record their movements, their relationships, and their preferences ("likes") to be tabulated and accumulated in "the cloud." Technology has enabled an immense industry in harvesting user attention, which we might call the "attention economy." This has eclipsed the economy of the Information age much like the rise of industry in the nineteenth and twentieth centuries eclipsed the agricultural economy.

This evolution of citizens, from field hands to factory hands to eyeballs, is perhaps the greatest threat to democracy today. By limiting participation in the polity simply to a limited array of human capabilities, whether consumer choices or attention on Facebook, the entire edifice of political participation is devalued.

The defining architecture of these new enclosures is the "platform"—the space on which all other devices rest. Amazon, for example, is more than a bookseller or an advertiser, a movie producer, or grocer: it is a platform on which numerous other businesses can operate, a toll good that is proving the phenomenal success of its innovative business model. "Platforming" represents a twenty-first-century business model, in which success comes not from production but from connection.

Similarly Facebook, which started out as a network for exchanging personal information, is now a platform for hundreds of thousands (at least) of "filter bubbles," hermetic conversations that do less to inform their participants than to confirm their prejudices. A filter bubble is a club good; it can exclude those who do not share its prejudices, but it is low in subtractability: the only limit on how many can join are those artificially imposed by the platform—for example, Facebook's limitation of five thousand "friends." This new public square encompasses billions of "users" with millions of niche conversations and almost no presence of authority to maintain civility (McNamee 2019). Thus, at the expense of many other social roles (citizen or kinsman or political follower or ardent lover), social participation acquires a "clubbishness" at the expense of public activities.

Just as the enclosure movement of the sixteenth century onward led to more efficient use of agricultural resources at the expense of domestic life, so too the "platforming" not only of commerce but of many other aspects of contemporary life—entertainment, politics, religion, communities, education—leads to a more efficient use of attention and optimizes those aspects that can be captured (and measured and monetized and marketed) at the expense of many others including shared fellowship and sacrifice. Just as entertainment is captured through "streaming" services, at the expense of the communal experience of actual theater attendance, so too "megachurches" such as the Abundant Living Faith Center in El Paso, Texas, with more than twenty thousand parishioners, and hundreds of other "megachurches" have become the seedbeds for today's evangelical movement, capturing reverence and devotion shared by thousands. Most of these have an internet presence, but something is lost when prayer and devotion are just a matter of a couple of mouse clicks at the kitchen table.

Attention and desire, of course, have existed throughout human history, but it is only in the twentieth and twenty-first centuries that the possibility of arousing and harvesting attention and desire on an industrial scale became the foundation of a new economic constellation; this is summarized in the prevalence of branding as a dynamic not only in the economy but also in political life through "nation-branding," as discussed in the previous chapter, and the assessment of political personalities and movements in terms of their "brand." How this new economic constellation might be part of the common good is a substantial question. These new enclosures, in other words, are not just about enclosing and monopolizing natural resources, but also about enclosing and monetizing the raw material of culture—memories, attention, shared images such as landscapes, and shared attitudes such as reverence and patriotism, which underlie democracy.

In sum, in this chapter I have considered the different coordinates of citizenship in the internet age, and how technology affects, alters, and undermines the common good of citizenship. I focused on two key resources in the internet age, attention and desire, as part of the foundation of a new economy. One consequence of this is that *organized* culture increasingly eclipses traditional or patrimonial culture as the shared experience of citizens everywhere around the world. This has resulted in an opportunity for new enclosures, for a new engrossment of the raw material of the new economy. The tension between these new enclosures and the "-scapes" that define a democracy are considered in the next chapter.

## Notes

1. Like so much else, privacy legislation in the age of the internet is focused more on harm to consumers than on harm to citizens. The Electronic Communications Privacy Act of 1986 allows the federal government to access digital communications, although no warrant is required for information more than 180 days old. The Cyber Intelligence Sharing and Protection Act of 2015 was opposed by the Electronic Frontier Foundation for its inadequate privacy protections. See the Conclusion for more on the "electronic frontier."
2. The safest form of travel in terms of accidents per passenger mile is flying. One could argue that if automobile drivers were trained and screened as rigorously as aircraft pilots, automobile travel would be similarly quite safe. However, assumptions about entitlements to automobility (i.e., who is entitled to use the commons of the public highways) and urban (and suburban) design are so thoroughly woven through contemporary society, that massive protests would greet any such institutional efforts to make driving safer. Tinkering around with the technology of cars and traffic safety is socially acceptable, even if the consequences are unseen.
3. The concept of organized culture is developed further in my article "Negations and Ambiguities in the Cultures of Organization," which was published in Mats Alvesson's *Classics in Critical Organizational Studies* (2011).
4. My point here is not that the internet is in any way a cause of terrorism, but rather that it multiplies opportunities for misunderstanding and betrayal, sometimes with deadly results. Even in the face of widespread campaigns against disinformation and "alternative facts," millions around the globe form the conclusion that if some assertion is "on the internet" it must be true. A raving drunk in a bar is ignored, or perhaps ejected by the bouncer,

but if he is raving on the internet, someone, somewhere around the world, will take him seriously, and give him a platform. The business model of Facebook is built on just this dynamic.

Chapter 6

# Democratic Vistas

Shared perspectives, sometimes identified as "-scapes," are one of the most important elements uniting a community, a self-identified grouping that asserts "we have something in common." In *Understanding Knowledge as Commons*, Hess and Ostrom (2007) identified *sunsets*, or more generally landscapes, as public goods. More broadly, we might suggest that "-scapes," the shared perspectives that unite a community, are exemplary public goods. As Arjun Appadurai suggests, these are the multiple dimensions of global flows, including ethnoscapes, mediascapes, technoscapes, financescapes, and ideoscapes:

> These landscapes are thus the building blocks of what (extending Benedict Anderson) I would like to call *imagined worlds*, that is the multiple worlds that are constituted by the historically situated imaginations of persons and groups spread around the globe. (Appadurai 1996: 33)

Not only landscapes but also ethnoscapes, mediascapes, and the other "-scapes" are *shared* perspectives, meaning that they unite a community and thereby create a shared feeling that "we have something in common." We can note that each of these is a technological construction. Although the ethnoscape of the Nuer was constituted by the Nuer and the Dinka, in the contemporary world the entire array of ethnicities, lifestyles, and media images that one encounters is constituted by the communication technologies and social media at hand. *Images* of immigrant hordes from the Global South loom much greater in the imagination of those who have seen them on social media than those who actually live near the southern border. And further, as technologies evolve, these "-scapes" evolve, and shared perspectives must be renegotiated every few years. For example, "bot farms" (servers that automatically deploy "bots" or automated programs on the internet) played no role in America's national politics before the current century, but now pose a major concern with regard to election integrity. The nuclear arms race of the twentieth century is now, in the twenty-first century, replaced by a digital arms race, with Russia's Internet Research Agency deploying armies of bots and trolls to pollute the new public square, damaging its value irreparably. More generally, one might say that the pollution of the public square has gone global.

In this chapter, I will examine these shared perspectives that make up a democratic society in a technological age. Foremost among them is the city itself (Section 1), and after that the facts and imaginations of wealth (and poverty; Section 2). Public goods (Section 3) and the urban commons in general take on a unique character in a neoliberal age that seeks to devalue the common good. Civic life, consisting of the ethnoscape, republicanism, and geographic stability, *engages* citizens and acquires new challenges in a technological age.

An important part of any public good is its *representation*: less in terms of some artist's sketchbook and more in terms of the *shared* images that the community holds, whether at court, or in the morning newspaper, or in the civic square. As discussed above in Chapter 1, a defining feature of technology is *autonomous representation*, representation that is independent of the actual object or implement. So too an important part of a republic is its representation, not only in the tomes of jurists and the halls of Congress, but in the daily lives of citizens. As private goods become ideologically ascendant (see Chapter 2), representations of public goods are increasingly contested and fragmented, as memes replace orators' ringing declarations and screenshots crowd out throngs in the public square. Life on the screen creates a superficiality to the common good impossible to imagine in traditional, face-to-face gatherings.

To understand in depth this superficiality and its consequences, we must consider two "-scapes" that have received considerable attention of late: ethnoscapes and financescapes. As flows of migrants and refugees increase, not only in the Americas but all over the world, portrayals of "aliens" have hardened, often on social media. The role of technology in redefining the urban ethnoscape is considered in the first section of this chapter. Similarly, as complex, exotic financial technologies have multiplied, offering promises of riches with little effort or risk, staid financial institutions, whether Wells Fargo or Drexel Burnham, have traded on the public good of "trust" (which was often incorporated in their name, such as "Bankers' Trust") to swindle millions of homeowners with predatory lending and nearly wrecked the world economy, as described below in Section 2. The role of technology in counterfeiting "trust" is a major story in today's financescape, as is the role of social media in representing, or perhaps creating, contemporary ethnoscapes, notably cities and the diversity and monumentality they represent.

Cities and civilizations are perhaps the quintessential commons in contemporary society, creating spaces for the circulation of peoples, ideas, and wealth. This circulation, as Jane Jacobs describes in *Cities and the Wealth of Nations* (1984), creates the opportunity for economic and other forms of diversity. Cities are as much an architectural as a political creation, and advances in construction technology and public health have enabled cities to evolve from the pestilential slums of the Middle Ages into the crown jewels that are Paris, San Francisco, and St. Petersburg. By way of contrast, municipal decay, whether in Flint, Michigan, or Chicago, points to the institutional neglect that is endemic in a technological society.

Just as architectural advances created new urban possibilities, so too technological advances create new opportunities for free-riding on the urban commons. Cities are about more than jamming thousands or millions of people together into small spaces; they are about a new view of the common good, in which the virtues of citizenship create benefits for all. Foremost among these benefits are the diversity of cities and their surrounding regions. Economists recognize that a diversified, import-replacing economy has greater potential for adequate livelihoods than single-crop regions or single-industry economies, which are dependent on a distant metropole.

In Section 1, I will describe the role of social media in creating today's imagined ethnoscape, and in Section 2 I will examine the role of technology in subverting the patrimonial forms of authority that previously underlay financial institutions. Both of these pillars of the common good, the ethnoscape and the financescape, are undermined by technological advances.

Just as print capitalism challenged the boundaries of literary works, so too digital globalism challenges the boundaries of privacy. Section 3 describes the dialectic between private efforts and public appreciation evident in both community parks and expressive works. Andrew Newman in *Landscape of Discontent* (2015) describes the efforts of citizens in northeast Paris to create a community park, and the entire history of literary and artistic production creates public goods, albeit with new meanings in an age of digital globalism.

Section 4 describes the changing meaning of citizenship in the era of digital globalism, building on Benedict Anderson's (1983) description in *Imagined Communities* of the emergence of nationalism in an era of print capitalism and its connection to the Gutenberg Press. At the close of the twentieth century, a new form of business was created, which was based less on producing and distributing goods and services and more on harvesting attention ("likes") and networks ("friends"). I am calling this new form of business *digital globalism*, in order to emphasize the underlying (digital) technology and the resulting (global network) scale. Although we typically think of business as engines of "the national economy," in the current era of digital globalism, footloose business has slipped these surly bonds and has been more about creating and aggregating new forms of value not captured in the statistics of "the economy" or "Gross National Product." The networks and eyeballs harvested by this business defines more of our lives every day. How these new commons engage citizens and subjects, less in terms of economic returns and more in terms of moods and motivations, will be described in the final section of this chapter.

## Representing the City

A substantial body of history, literature, social science, and even engineering interrogates the nature of the city. For most of recorded history, cities, particularly monumental cities such as Chicago, Paris, and Detroit, have been regarded as the pinnacles of civilization, a crowning achievement shared by all of humanity. However, if not properly governed or if neglected, cities and civilizations can degrade.

Chicago, Carl Sandburg's "City of the Big Shoulders," and home of the "Chicago School" that dominated American sociology in the first half of the twentieth century, has been a throbbing commercial hub; located at the foot of Lake Michigan where rail lines and Great Lakes transport converge, it brought together the agricultural bounty of the Midwest, the emerging industry of the Great Lakes states, and the emerging economy of derivatives (on the Chicago Mercantile Exchange), to create an unprecedented center of prosperity not on the coasts but uniquely in the center of the continent.

Paris, the "City of Light," with its architectural monuments, its role as a center of fashion, arts, and learning, and its cultural imprint on writers and scholars everywhere, has left its mark on architecture, engineering, and technology.

Finally, David Maraniss's *Once in a Great City: A Detroit Story* (2015), written in the wake of Detroit's 2013 filing for bankruptcy (the largest municipal bankruptcy in American history), recounts the numerous contributions that Detroit has made to American culture: from the origination of two musical styles (Motown and hip-hop), to the automotive industry that became the foundation of the American middle class, to the anchor of the American labor movement in the United Auto Workers, a major engine of the civil rights movement in the 1960s, to world-class museums and orchestras, and notable architecture. "The Arsenal of Democracy," Franklin Roosevelt's characterization of Detroit's industrial base, was central to winning the war against Germany and Japan. In the 1970s, Detroit was a focus of progress in civil rights. Yet three decades later, after years of inattentive management, the city filed for chapter 9 bankruptcy, a major disgrace. No one was governing the urban commons.

The city is a fairly recent invention in human settlement. Homo sapiens has ranged across the globe for roughly the last 300,000 years, but only in the waning 11th hour of this history did urban settlements make an appearance. The earliest cities were sacred shrines and later formations for projecting the power of priests and warlords.

From the very beginning, the city was far more important than simply jamming hundreds or thousands of people into small precincts; it was about a new conception of power and a new conception of shared humanity, in which the ultimate public good, the city, was a source of pride for all and *for citizens*, the rightful possessors of the city, who do not simply occupy it but actually build it. Perhaps the greatest shared value of the city is its *ambience*, and the ambient commons of unstructured information is often what gives a city its vitality. Enclosures of the ambient commons, whether through garish billboards or surveillance cameras, saps this vitality (McCullough 2013). In contrast to the monumentality of the Lincoln Center or the Palais Garnier in Paris, where artistic creations are displayed, the beat of Greenwich Village or the vibe of night clubs in Harlem is where artistic creativity originates. By suppressing this informal vitality of the ambient commons, a society suppresses its future.

Cities, of course, are more than just creativity. Diversity, monumentality, civility, and productivity go into the making of cities. A city is perhaps *the* archetypal ethnoscape of the contemporary world, and the contrast between urbanites and rustics eclipses ethnic and national distinctions in today's world. Whether the rustics are called "hillbillies" or "*péquenauds*" or "деревенщина," around the world, or at least in its civilized quarters, they are seen as unsophisticated and ignorant.

Social media breaks down the urban ambience, substituting images on small screens for the cityscape. Many city dwellers are tethered to their "smartphones," oblivious, or at least less aware, of their cityscape, a narrowing of perspective that used to happen only among rustics in the countryside. The *character* of the city changes when the spontaneous interactions of pedestrians with each other is replaced with eyes fixated on small screens. Facebook pages substitute for neighbors, and create "friends" who have never met. The "collective effervescence," Durkheim's (1965) characterization of the shared feeling of congregations that is at the heart of the religious experience, or of political rallies, or of family celebrations, dissolves into solitary absorption on the smartphone.

In sum, the cityscape, a crowning, collective achievement of human history and an architectural and technological triumph, is now dissolving between the twin forces of technological absorption and institutional neglect. The twentieth-century devolution of the common goods of prosperity and public goods into absorption with private goods is a subject to which I now turn.

## Wealth and Poverty

In 1958, John Kenneth Galbraith (*The Affluent Society*) took note of the paradox of "poverty in the midst of plenty" in what was supposed to be a wealthy society. For hundreds of years, as Galbraith observed, American society had placed an emphasis on private wealth, often to the neglect of public goods such as infrastructure, education, and public order.

This valorization of private goods and the market, begun perhaps with Adam Smith, goes contrary to tens of thousands of years of human experience. Throughout human history, most values, most goods, have been public, common pool, or club goods, with private goods forming only an insignificant corner, perhaps the king in his castle with his chest of gold, or the peasant in his hut with his personal wardrobe. The *commons* that the peasant cultivated was a common pool resource, shared with other villagers, just as the king's castle was a club good shared with his dynasty. The skills of a craftsman, or the market knowledge of a merchant, were club goods acquired through apprenticeship in the guild. So too the comradeship of warriors or the sodality of charitable organizations were club goods, reinforcing a sense that "we are special." All goods depend on shared goods. This is an easy demonstration: even emblematic private goods, such as doughnuts (Hess and Ostrom 2007: 9), depend on state regulation (in America, the Pure Food and Drug Act) to assure their safety, and the functioning of markets in today's society depends on the rule of law and the availability of courts to enforce contracts. We now take this for granted, but before Upton Sinclair's *The Jungle* (1980) factory-produced industrial food was often suspect. Likewise personal computers, which Hess and Ostrom similarly identify as private goods, depend on a vast architecture of standards, quintessentially public goods. One might say that there is no such thing as an exclusively private good, other than something made by a hermit in his cave. All other goods are in some manner or other shared; even if this is only through a market mechanism, the rule of law that guarantees ownership, or only with family and kin. We can observe that the market is perhaps the oldest and ultimate public good, and the manner in which medieval towns designated certain days as market days bears witness to the market as a public institution.

Economists often point out that contemporary society is more "prosperous" than its historical predecessors. This is true only insofar as one confines an understanding of "the economy" to the market-mediated circulation of private goods and services, excluding both unpaid domestic labor (a necessary part of the ethnoscape) and developmental labor including the engineering effort to create new goods such as the educational commons that I describe later and the educational labor needed to create new workers, none of which figure into the statistics of "Gross Domestic Product." Time spent in a classroom or a laboratory is not reckoned in these statistics, although both clearly improve the *productivity* of other activities that are so accounted. It also excludes the production of the rule of law or safe streets (public goods) as well as the production of club goods such as reputations and memberships. Family solidarity exercised on feast days and family celebrations, and in fact the entire apparatus of religious institutions, higher education, and nearly all services of government are public goods or club goods, which are not (or should not be) for sale, and hence are not counted as part of "Gross Domestic Product."

Whenever one has a complex system with multiple variables (private goods, public goods, and common pool resources, for example), optimizing the system for one single performance variable and ignoring the rest inevitably improves the performance of that variable, although usually at the expense of the other, unmeasured variables, which are characterized by economists as "externalities." It would be like building an internal combustion engine for maximum horsepower (a single performance variable) at the expense of fuel consumption, weight, size, emissions, and even cost. It might be a powerful engine, but no more than an idle, workshop curiosity. The entire *art* of engineering has been expressed in the knowing of how to manage and optimize these trade-offs, between (for example) size and cost or emissions and weight, through what engineers refer to as "trade studies," to build something that is actually useful. This requires balancing all the variables that must come together in the final, engineered product. So, too, optimizing "the economy" solely for private goods may produce impressive statistics for "Gross Domestic Product" (measuring private goods), an idle, academic curiosity, but at the expense of public goods (such as infrastructure), club goods (such as educational institutions), and even common pool resources (such as the environment), as well as at the expense of overall resilience. This skewing has largely been the story of the American economy for the last 40 years, ever since the beginning of the neoliberal era. Smart investors know that a diversified portfolio can better withstand the ups and downs of business cycles. Likewise, a diversified institutional portfolio of public, private, club, and common pool resources can better withstand the ups and downs of unexpected events, wars, famines, natural disasters, and pandemics.

This optimization of the entire complex of goods and services, public and private, for private consumption has been the story of economics over the past three hundred years, ever since Adam Smith, as private goods were measured and public goods were slighted. This has resulted in the improvement of private performance, although at the expense of the common good, whether the impoverishment of domestic life or a withering of democracy. And further: common pool resources, like club goods and public goods, are not marketable, so it is complete nonsense to ascribe a "price" to them, at least not until they are privatized and placed on the market. Thus, any comparison of the "affluent society" with earlier societies, implicit in Galbraith's (1958) title *The Affluent Society*, rests on the category error that the only goods worth counting are private goods.

In America today, one representation of private affluence is home ownership, and America has placed more emphasis on home ownership than have other industrial societies. "A man's home is his castle" suggests not only that he is a sovereign within its four walls, but that home ownership is the ultimate private good, and financing home ownership and the social individualism that it represented was for the common good as understood at mid-century. The cityscape of a suburban neighborhood with tidy homes and well-manicured lawns is emblematic of prosperity.

Beginning in the 1980s, however, for a variety of reasons, not the least of which was the deregulation of financial services and the celebration of the "free market," following Friedrich Hayek (1944) and others, home ownership took on a different color, and predatory lenders and "mortgage originators" discovered that they could swindle millions of homeowners. Prior to the neoliberal turn of the 1980s, most mortgages were written by banks and savings and loan institutions, who held onto the note and thus had some skin in the game. "Mortgage origination" became a new business from the 1950s onward, in which mortgage originators wrote mortgages backed up by overvalued property, mortgages that they then sold to hedge funds, pension funds, and other financial institutions where the hand of regulation was slight. "Flipping houses" became a new business model, as it was nonexistent before the current century, and took off as a model for encouraging real estate speculation. The resulting Great Recession is a recent and familiar story.

Similarly, "private equity," a business model that scarcely existed before the neoliberal turn, like its predecessor in the leverage buyout industry lines the pockets of executives and shareholders by flipping overvalued companies: using (typically) borrowed money to buy a controlling interest in shares, then divesting the company of underperforming assets and taking the company private. Private equity has resulted in the loss of more than a million jobs, supposedly in the name of efficiency but at the expense of the common good (Baradaran 2017).

The enabling role of technological developments in these stories is a tale that has thus far not been told. Traditionally, loans were made on the basis of the assessed valuation of the property, the borrower's income, and the borrower's credit history. The borrower's (informal) reputation in the community also counted. Reputation is a club good. As the instruments of calculation were improved (that is, became more complex and opaque), lenders were able to bend these rules, and justify loans that they knew the borrowers would be unable to repay. Why a lender would make a loan that he did not expect to be repaid has puzzled some commentators, but when the loan is backed by the deed to an overvalued property, it makes good business sense to loan more to the borrower than he can afford to repay and, after a few months or years when the borrower defaults, foreclose on the property. This business model fueled a bubble that burst in 2008, leaving millions poorer than before.

"Financial engineering"—a concept that scarcely existed before the advent of the neoliberal era—became a new business model. The creation of complex and opaque financial instruments and practices changed "finance" from *investment*, whether in factories or homes, or productive resources, into *speculation*, suggesting that "wealth" is no longer a true measure of the common good. The creation of a speculative economy measuring in the *trillions* of dollars, overshadowing the "real" economy of goods and services, created what we might call an "anti-commons," a shared hazard, less of a meadow than a swamp, where snakes and alligators and predatory lenders and unscrupulous stock jobbers lurk, contrasted to the classical commons of shared productive resources.

Part of the bursting of the bubble was due to the fact that financial markets were increasingly automated—that is, rendered opaque. The classic image of the trading floor at a stock exchange, where traders in the pits in brightly colored jackets waving wildly ("Buy!" "Sell!") strike face-to-face deals, has almost completely been replaced by machines and algorithms that strike deals, in the ether in milliseconds, just as haggling in open-air markets has been replaced by Amazon. As described in Alex Preda's "Machineries of Finance: Technologies and Sciences of Markets" (2017), finance has gone from being a liquidity supplier (enabling the flow of goods, services, and capital) to being the main game of the economy, with financial flows eclipsing by an order of magnitude the flow of goods and services. The resulting "finance curse" (Shaxson 2019) immiserates millions if not billions, to the puzzlement of the guardians of the status quo. How can wealth be a curse? This, too, is an enclosure. Just as an abundance of natural resources can often lead to the "resource curse" in which resource-rich nations such as the Congo or Chile or Venezuela fail to develop institutions to govern their common resources to the benefit of all, so too the net result of an accumulation of financial resources has arguably left large segments of the world poorer, a fact that does not show up in any statistics about the "Gross Domestic Product."

An untold story behind the Great Recession has been the role of financial technology, or "fintech" (a term that did not exist before 1980), in inflating the bubble. New financial instruments, such as collateralized default obligations and credit default swaps, emerged on the scene, and were deployed by staid financial institutions all over the industrial world. Tax havens, whether in Luxembourg, Switzerland, Jersey, or the Cayman Islands, became the ultimate destinations for trillions of dollars, pounds, and euros, a squirreling away of wealth that has no connection to the common good. I do not intend to state that this pursuit of tax havens was a product of technologies such as "fintech," spreadsheets, and the internet; the collapse of empires (French, British, Soviet, and then American), imperial overreach, and the collapse of Bretton Woods as described in the next chapter was equally a part of the crippling of national economies. The net result of financialization, however is mass immiseration, far from the common good. Nicholas Shaxson, in *The Finance Curse* (2019), describes how the global accumulation of wealth, the dark side of globalization, makes the world poorer.

A critical understanding of technology will help us understand how amassing private wealth can produce widespread poverty. Charles Perrow (1984) describes "normal accidents" as the expectable outcome of industrial systems that are complex and tightly coupled: when a system is tightly coupled, normal operational deviations ramify throughout the system, rather than being buffered by loose coupling. When it is excessively complex, tracing these ramifications becomes difficult, particularly at moments when time is precious. Perrow began his analysis with an examination of the Three Mile Island disaster, yet applied it to aircraft, petrochemical plants, and other technologies. Similarly, Perrow's ideas are applicable to financial structures: the rise of "fintech" systems that are tightly coupled and opaque has contributed to several notable financial crashes, notably the housing bubble at the beginning of the twenty-first century.

The tendency of financial markets (and now residential markets) toward cycles of boom and bust represents a dark side of private goods. In the wake of the stock market crash of 1929, a wave of "short-selling" (a concept that scarcely existed before the twentieth century) emerged—borrowing an asset to be sold, hoping that the price will fall to permit the "investor" to cover his short and give back the borrowed shares and keep the difference between the (higher) price at which they were sold and the (lower) price at which they were bought. "Shorting" became a commonplace business model after the Great Crash, and has made a comeback at the beginning of the twenty-first century. To "short" an asset is to bet on its failure, and an overvalued security becomes not a private good but a public hazard. From a private property viewpoint, "shorting" perhaps makes good business sense, but it is clearly inimical to the common good.

In sum, even something as simple or obvious as household wealth is a social construction, depending on social conventions and shared norms; "Gross Domestic Product" is a very recent invention, coming out of the rise of the nation-state in the ashes of imperial dominions (Lepenies 2016). Wealth, even when aggregated, is not the same as the common good, and in fact is more typically inimical to the common good. As the custodians of private wealth become wealthier and more powerful, the caretakers of public goods, including (but not limited to) governments and nongovernmental organizations, wither away. Anti-government ideologues free-ride on the public good that government supports.

A recent alternative perspective to "Gross Domestic Product" is the concept of "Genuine Progress Indicator" (GPI), which expands on GDP to include such social goods and externalities as income inequality, costs of underemployment, costs of pollution, the value of higher education, and public goods such as highways and streets (Kubiszewski et al. 2013). The inventor of GDP, the economist Simon Kuznets, noted in 1934

> the welfare of a nation can scarcely be inferred from a measure of national income. If the GDP is up, why is America down? Distinctions must be kept in mind between quantity and quality of growth, between costs and returns, and between the short and long run. (Kuznets 1934)

When we expand our concept of the "common good" to include non-private goods, we discover that often technology has detracted from the common good. Obvious examples are externalities (which, by definition, are not calculated into accounts) such as pollution and a degraded quality of life; less obvious examples include the erosion of privacy through surveillance technologies and the fracturing of community solidarity into tribal competitions. An exclusive focus on private goods, which typifies most policy discussions in America, subtracts from the common good.

In sum, the injection of technology into financial institutions and calculations, while possibly making them more efficient, has also made them less transparent and more fragile. *Finance* is a substantial, institutional edifice that can be undermined by technology and diverted from its institutional objectives toward supporting only private goods. A similar dynamic obtains for public goods in a technological society.

## Representing Public Goods

In today's society, public goods are increasingly contested, and even goods that at one time were "of course" public—municipal gardens, sidewalks, open-air markets—are increasingly enclosed. The images that we have of public goods, whether urban commons or expressive works, are increasingly the locus of this contestation. For an example, we might consider the Jardin d'Éole described by Andrew Newman in *Landscape of Discontent* (2015). Built in an abandoned railroad yard in northeast Paris, this garden became a site of contestation between immigrant groups organized to manage the "urban commons," and the government as represented by the Direction des Espaces Verts et de l'Environnment. In the mix were also ideas of civic responsibility and "the republican notion of public space as a common good for all furnished by the state" (Newman 2015: 149). Landscape architecture, in Newman's words, "naturalizes *patrimoine*" (a totemic trope worth noting), yet the use of electronic surveillance results in an "enclosure of democratic commons" (2015: 137). "The demand for the park had its roots in an attempt to recast *what the city is* for at a basic level (sustaining life as opposed to extracting value) and radically imagine *who the city is built for*" (2015: 61). Settled arrangements among immigrant communities and deeply held notions in French heritage are upended by technology, including facial recognition systems. Similarly in "Gatekeepers of the Urban Commons," Newman (2013) describes how "monitoring and controlling the social composition of the urban commons" (2013: 947) becomes a form of civic engagement for middle-class Parisians, which is made more acute by the presence of West African and Maghrebi immigrants. "The commons" is often less attainable when those on the commons feel that they have little in common.

In addition to public spaces, public goods include cultural productions, whether books, cinema, or musical performances. Prior to the Industrial Revolution, there was no legal protection for expressive works, in part because print capitalism was nonexistent. Stationers' guilds might hold books closely (a sort of private copyright), but there was no public order. With the Statute of Anne in 1710, the first legal protection for books, which was vested in authors rather than in publishers, protected expressive productions. Article I, Section 8 of the American Constitution makes it clear that the purpose of patents and copyrights is to promote the advancement of science and the useful arts by giving the inventor or the creator a *limited* period of protection. With the growth of what we might call the "culture industry" (primarily Hollywood, but also other cultural productions on an industrial scale including mass media), there were efforts to enclose this emerging commons, culminating in the Sonny Bono Copyright Act of 1998. Among the primary drivers of revisions and extensions of copyright since the first copyright act in 1790 have been the increasing availability of media (beginning with audio recording [the gramophone] and extending through motion pictures to digital media and now thousands of sites on the internet) to capture and preserve expressive productions. With the rise of this culture industry, the dividing line between knowledge and ideas, on the one hand, and their expression, on the other, is increasingly blurred. Technology has once again blurred the boundary between public and private goods.

Knowledge, of course, is perhaps like education, the ultimate public good. It is neither excludable (other than secrets) nor depletable; but the representation of knowledge, whether in prose or poetry, is protected, in order to encourage creativity. As technologies of knowledge representation develop, creativity is ring-fenced and cultural growth is stifled. Knowledge and the arts are public goods, whose production and development *always* occur in a commons, whether an academic seminar or a night club performance. I am drawing a strong distinction between the idle musings of one's mind, on the one hand, and *shared* discussions and insights, on the other, only the latter of which could truly be called knowledge; likewise, my scribblings on a sketch-pad versus a rough or finished drawing that I *share* with my friends is the distinction between a private good and a public good. The scholar or composer sitting at her desk would not say that her composition was complete until it had been presented or performed. Yet with the growth of the internet from 1995 onward, issues of free-riding, congestion, overuse, and pollution, which have plagued common pool resources for centuries, began to plague the knowledge commons. The "second enclosure movement," in the words of legal scholar James Boyle (2002), began staking out new possibilities for industrial development.

In sum, as can be seen both in the Jardin d'Éole and in the history of copyright protections, there is an important dialectic between private production and public appropriation, with each dependent on the other: public goods such as useful knowledge or urban parks require private protection whether through copyright laws or citizens' vigilance, and private goods in today's society require protection from the state. Devaluation of either side of this dialectic, whether in the Soviet economy of the twentieth century where everything was made "public" (i.e., the property of the state) or in the neoliberal turn in today's society where traditional public goods, including schools and streets, are privatized (i.e., enclosed), invariably fractures and immiserates the society, even if it may benefit a small elite (the "one percent," or Communist Party apparatchiks). The test of a first-rate society is the ability to embrace two opposed civic orders at the same time, and still retain the ability to function.[1]

As mechanical reproduction became ascendant, first with the printing press and later with cinema and then the internet, contests over who can control knowledge and images became heated. When media was a business on the fringe in an industrial economy dominated by hard goods, this was scarcely an issue, and copyright terms were 40 years beyond an author's death. But as Hollywood and motion pictures turned media into a major force, copyright terms were extended to 75 years beyond the author's death, thus privatizing what had previously been a public good. As software and computer technology extended the (potential) range of copyright protection, enclosing the instruments of the new economy, a substantial body of work centered on the Free Software Foundation argued for the abolition of copyright for software. This push-and-pull of intellectual property protections in multiple domains is driven both by technological advance and institutional decline.

## The Elementary Structures of Civic Life

Having discussed how public goods are represented through knowledge and culture and their place, or not, in the commons, we turn now to how *citizenship* can be a shared and valued attribute as part of the structures of civic life. Citizenship is perforce a *shared* attribute. Citizens can engage to varying degrees with their consociates, but Robinson Crusoe was not a "citizen" of his island. Precisely what is shared, what rights and obligations, is a thorny question, with various parties arguing for ancestry and birthright and race; for many years, those of African descent were only "second-class citizens" and others of non-European or even southern European ancestry were suspect. "Naturalization," a totemic ritual and trope that conferred citizenship on aliens, turned something that was supremely cultural into something that was "natural."

By citizenship, in brief, I refer to an individual's relationship to the state. In the Middle Ages, the king's *subjects* were not *citizens*. Defining the contours of citizenship has been an open contest for nearly all of America's history, as indeed it has been for every other modern nation. "Birthright citizenship" is today hotly contested with the arrival of undocumented immigrants. The legal contours of citizenship have always been a front-burner debate, with numerous books discussing what it means to be a citizen.

Part of citizenship is a new ethnoscape, in which the world is divided into fellow citizens and aliens. Before the arrival of modern transportation and communication technologies, the ethnoscape was but a minor issue, more of a concern to kings fighting their wars than to their common subjects. People just were not traveling or migrating in large enough numbers to pose a problem. As citizens from all over the world began mingling, not only in America but in every country in the world with a major industrial city, deciding who was entitled to the live in a country and who was entitled to the benefits of citizenship became pressing issues. For example, in the late nineteenth century in the United States, debates about citizenship culminated with the passage of the Alien Exclusion Act of 1924, which severely limited immigration into the country from parts of the world other than northwestern Europe.

A second part of citizenship is republicanism. Citizens are *not* subjects of a monarch or president; there is a substantial difference between submission to an autocrat and the mutuality and engagement of self-government. This is, or should be, obvious and noncontentious, except for the fact that "voter suppression" and its first cousin, gerrymandering, are burning political issues, and autocrats are on the rise around the world, including in many "civilized" nations. Computer technology puts voter suppression and gerrymandering on steroids, using precinct-by-precinct registration and polling data to "crack and pack" political opposition, a fact that the Supreme Court, stuck in the twentieth century, does not see as problematic. The "race between education and technology," noted in Chapter 3, is also a race between citizenship and technology, with "Moore's Law" of technological acceleration suggesting that the deck is stacked against the common good. More generally, one can imagine numerous technological means to undermine the fundamentals of citizenship, fundamentals including residence, identity, and civic rights.

A third feature of citizenship is geographic stability. Although tribal populations are today considered citizens of the territory in which they dwell and roam, in fact their tribal status is as *members*, not "citizens" of the tribe. To characterize someone or oneself as a "citizen of the world" is little more than a pretentious trope. Some nations allow "dual citizenship," where one can claim citizenship both of his or her parents and of the native land, sometimes after difficult negotiation, but any notion of quadruple citizenship would be nonsense. Exclusivity, with some marginal adjustments, is a feature of citizenship.

Finally, to be a citizen means that at least nominally one commits to obedience to the laws and norms of the nation and the city. How these are learned, and how they are codified, both formally and informally, is an ongoing question. "Good citizens" do not litter the streets or disturb the peace, even in the absence of police enforcement. As educational institutions from grade school onward place less emphasis on humanities and civic education, and more emphasis on science and technology, the understanding of shared citizenship withers.

A question before us is how these cold qualities engage, so that they become more than simply bureaucratic rules and regulations, and become actual values that inspire all to be "good citizens." What does it *mean* to be a citizen? In part, the answer is wrapped up in nationalism, but nationalism is a recent force in human history; citizenship is a more ancient quality. Those who proudly proclaimed "*civis romanus sum*" (I am a Roman citizen) were stressing with pride a tie with a state or an empire, not a nation. Yet the question is now: how is citizenship *viewed*, not as an abstract legal doctrine but as a burning quality in quotidian lives?

Citizenship is a *club* or *toll* good, with the attributes of excludability and nondepletability that Elinor Ostrom (1990) identified. Considered as a club good, we can see that taxes, in the words of Justice Holmes (see Chapter 2), are the price one pays for civilization, and that free-riding, the legal or illegal evasion of taxes, is the antithesis of republican virtue. Bragging about tax avoidance strategies (such as transferring income or assets to low-tax jurisdictions, or exploiting questionable deductions) is an admission that one is embarrassed by citizenship and public life, a failing that has afflicted several prominent national leaders in the past 40 years.

The Industrial Revolution added new dimensions to citizenship considered as a legal construction. Whereas previously one's participation as a citizen related primarily to civic affairs whether politics or municipal celebrations, today one's economic role, as a producer and a consumer, is equally important, maybe even more so if the media is any guide. A "good citizen" contributes to the national economy, not only by working hard but also by consuming hard.

The manner in which citizens have been *engaged* with the state is related to the tools through which that engagement is enacted. For most of history, those tools were primarily the tools of warfare, and defending the sovereign was part of the obligations of citizenship, and vice versa. With the Industrial Revolution, and the rise of industrial technology, for most citizens a new set of obligations—producing and consuming, and a new science of economics to rationalize them—eclipsed military obligations. This new technology was distinctive because it was scalable and diffusible in ways that earlier tools were not; a key characteristic of modern technology is that it is the subject of *autonomous representations*, as previously noted, whether in the form of standards or instructional manuals in ways that earlier tools were not. One consequence of this autonomy is that technology uniquely bestrides the narrow earth, eclipsing numerous social formations based on territory and locality, including the state and citizenship.

An emerging industry after World War II was the creation of tax havens in small jurisdictions, whether the Cayman Islands or Luxembourg, where the wealthy could hide their money. An entire shadow economy of dirty money, such as the proceeds of drug deals or illicit currency transfers, has emerged in these locales, and a hidden business in "money laundering" offers to make dirty money clean, no questions asked. Increasingly, technology has made it possible for the wealthiest to free-ride on their civic obligations, an opportunity not available to the masses. The commons of citizenship is undermined by the free-riding of some of the most powerful members of society.

Modern technologies probe the boundaries of citizenship. Unlike in earlier times, citizens today are not rooted in specific locales, but can potentially range over the entire world. Discussions that were once confined to the city square are now on Facebook and Twitter, and echo instantaneously around the world, engaging both citizens and noncitizens with simulacra of familiarity that are mostly a source of confusion.

Four features of contemporary technology probe the boundaries of citizenship. Once again, scale is at the top of the list, the fact that many technologies are almost infinitely scalable. Unlike earlier systems, the internet and related systems are no longer rooted in laboratories or factories or open fields, but rather extend over the entire world. However, once in the wild (so to speak) they take on a different meaning, more as a coercive force than as an instrumentality or a means to an end, acquiring greater potential to ride mankind (in Ralph Waldo Emerson's phrasing). Prior to the twentieth century, sorting out the ethnoscape was straightforward, if not always edifying; in today's melting pot, the ethnoscape is not only of bodies but also of images and evanescent whispers, and figuring out who is a fellow citizen and who is a bot becomes a challenging political calculation.

Today's financescape is also technologically challenged, transforming patrimonial authority into technocratic authority. Historically, finance represented patrimonial authority, and banks such as Morgan Trust and Wells Fargo, embodying family names, enabled banks to trade on that trust; after the 1930s, they did so with the backing and regulation of the federal government. In the late twentieth century, regulations were loosened, including in 1999 the repeal of the Glass-Steagall Act, legislation from 1933 that separated commercial banking from investment banking, which was a major turning point leading up to the Great Recession in the next decade. Financiers then were able to obscure the terms of their contracts, with the result in the beginning of the twenty-first century of an explosion of predatory lending that nearly wrecked the world economy. The role of technology in transforming financial relationships and thus enabling predatory lending is obvious; business relationships that once were based on a handshake and family name could now be conducted entirely online, and "looking the borrower in the eye" became a quaint anachronism.

Closely related to this is the modernist, futuristic aesthetic of technology noted in the previous chapter. Modernism presents itself as a universal aesthetic:

> To be modern is to find ourselves in an environment that promises us adventure, power, joy, growth, transformation of ourselves and the world—and, at the same time, that threatens to destroy everything we have, everything we know, everything we are. (Berman 1982: 15)

This creative destruction suggests that we have slipped the surly bonds not only of space but also of time. Italian futurism, a movement in the first half of the twentieth century, glorified speed, collision, and technology. The *Futurist Manifesto*, also titled *The Joy of Mechanical Force*, celebrated these central elements of modernism. If the "-scape" of the commons, broadly defined, is rooted in a particular time and locale, then futurism does not so much degrade the commons as smash it to bits. Celebrations of disruption (Bower and Christensen 1995) are celebrations of an antisocial existence, now only not initiated by street-corner punks but by leading institutions. The project of this disruption, of course, is not so much ill-defined "progress" as it is an imperialistic concentration of technological power.

Finally, in the current century, technology has given us the capability to translate both features and "-scapes" into an almost infinite variety of registers and discourses, so that what once was confined to localities or in-person interaction now can be stored in a database almost anywhere. At the top of the list, of course, is facial recognition technology, so that with closed-circuit television (CCTV) cameras, an ultimate private good, one's facial aspect is now appropriated by the state. Other private goods, whether shopping histories or genomes, are increasingly stored in government or corporate databases (e.g., ancestry.com). Even attention, as noted in Chapter 5, is mined and marketed via Facebook and Google.

Classically, the epitome of urbanity was the *agora*, the gathering place for merchants, athletes, orators, and preachers. Although in today's cities the *agora* has been largely replaced by sports stadiums, theaters, and shopping malls, in some of the greatest cities it remains, whether in Times Square in New York City, the National Mall in Washington, DC, Grosvenor Square in London, or Tiananmen Square in Beijing. These twenty-first-century *agorae* are often considered the epitome of these cities, and one cannot claim to have visited New York City until he or she has seen Times Square. *Agorae* inspire and breathe life into citizenship, and sports stadiums and theaters for many are the essence of urbanity. In sum, some of the core features of technology—scalability, transformation, modernism, and translation, as described in Chapter 2—can be seen as direct assaults on the common good, as the experience of a public gathering is replaced by the grubby consumption of screen time, and political leaders' ringing orations in the open air are reduced to 280-character tweets.

A dystopian challenge would be to imagine an urban commons with CCTV monitoring, with "eyes on the street" (Jacobs 1961) not from front porches but from facial recognition systems halfway around the world. All of this is technologically possible today, but it would distort the meaning of the commons beyond all recognition: more like a prison on a global scale than a rural meadow. The growth of the modern surveillance state, whether exemplified in schools, hospitals, or prisons, is roughly coincident with the modernist fetishizing of technology (Foucault 1975).

In sum, civic life in a technological age acquires a completely different character from that of the Romans or even most of the modern era, with ethnoscapes and surveillance replacing the classical public square. Increasingly, one's role as a citizen, whether as a taxpayer, a participant in civic discussions, a neighborhood resident, or a consumer, is mediated and transformed by technology. Just as Amazon has usurped the place of brick-and-mortar shopping, and chat rooms have displaced town hall discussions, so too citizenship becomes *less* engaging as it is increasingly online.

## The Poetry of the Commons

Is "the commons" today mere preindustrial nostalgia, whose evocation is less that of Thomas Gray's "Elegy in a Country Churchyard" (one of the best-known poems in the English language) and more that of semiliterate doggerel of advertising slogans?[2] Or can we find places where a vision of the commons, however named, engages citizens and is an important part of their lives? As society becomes increasingly urbanized, the commons is increasingly an urban commons, and urban vitality and ambiance are as much a common pool resource as is the atmosphere or a country meadow.

Jane Jacobs, perhaps *the* preeminent scholar of urban culture, has argued in *Cities and the Wealth of Nations* (1984) that cities and the diversity they embrace are essential to national prosperity; obviously a rejoinder to Adam Smith's *The Wealth of Nations*, Jacobs argued that diversity, rather than rigid order, is the foundation of vitality. In her best-known work, *The Death and Life of Great American Cities* (1961), Jacobs argued against the rational order of Robert Moses and LeCorbusier to suggest that the city is a commons, in which the cityscape ("eyes on the street") is a source of vitality. In the 1950s, a movement of "urban renewal" attempted to remake cities such as New York and Chicago, replacing mixed-use neighborhoods with rigidly zoned, racially and socioeconomically uniform settlements. Jacobs argued that mixed-use districts had a vitality and a liveliness that the "rational" order of Moses lacked. Part of this vitality was what Jacobs called "eyes on the street"—an open-air commons, rather than isolated families, maintained safety and created a sense of community and a vital economy:

> The more successfully a city mingles everyday diversity of uses and users in its everyday streets, the more successfully, casually (and economically) its people thereby enliven and support well-located parks that can thus give back grace and delight to their neighborhoods instead of vacuity. (Jacobs 1961: 111)

A city is a commons, albeit one that is contested by numerous interests—neighborhood, corporate, and everything in between. Although private dwellings and offices are private spaces, the controlled aggregation of these, along with parks, monuments, shopping malls, municipal buildings, schools, transit systems, and all the infrastructure of urban life, is a common pool resource, the vitality of which is central to the vitality of the nation. Efforts to privatize these, whether by selling off curbside parking spaces, or transit systems, or schools, are a twenty-first-century form of enclosure that may (but more typically does not) result in greater efficiency but at the expense of the common good. Chicago's lease in 2014 of curbside parking spaces to a private consortium for $1 billion is widely regarded as a failure (Farmer and Noonan 2014); likewise, privatization of transit systems (primarily bus and rail) in Europe and the United States is an ongoing controversy (Winston 2010), and the privatization of public education attacks the foundations of a liberal democracy. All of these cases of privatization are part of the neoliberal enclosure movement.

Elinor Ostrom's distinctions (1990) among private goods, public goods, club goods, and common pool resources fails to capture the moods and motivations associated with each. These moods and motivations, whether identification or imperial assertion or self-possession, are no less important than the clearly demarcated distinctions of depletability and exclusivity with which she lays out different types of goods. Sometimes, these moods and motivations are obvious: "sunsets," which for Ostrom are emblematic of public goods generally, often evoke a wistfulness for a day (or, more poetically, an era) that is slipping into history. Similarly, doughnuts, identified as emblematic of private goods, are at times associated (figuratively) with overindulgence and obesity. A library, which Ostrom identifies as a typical common pool resource, is more than just a place for keeping books; libraries are associated with centers for learning and the advancement of knowledge, and the architecture of some of the world's best-known libraries evokes a dignity and a stateliness that suggests that a library is far more than just a storage locker, as seen in Philip Larkin's "Library Ode":

> So youth and age
> Like ink and page
> In this house join.[3]

Similarly, leading cities from Chicago to New York to Paris have evoked lyrical representations. For but one of numerous examples, Carl Sandburg wrote about Chicago:

> Stormy, husky, brawling,
> City of the Big Shoulders.[4]

Sandburg contrasted "Hog Butcher for the World" to "little soft cities," evoking a masculinity that other cities lacked.

None of these are logical statements. Instead, their meaning is primarily *poetic*, following Kenneth Burke's distinction between "semantic" and "poetic" meaning (Burke 1973). Although semantic meaning is a matter of factual or logical tests, poetic meaning is more a matter of attitudes, moods, and motivations, and does not admit positivistic truth or falsity. Rather, poetic meaning is a matter of social congruence, so that what is poetically true for one community might well be nonsense for another.

To grasp the poetry of the commons, we look not at the statutes that define different types of goods, but rather at the scenery, broadly understood, that is associated with it. Landscapes, for example, are archetypal public goods, yet, as described above in Chapter 2, it was not so until the Hudson River School of painters transformed the waste and howling wilderness of the seventeenth-century Puritans into the noble scenes of Romantic poets. Similarly, we might regard financescapes (Appadurai 1996: 33) as an archetypal representation of private goods, which went from being a private concern to being a public hazard with the financial crises of the twentieth and twenty-first centuries.

Poetically, an archetypal common pool resource is a country meadow or pasture, and the "tragedy of the commons" evokes the fate of shared natural resources. The term could equally be applied to the urban commons, and the moods and motivations associated with looking out over a peaceful, ecologically diverse meadow could also be applied to looking out over an ethnically diverse, peaceful neighborhood threatened by real estate speculators who are intent on flipping houses and crashing the real estate market. Neighborhood speculation is a business model that scarcely existed before 1980, yet it is now a major disruptive force, and some of the most powerful institutions in the economy thrive on predatory business models based on wrecking the common good. These predatory business models extend well beyond residential real estate to include some of the major institutions of the economy.

In America, the "frontier"—the boundary between civilization and pristine nature—is a commons, a figure that Vannevar Bush, President Franklin D. Roosevelt's science advisor, drew on in his memorandum, "Science, the Endless Frontier," which created the charter for public investments in science, thus making scientific advancement into a public good. In America, in contrast to European nations, the "frontier" is less a national border then a boundary between civilization and the wilderness, beckoning exploration. Frederick Jackson Turner (2014) created the canonical statement of this in *The Frontier in American History*, which was published in 1893, the same year that the Census Bureau declared that the frontier was closed. So, too, the frontier in the American imagination has been used as a metaphor for every wilderness, from space (the "final frontier") to the internet (the "electronic frontier") to the challenges of a postwar generation (John F. Kennedy's New Frontier). Beyond the frontier is the "state of nature" awaiting colonization. Other nations have their own frontier imaginaries, whether Russia, France, or China, the latter with the Wild West of the Uighur.

In every case around the world, the frontier imaginary is in invitation to colonization, with indigenous peoples ("savages") subjected to the advance of civilization. Although this colonization is as old as history, it acquired greater force and vigor with modern transportation and military technology.

Club memberships are archetypal club goods, and the rituals associated with these, including initiation and other rites of passage, evoke the sense of belonging and exclusivity that are typical of club goods. These rituals convey the mood "we are special," whether in the rituals of a fraternity initiation or a university commencement or a naturalization ceremony for new citizens. A university degree is a club good, albeit one that is debased when for-profit "universities," existing only on the internet, sell their certificates. Mediascapes today are associated with tribal identities, and the explosion of different media on cable and the internet has splintered the "imagined community" of the nation into a host of imagined foraging bands jammed together inside the borders of a single state, or perhaps of caravans invading from the South.

The commons of airspace is a club good, and its celebration in the poem "High Flight" by Royal Airman John McGee is perhaps unparalleled in the poetry of the commons:

> Oh! I have slipped the surly bonds of Earth
> And danced the skies on laughter-silvered wings;
> Sunward I've climbed, and joined the tumbling mirth
> Of sun-split clouds,—and done a hundred things
> You have not dreamed of—wheeled and soared and swung
> High in the sunlit silence. Hov'ring there,
> I've chased the shouting wind along, and flung
> My eager craft through footless halls of air.
> Up, up the long, delirious burning blue
> I've topped the wind-swept heights with easy grace
> Where never lark, or ever eagle flew—
> And, while with silent, lifting mind I've trod
> The high untrespassed sanctity of space,
> Put out my hand, and touched the face of God.[5]

When the space shuttle Challenger crashed in 1986, President Ronald Reagan, in his address to the nation, took note of how the astronauts had "touched the face of God."

These "-scapes" reinforce each other, so that media portrayals of immigrant hordes (an imagined ethnoscape) add rigidity to an exclusivity of the already tribal identity of racist politics. Conversely, frontiers like space or the internet or revitalizing cities beckon adventurers to create new commons. Or to state the point most bluntly, in an age of mechanical reproduction and challenging frontiers, we have the opportunity to create, or to destroy, the new commons genuinely understood. We can maintain and reinforce the idea of the commons as a supportive space open for all eyes to enjoy and even to explore. Or, we can use our media to portray immigrant hordes that threaten our commons, promoting rigidity and exclusivity that lead to tribal identity and racist politics.

The work of art in a technological age, following Walter Benjamin (2015), is the representation of goods, public, private, club, and common pool resources. Poets and painters, no less than jurists and policemen and neighbors' eyes on the street, create the commons, less as a physical entity and more as a shared resource creating a sense of community. The visual aspect of a library, as evident in Larkin's "Library Ode" quoted above, which we might name the "biblioscape," evokes a community of scholars whose words echo across the ages. In a democratic society, the ethnoscapes, mediascapes, and financescapes, and yes, even the technoscapes, form the fabric of the community. The enclosure, pollution, and usurpation or abuse of this fabric through free-riding, misrepresentation, and predation by the powerful members and institutions of society degrades the common good.

## Notes

1. "The test of a first-rate intelligence is the ability to hold two opposed ideas in the mind at the same time, and still retain the ability to function" (Fitzgerald 1945: 69).
2. For the full poem, see https://www.poetryfoundation.org/poems/44299/elegy-written-in-a-country-churchyard (retrieved 1 September 2021).
3. For the full poem, see https://allpoetry.com/Library-Ode (retrieved 1 September 2021).
4. For the full poem, see https://www.poetryfoundation.org/poetrymagazine/poems/12840/chicago (retrieved 1 September 2021).
5. See https://nationalpoetryday.co.uk/poem/high-flight/ (retrieved 1 September 2021).

Chapter 7

# Building Institutions for a Technological World

We live in a technological world. In the nearly 60 years since Jacques Ellul first published *La Technique: L'Enjeu du Siècle* (*The Technological Society*) (1964) the world, or more accurately our imagination of the world, has become dominated by the machine, and other imaginaries, whether reverence or friendship, have faded into the background. The boundaries of our experience, and our understanding of our place within it, are today defined by the machine. The coordinates of our experience, even for the most remote villages, are defined by technological devices, whether the factory or the media or the internet. As obvious as this statement is, it is entirely silent on who the master is of the technologies that define the coordinates of our existence. With whom we communicate, associate, and worship, and whom we give our loyalty to, are subtly shaped by the technologies with which we live. If "things are in the saddle," in Ralph Waldo Emerson's words, who shapes the things?[1]

In this chapter, I will examine six technological systems where national and international collaborations have successfully created a republican order, providing safety, security, and communal adequacy for the users and for the larger society. By "republican order," I understand the mutuality that is the opposite of "imperial order," the domination of throngs of subjects or users by a single power. Some of these republican orders, such as E-Estonia, are confined to small countries, whereas others, such as Eurocontrol (European Organisation for the Safety of Air Navigation, stylized EUROCONTROL) and the Aviation Safety Reporting System, span continents, yet hinge on tightly defined communities of users. In every case, there is a sober assessment of the technologies' potential and limitations, which is far from the idolization of technology that pervades so much of contemporary society. There is also a solid foundation in preexisting communities or groups that used the technology for their own ends. Technology supports the common good only insofar as there is a *community* that agrees upon the good.

My examination will cover six broad technologies: infrastructure and industry (including roads and bridges, and waterborne transport), air transport, national appropriation of the internet (E-Estonia), social media generally, finance, and the high seas. The first of these is infrastructure and industry, and I note here that regional development (for example, the Tennessee Valley) is closely connected with industrial development. I will then examine air transport and the cooperation of the international aviation community in assuring its safety. Next, I will look at the internet, as adopted by E-Estonia and social media, which are examples of newer commons. I will focus both on national and international initiatives for governing club goods such as airspace, common pool resources such as power grids, and the artificial commons of the internet. Finance has become a commons, or more accurately a club good, as I will detail in the next section. Finally, the International Law of the Sea is an example where nations around the world have (mostly) abandoned hostilities to conserve a commons, although in the South China Sea this is now being threatened by the technological developments of man-made islands and cell phones. In all of these cases, the absence of a single, dominant player, and the obvious benefits of cooperation (or hazards of lack of regulation), compelled a diversity of parties and nations to come to an agreement on how these commons should be governed. The successful governance of these commons in the face of technological challenges bears out Elinor Ostrom's (1990) eight criteria.

Infrastructure, embracing both transportation and urban services (power grids, water supplies, disposal of waste, broadband service, and highways) has come to define a commons just as much as the ecology of a mountain meadow. In both cases, the principles of good governance (clear boundaries, gatekeeping, monitoring, collective choice arrangements, among others) are required, and increasing attention paid to the governance of infrastructure is testimony that this is one of the leading issues in the governance of the commons (e.g., Frischmann 2012; Anderies et al. 2016). Yet the ongoing *neglect* of infrastructure, as documented by the American Society of Civil Engineers, suggests that this is another area in which the race between technology and institutions is being lost.

Air transport, as noted in Chapter 4, depends on an artificial commons, airspace. When Charles Lindbergh flew from New York to Paris in 1927, air traffic was not a concern, but less than 20 years later, with the skies becoming overcrowded, and new technologies testing their limits, developing the resources to maintain air safety became an ongoing concern. Foremost among these is the Aviation Safety Reporting System, a voluntary monitoring and compliance mechanism.

The crown jewel of international institution-building may be the International Law of the Sea Treaty, described below, passed by the United Nations in 1956 (also known as the United Nations Convention on the Law of the Sea or UNCLOS). Prior to this, maritime regulation was nonexistent, with coastal waters out to three miles from the coast—the maximum range of a cannon—being under national jurisdiction. Anything else on the high seas was in a no-man's land. As navigation improved and harvesting technologies (for maritime life) evolved, protecting the seas' biodiversity from overharvesting and protecting shipping lanes from competing traffic became a shared concern among maritime nations, and the Treaty presents a durable protection.

If the International Law of the Sea Treaty is a settled arrangement, governing a newer resource, the internet is still a work in progress. The internet resembles less a village green than a medieval city, where public order depends more on parades of armed retainers than the accepted rule of law. On the internet, weaponized trolls, deepfakes, and the good intentions of Google, Twitter, and Facebook are the primary deterrents. In between these two options, of the rule of law and balance of power, are numerous other technological commons where interested parties probe the boundaries, and yet where underlying institutions are sufficiently resilient to maintain order. These include library resources and new media in the entertainment industry. The objective of this chapter is to understand how the unique properties of technologies beyond instrumentality, including scalability, transformability, autonomous representation, and even the modernist aesthetics of technology, challenge the common good.

I aim here to demonstrate that even in a technological society Ostrom's (1990) eight principles for governing the commons ("clearly designed boundaries," "congruence between appropriation and provision rules and local conditions," "collective choice agreements," "monitoring," "graduated sanctions," "conflict resolution mechanisms," "minimal recognition of rights to organize," and "nested enterprises") are still valid, albeit more challenged by the unusual capabilities and unexpected aspects of technology. Technology, as I describe in Chapter 3, is far more than sophisticated tools: technologies have capabilities of scalability and portability, translation of forces and energy, and associations with magic that simpler tools lack. In a technological society, governing the commons is more challenging yet also more critical: the trade-off between "monitoring" (Ostrom's fourth criterion) and privacy, or the boundaries of nonphysical commons such as the internet, becomes much more challenging as technologies both create and probe those boundaries. Ostrom identified "clearly defined boundaries" at the top of the list of requirements for governing the commons; in a technological society, these boundaries become porous, amorphous, and even invisible.

## Power Grids, Supply Chains, Industrial Regions

Part of the *magic* of common goods is that they are almost invisible: like the air we breathe, or the safety of our streets, we can pass our days without giving them thought. It is only when they break down, like an airplane falling out of the sky, that we become alarmed. Leading the list of taken-for-granted common goods is the way we power our lives with electricity. Electricity, at least for domestic purposes, is a toll good, meaning that exclusion is easy, but it is not very subtractable; with distributed generation, utilities can ramp up production to meet increased local demand. The *power grids*, through which energy is distributed, on the other hand, are common pool resources, similar to irrigation systems (cf. Hess and Ostrom 2007: 9), and over the past century great progress has been made devising interconnections among electrical utilities so that municipalities in the lower 48 states (excepting Texas) can share loads, rather than simply depending on local generation capacity. Parallel to this interconnection has been the extension of electrical service into nonmunicipal areas, which began with the Rural Electrification Administration (REA) in 1935, but which was not completed in some remote corners until the 1960s.

The first municipal electrical generating station was the Pearl Street Station in New York City, which was built in 1882. For many years, electricity was a municipal affair, with generating stations supplying the city and farm families lighting their homes with candles or coal oil lamps until the REA brought electricity to America's farms and villages. A precursor to the REA was the Tennessee Valley Authority (TVA), which was created as one of the first projects of the New Deal. As told in the book written by its first chairman, David Lilienthal, *TVA: Democracy on the March* (1944), the TVA overcame the opposition of the "Power Trust" to bring not only electricity, but also industry and improved farming methods to millions in what had previously been a barren region. Published at the height of World War II, this book celebrated regional development and unlimited electric power as the key to prosperity. Along with the Bonneville Power Administration (BPA) in the Pacific Northwest, the TVA did in fact bring renewed prosperity to millions of Americans; some 30 years later, it provided a model for the Appalachian Regional Development Commission and similar regional development authorities around the country. Regional economies, whether the Tennessee Valley, Route 128 near Boston, or Silicon Valley, are now recognized as *the* engines of prosperity. In the current century, *supply chains*, knit together by newer materials management systems, are essential to industry.

The TVA built 30 dams on the Tennessee and Cumberland Rivers, controlling the flow of the former and providing hydropower to ten million inhabitants of the Tennessee Valley and to ships navigating up and down the Tennessee River. A similar number of coal, natural gas, nuclear, and solar power plants supplement the original hydroelectric vision. Starting with the original dam at Muscle Shoals, the TVA provided fertilizer that rejuvenated worn-out lands, and turned a barren wasteland into one of the most productive agricultural regions of the country. With a system of locks and dams, it facilitated commerce, supporting industrial growth. The Tennessee River and its tributaries are one of the major arteries for commerce in the southeastern United States.

From the very beginning, the TVA was about more than simply power generation and flood control. Working with agricultural extension stations, it promoted improved farming techniques and forestry and soil conservation. It discovered aluminum-rich ores, the mining of which it promoted and which contributed to the war effort, as aluminum was needed for aircraft. Lilienthal presents a heroic vision of reclamation, which is now led by technologists:

> There is almost nothing, however fantastic, that (given competent organization) a team of engineers, scientists, and administrators cannot do today. ... When [builder and technicians] have imagination and faith, they can move mountains; out of their skills they can create new jobs, relieve human drudgery, give new life and fruitfulness to worn-out lands, put yokes upon streams, and transmute the minerals of the earth and plants of the field into machines of wizardry to spin out the stuff of a way of life new to this world. (Lilienthal 1944: 3)

Ideologically driven efforts to privatize the TVA and Bonneville—a twenty-first-century enclosure movement—have foundered on the rocks of economic impossibility: privatizing them would benefit no one beyond a handful of oligarchs, and would cost ratepayers and taxpayers billions (Conca 2018, for example). It would destroy one of the most enduring legacies of Franklin Delano Roosevelt's New Deal, as well as the foundations of regional prosperity in both the Tennessee Valley and the Pacific Northwest.

Electricity, as noted above, is a toll good, meaning that it is not very depletable.[2] Power grids, on the other hand, are common pool resources enable local utilities to share power and avoid transmission loss across long distances. The Southeastern Interconnection for example, enables load-sharing among 13 states from Florida to Missouri. As such, power grids are *the* foundation for broad prosperity throughout society, so much so that we scarcely give them thought, unless they fail. In 2021, Texas, which had declined to join the Western Interconnection, instead going it alone, experienced massive statewide power failures.

Power grids, and infrastructure more generally, once extended into the countryside, have come to define a new form of commons, the region, defined here as a self-conscious, contiguous geographical expanse encompassing multiple jurisdictions with an integrated, diversified economy. Regions can be based on landscape, shared heritage, transportation infrastructure, or shared resources, but have the characteristics of diversity and import substitution that enable them to be largely self-sufficient. Regional development, such as that of the Tennessee Valley, exemplifies all of the features of a well-governed commons that Ostrom identified, only now on a much larger scale than a village meadow: "clearly designed boundaries," "congruence between appropriation and provision rules and local conditions," "collective choice arrangements," and the rest. The TVA and the BPA prove that it is possible to govern an industrial commons, less through autocrats such as Samuel Insull, head of the "Power Trust," and more through the balanced agreement of a plurality of diversified industry partners.

Generalizing from this development, we might think of an *industry* as a commons, embracing not only factories and firms, but also skills, markets, and industry knowledge available only to insiders. As Charles Perrow has written in *Complex Organizations: A Critical Essay* (1974), an industry can consist of both public and private entities, universities, and even voluntary associations and public agencies. The agricultural *industry*, for example, includes the land-grant universities, and personnel and information circulate among agribusiness and the Farm Bureau and farmers' associations, and a host of suppliers and customers including some of the largest agribusiness firms such as Cargill and Monsanto. It includes factories that produce foodstuffs and supply chains that distribute them. The financial *industry* embraces not only banks and financial institutions (the so-called "FIRE" economy of finance, insurance, and real estate), but also regulatory bodies. Business schools and advocacy organizations such as the Financial Services Roundtable, the Federal Reserve Bank, and leading financial institutions form a self-conscious community with stewardship over the backbone of the American economy.

My own experience in the software industry might serve as a good illustration of the idea of an industry as a commons. In the course of a decade-long career, I worked with a small software startup that worked closely with both government entities such as the US Air Force and with corporate customers such as General Motors and IBM, as well as with academic institutions. At times, I was the contract manager, and at other times I was the customer. What brought us together was a common "techie" subculture, closely allied with the defense industry, which had billions of dollars of corporate and government funding flowing through it. As an anthropologist, I understood the importance of cultural adaptation, and developed a number of tricks and tools to "fit in" with my customers and suppliers, and so forge long-standing business relationships, several of which endure even to this day. These tricks and tools included the use of acronyms, which are frequently boundary markers. They also served as references to mutual acquaintances and as shared reference points, all of which convinced both customers and suppliers that I was part of the community. Familiarity with shared narratives, such as the launch of a new program (for example the CALS program, Computer-Aided Logistics System) convinced customers that I was one of the "gang." Eventually, an Air Force contract, with Wayne State University as my subcontractor, opened the door to my resumption of my academic career in 1995.

In sum, analyzing an industry as a commons reveals multiple hidden dynamics, not the least of which is both the industry subculture and boundary markers such as acronyms, and some of the dynamics that give the industry vitality (such as informal collective choice arrangements through trade associations). Governing and growing the industrial commons is an important issue in a technological society.

A region, whether the Tennessee Valley, Silicon Valley, or Route 128 around Boston, embraces not only multiple enterprises, both public and private, but also a distinctive subculture that is essential to its vitality. Both regions and industries embrace local knowledge, whether that of industry practices or the regional landscape, that those outside the region or industry are scarcely aware of. This local knowledge is a club good that only those in the region or the industry possess.

The American folk singer Woody Guthrie, hired by Bonneville Power Administration in 1941, wrote what is perhaps America's best-known folk song, "This Land Is Your Land":

> This land is your land, this land is my land
> From California, to the New York Island
> ...
> This land was made for you and me.[3]

This celebration of the landscape and the common good is perhaps unparalleled. Regions, like the cities that Jane Jacobs (1961, 1984) celebrated, combine (import-substituting) economic diversity with a strong sense of attachment, meaning that residents of the region have some commitment to working toward the common good. The TVA and the BPA were not government impositions so much as they were (government-created) commons welcomed by all except perhaps the "Power Trust."

Would-be monopolies, whether Samuel Insull's "Power Trust" (which at its height controlled electric utilities in 5,000 cities and towns in 32 states) or Kenneth Lay's Enron, both of which were technological empires in the twentieth century, or Google in the twenty-first, are enclosure movements, engrossing not simply upland meadows but entire industries and regions. In the past, democratic societies have broken up or regulated such enclosures. The possibility of regulating such monoliths as Google, Twitter, or Amazon for the common good is an open question.

In sum, the scaling up and monopolization of numerous industries, whether electric power in the twentieth century or attention-harvesting via the internet in the current century, represents enclosure: that which had previously been a commons has become an empire. The place of such technological empires in a democratic society is an open question.

## International Air Traffic

In 1960, only three years after the initial formation of the European Customs Union, 41 nations in Europe agreed to create the "Single European Sky" (SES) in recognition of the increasing volume and importance of air transport for global commerce. Although Great Britain and France initially refused to comply, largely for reasons relating to military aviation, eventually all of Europe plus affiliate members Israel and Morocco joined the effort. Eurocontrol thus created a commons that transcends national borders, although it is at times challenged by cultural and linguistic boundaries or natural disasters: a mid-air collision over Überlingen, Germany, in 2002 was a consequence of German and Russian pilots reading differently the instructions from air traffic control (a human voice) and an automated Terminal Collision Avoidance System (TCAS). Similarly, a volcanic eruption at Eyjafjallajökull, Iceland, in 2010 stranded millions of passengers worldwide from 15 to 23 April 2010. International air traffic occupies a commons that did not exist before the twentieth century, yet it is now nearly the perfect embodiment of governing a technological commons.

Eurocontrol consists of several embedded agencies, including the Maastricht Upper Area Control Center; the Network Manager Operations Centre, which coordinates flight plans and actual traffic; plus research and training facilities including the Eurocontrol Experimental Centre and the Institute of Air Navigation Services. For example, the Maastricht Upper Area Control Centre provides air traffic control over 41 member states in Europe and the Near East (including Turkey and Israel), and the Eurocontrol Experimental Centre conducts air traffic management research and simulations.

Eurocontrol is a nearly perfect embodiment of Ostrom's eight criteria most notably the eighth criterion, "nested enterprises." This nesting is facilitated in large part because there is both an absence of military hostilities among the 41 members and a strong identification with the resource, airspace. Airspace is a club good, and airmen—not only pilots, but anyone in the industry—has a strong identification with a common good. This bonding results in large part because of the dramatic and spectacular consequences when an airplane falls out of the sky; hence the entire industry is pervaded by a *safety culture* that is a model for other hazardous industries such as hospitals. Key elements of this safety culture, which neatly match Ostrom's eight criteria for commons management, include "clearly designated boundaries," "monitoring," and "graduated sanctions."

One of the key institutions for monitoring airspace in the United States is the Aviation Safety Reporting System (ASRS), which was created by the Federal Aviation Administration and managed by the National Aeronautics and Space Administration (NASA) in 1976 at roughly the same time that commercial air transport was being deregulated. The ASRS is a voluntary compliance system under which any operational personnel can voluntarily report a safety deviation, whether an altitude bust or a near miss or a miscommunication with air traffic control, and by voluntarily reporting the incident they can avoid sanctions. The reports are accumulated in a database, which is used to identify and analyze safety trends. The ASRS has been used as a model for safety monitoring in other industries, including rail transport, medical institutions, firefighting, and offshore petroleum.

The ASRS is a subset of a general pattern of Flight Data Monitoring (FDM) as established under the Chicago Convention of the International Civil Aviation Organization (ICAO), a United Nations agency founded in 1947 that coordinates and harmonizes operational practices among 193 member states. FDM is successful in large part because it represents the intersection of two clubs, the aviation community and the international community. Although the international community has many disputes, frequently related to territorial disputes, international law, terrorism, and rogue nations, air safety is one area that all can agree upon. The development of institutions that effectively govern this commons has been a sterling success, and has been replicated in other regions and industries. Recent civil aviation incidents, notably the two crashes of a Boeing 737 Max 8 in 2019, typify pushing of envelope[4] with technological improvements, in this case attitude control. In conclusion, the international aviation community has risen to the challenge of monitoring and improving flight safety, although the technological community continues to test those limits.

## E-Estonia: Technological Leadership from a Small, Baltic Nation

If the internet is a Wild West or the "electronic frontier," then an outpost of civility is the Baltic nation of Estonia, a country founded in the nineteenth century, independent until the 1930s, and then from 1940 to 1991 part of the Soviet Union, a period known as the Era of Silence. Estonia achieved independence after the "singing revolution" on 10–11 June 1988, in which a human chain of approximately two million people, stretching from Tallinn to Vilnius, defied Soviet troops and tanks, and ultimately led to a declaration of independence on 16 November 1988, slightly less than 50 years after the Soviet Union overran the Baltic states. Perhaps due to the temporal coincidence of Estonian independence and the birth of the internet, from 1991 onward Estonia has harnessed its national destiny to electronic communications, as described on their website, "to build a fully functioning country from scratch, while knowing we cannot afford the bureaucracy of a developed democracy."[5] E-Estonia is a nearly perfect illustration of the possibilities of governing a technological commons.

E-Estonia consists of multiple services, including e-banking (launched in 1996), e-cabinet meetings, m-parking (paying for parking using mobile phones), eSchool (enabling parents, students, and children to collaborate online), a digital ID card, bus tickets that can be used via mobile phone, an electronic land registry, internet voting, public safety, a land registry, and a business registry. The infrastructure of E-Estonia is called "X-Road," a platform for nearly all public services, receiving more than 500,000 queries yearly. *Wired* magazine in 2017 called Estonia "the most advanced digital society in the world." As a small country lacking abundant natural resources, living in the dying embers of a totalitarian empire, Estonia has been forced to innovate, and is widely recognized as the most entrepreneurial country in Europe. In 2000, the Estonian government declared internet access a "human right."

The objective of E-Estonia is to build a digital society by facilitating citizen-government interactions through electronic media. It offers more than 600 e-services to citizens and more than 2,000 to businesses, thus resulting in less red tape and administrative overhead. E-Estonia includes e-Residency, a transnational digital identity, and currently there are more than 1,500 Estonian e-Residents in 73 countries in Europe and around the world. Nearly all Estonian schools are online, and cabinet meetings are paperless; the country has a free Wi-Fi network covering most of the country, and uses e-voting, a technology that challenges other, supposedly advanced, countries. Tax returns are made online, taking most taxpayers about five minutes to complete.

Estonia might be considered the obverse of the resource curse, the fate of nations such as Saudi Arabia and Venezuela that are "blessed" with abundant natural resources (Sachs and Warner 1995; Ross 1999). Nations such as these can live off of their natural resources, without feeling the compulsion to develop institutions; dictatorships, corruption, and oligarchies are the fate of resource-rich nations such as Nigeria and Chile. In contrast, resource-poor nations such as Denmark have developed strong democratic institutions. Although the "resource curse" has engendered a substantial debate over the past 20 years, too extensive to explore here, it is clear that Estonia's resource poverty, combined with democratic institutions, has made it a leading light, an example of using technology for supporting the common good. Forced to innovate, and committed to the common good, Estonia is an exemplar to democratic societies of the possibilities of technology for advancing public institutions and democratic ideals.

## Social Media

Perhaps the ultimate private good is privacy, which now can be easily violated on the internet commons. Private information can be shared, but if it is too widely shared, it is no longer private. A substantial body of jurisprudence examines issues in privacy, but the technological threats to privacy beyond phone tapping and hidden cameras burst onto the scene with the internet, search engines, and social media. Most users do not care if their personal information, including shopping history, "friends," and "likes" and travel routes are aggregated into databases by Google and Facebook; the convenience of the internet for many seems to be a (possibly Faustian) bargain. But the threats to democracy from internet platforms such as Cambridge Analytica are only beginning to be perceived, and the threat not only to the common good but to democracy itself is now emerging. The internet-enabled corruption of democratic institutions, as "public servants" acquire the tools in social media for promoting their "brand," and as demagogues with Twitter megaphones substitute attention-seeking for governing, is perhaps *the* technological drama of the twenty-first century.

Is personal data a private good? Data presents a unique challenge to the concept of shared resources. On the one hand, data is not depletable: like club goods and toll goods, tabulating or using data does not subtract from the entire reservoir. On the other hand, with social media, data is not excludable, or more accurately, social media such as Facebook and Twitter have as their business model not simply harvesting user data but also manipulating user behavior. Attention has become a common pool resource, and social media work has become an enclosure, harvesting attention and selling it to advertisers. Although the *boundaries* of privacy vary widely among cultures, it is clear that privacy, however bounded, is a private good. When that which should be private is broadcast on the internet, it is no longer private.

By now, it has been well documented how Facebook works against the common good (McNamee 2019) in terms of creating filter bubbles, spreading rumors, and enabling companies such as Cambridge Analytica to corrupt elections. An open question is whether this negative impact is simply due to the inattention of Facebook's executives, or whether it is inherent in the very nature of social media. Social media exploit the fact that all over the world people are careless with their personal data, with not only identity data such as social security numbers but also shopping history, travel plans, and friendships.

It is my position that this corruption of the commons through social media is inherent in the character of those media: several of the critical features of technology that I identified earlier, including scale, transformation, and translation, do not simply enable the harvesting of personal data, but in an unregulated environment quite nearly mandate corruption of the commons. Circulation of personal data, for example, before the era of the personal computer, was primarily a matter of gossip circles, embracing (at most) a few dozen participants; tabloid newspapers might traffic in gossip about celebrities, but for the average citizen there was no issue of his or her personal preferences ("likes") going viral. On Facebook, however, "likes" and "dislikes" are collected, aggregated, cross-tabulated, and ultimately sold to advertisers. "Likes" are now scalable. The corruption of the commons through social media reached an apogee in the events of 6 January 2021, in which an armed mob stormed the US Capitol, seeking to overturn the recent election. Thousands of Trump followers, convinced on social media that the election had been corrupted, assaulted the Capitol in an insurrection that left five dead and many more wounded. The fact that these rumors exploded over the internet, resulting in the first attack on the Capitol since the War of 1812, and that even since many in the right-wing filter bubble see this as unproblematic, suggests that the internet is tearing us apart.

In the marketplace, "likes" can be translated into consumer preferences and monetized by advertisers. If I "like" golden retriever puppies, for example, it is no more than an idiosyncratic datum. If tens of millions of Facebook users register their "likes" for golden retrievers, cocker spaniels, and dachshunds, when cross-tabulated with other demographics, including browsing history, zip code, automotive purchases, and other "likes," advertisers have a powerful tool for targeted advertising—an enclosure of attention. Further, by tracking and mapping our "friends," Facebook creates a powerful resource for charting paths of influence within our social circles. Many have had the discomforting experience of a pop-up ad that seemed targeted to them based on recent browsing. Although the exact algorithms for targeting are closely held trade secrets, the general pattern of targeted advertising on the internet, based on "friends" and "likes," is no secret. These pop-up advertisements echo a recent purchase. In sum, it is the very character of technologies of social media, and not simply the inattention of the executives of Google, Facebook, and the others, that violates the common good of personal privacy.

In Europe, reflecting the technological maturity of the 28 members of the European Union, which is built on a substantial history going back before the 1957 Treaty of Rome and the 1992 Maastricht Treaty, the General Data Protection Regulation (GDPR) in 2018 put strict limits on how platforms such as Facebook could aggregate and share their users' data. Companies have to get users' permission before they target ads based on shopping history, education, relationship status, and web-browsing history. The GDPR, enacted in 2019, limits companies such as Google and Amazon in their ability to micro-target internet users, and provides substantial penalties for violations. Whether or not internet users will avail themselves of its protections, or whether non-European nations can recognize this as a problem, are still open questions.

## Bretton Woods and the International Finance Community

In 1944, as World War II was still in full force, delegates from 44 nations gathered at a resort in New Hampshire to hammer out a postwar economic order. Mindful of the hyperinflation that had ruined the German economy during the Weimar Republic from 1918 to 1933, eventually leading to the rise of the National Socialist Party, over two days they completed an agreement that the participating nations base their currencies on the gold standard, initially pegged at $35 per ounce. This system held up for 27 years, until deficits run up during the Vietnam War forced the United States to abandon the gold standard and hence the Bretton Woods Agreement. The collapse of this international order meant that the club of international finance had now collapsed. The durability and fragility (in the wake of imperialistic adventures) of international agreements are illustrated by the story of Brotton Woods.

I use the term "club" here advisedly to indicate a group with a self-conscious and exclusive identity. Club goods, like toll goods, are exclusionary yet nondepletable, yet unlike toll goods they are available only to those who have a previously established identity as a member of the club, whether based on professional certificates, social class, totemic identity, or birthright. The possession of club goods, whether fraternity memberships or exclusive real estate, frequently becomes an identity marker for members of the club. Having a national currency that was easily convertible to the currencies of other club members was a token of membership.

For 30 years, Bretton Woods was a successful financial institution, which sought to stabilize international currencies and economies. The gold standard was a club good, which was owned by members of the international community. One objective of Bretton Woods was to restrict flows of speculative capital; rather than the "beggar thy neighbor" game, international prosperity was based on the idea of "we are all in this together." Subsequent efforts to recreate this order, most notably the World Economic Forum headquartered in Davos, Switzerland, have been buffeted by the seemingly opposed forces of globalization and populism, which are actually opposite sides of the same coin: With improvements in transportation and communication over the past 40 years (most notably air travel, the internet, and global media), petty despots, whether in Budapest, Rio de Janeiro, or Washington, DC, have found that they can use social media to build globe-spanning nationalistic movements.

With the collapse of this order, finance became a Wild West, and predatory financial institutions began to emerge. "Financial technology"—the tools and business methods useful to conquer, at least for private purposes, this Wild West—emerged, and currently dominate the financial landscape. "Fintech"—exotic financial instruments, including collateralized debt obligations, currency swaps, structured investment vehicles, and broad index secured trust offerings, represented the newest forms of "wealth." The production and circulation of actual goods and services in the world is vastly eclipsed by the production and circulation of financial derivatives that can create (and extinguish) "wealth" with the flick of a wrist or the click of a mouse. These are all speculative instruments, several links removed from real wealth. The *magic* of technology in the world of finance is in the fact that, aside from specialists, few understand where the "wealth" came from or disappeared to. It is notable that the deficits incurred by the Vietnam War—an imperialistic adventure that ended badly—were the stake driven through the heart of Bretton Woods. Imperialistic overreach, antithetical to the common good, always ends badly, a lesson of history that never is learned.

## International Law of the Sea

Perhaps the largest and most problematic common pool resource in the world is the high seas, covering 71 percent of the earth's surface, bordered by more than a hundred nations, and used by many more for navigation, commerce, and mineral extraction. As long as humanity has been venturing out onto the seas, whether the Mediterranean or the Atlantic and Pacific, there has been an evolving body of statutory and customary law governing the use of the seas. The earliest of these was perhaps the Byzantine *Lex Rhodia*, which was followed by law codes developed during the Middle Ages.

In the seventeenth century, technological improvements in navigation (notably, the compass) and exploration (notably, the discovery of the New World) led to escalating conflicts over the use of the high seas, which were initially resolved in the interest of the dominant maritime powers, Spain and Portugal. In 1609, the Dutch jurist Hugo Grotius published *Mare Liberum*, which established that the seas, like the air but unlike the land, were the common property of all:

> The air belongs to this class of things for two reasons. First, it is not susceptible of occupation; and second its common use is destined for all men. For the same reasons the sea is common to all, because it is so limitless that it cannot become a possession of any one, and because it is adapted for the use of all, whether we consider it from the point of view of navigation or of fisheries, which is considered the beginning of international maritime law. (Grotius 1609)

Advances in navigation, communications, harvesting, and mining technologies have challenged the notion that the sea is "common to all." In 1956, the United Nations held its first Convention on the Law of the Sea (UNCLOS), which established different types of waters, including:

- internal waters;
- territorial and archipelagic waters;
- contiguous zones;
- exclusive economic zones;
- international waters (outside territorial waters); and
- continental shelf.

The UNCLOS established obligations for protecting the marine environment and navigation on the high seas, and created the International Seabed Authority. Technological improvements continue to probe the boundaries of the convention. Most recently, China has been asserting a claim over a region of the various parts of the South China Sea, most notably the Spratly Islands, an almost uninhabited archipelago of hundreds of islands and coral reefs, territory also claimed by Taiwan, the Philippines, Malaysia, Brunei, and Vietnam. For most of their history, the Spratly Islands and the Paracels had value primarily as fishing grounds and for navigation; almost no natural resources other than guano used for fertilizer are found on these islands. Current military technology, however, gives the islands strategic value in conflicts among Taiwan, China, the Philippines, and several lesser powers; most

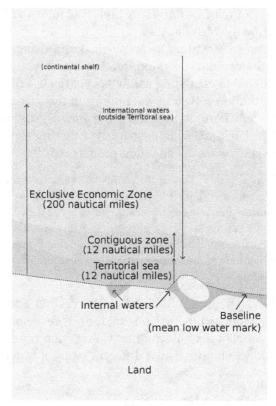

**Figure 7.1.** International Law of the Sea. Wikimedia Commons, public domain.

recently, a cell phone tower has been erected on one of the islands, extending communication.

The Law of the Sea may be considered both the greatest success of international commons governance and also the most challenged. The UNCLOS provides all of the eight features that Ostrom (1990) identified for commons governance ("monitoring," "clearly designed boundaries," and the others), yet several key features of contemporary technology challenge these. Most notably, the scalability of contemporary technology challenges the extension of territorial waters; Grotius could never have considered man-made islands, because in the seventeenth century the technology to construct these islands did not exist; today man-made islands probe the boundaries of this commons. Similarly, as mining technology improves, nations will have an incentive to extend their territorial waters to the edge of the continental shelf, and beyond, if only to collect royalties on undersea minerals. The "drama of the commons" (National Research Council 2002) is played out on the grandest stage of the high seas, and pointed contests between technology and the common good gives this dramatic force.

These six case studies (industrial development, air transport, E-Estonia, social media, finance, and the high seas) all document that it is possible to govern the commons in a technological age, but only if the society recognizes that it is a commons and gives it appropriate attention. In some cases, for example air transport, this depends on a select group to govern the commons, while in others (for example social media) the entire society must conclude that it has a stake in governing the commons. Whether a society is capable of scaling up such decisions calls into question its republican character in a technological world.

## The Republican Ideal

Although the character of the republic has been debated for several thousand years, it is generally agreed that a republic is different from an empire or a monarchy. Republican citizens have ceded some portion of their autonomy to a leader, who, in return, provides social order and stability; in contrast to the subjects of the crown, who are not citizens. Shaping the contours of citizenship and subjection has always been inflected by national identity and regime: The "People's Republic of China" reproduces the Qing and Manchu Empires, maintaining colonial outliers in Tibet and offshore islands as the "Middle Kingdom." Similarly, the American Empire today embraces colonial outposts in Polynesia (American Samoa), the Caribbean (Puerto Rico), and hundreds of military bases around the world and adventures on nearly every continent, even if, in the words of Daniel Immerwahr (2019), it is a "hidden empire." Imperialism and colonialism are fundamentally antithetical to the common good, yet now acquire force and vigor with contemporary technology.

Plato in *The Republic* described the ideal city-state, where concerns for justice and wisdom, rather than imperial conquest, ruled. Countries around the world, particularly in the modern era, have invented and reinvented republicanism, so that today nearly every nation embraces (at least rhetorically) the republican ideal. France founded the First Republic in the middle of a revolution, which was then overthrown by the Napoleonic Empire. The Fifth Republic, founded in 1958 by Charles de Gaulle in the wake of the collapse of the colonial adventure in Indochina (today Vietnam), stressed a strong head of state and a common culture; "multiculturalism," the assertion that different populations can or should express their own cultures within the boundaries of the state, is anathema to the vision of French republicanism.

A core part of republicanism is mutuality—the mutual agreement among citizens that "we're all in this together." Cultural divisions, aggregations of power, and surveillance technologies broadly understood to include all forms of enclosure, tribalism, or colonialism, undermine this mutuality. Stated bluntly, as discussed in Chapter 5, Facebook undermines the mutuality that is at the heart of republicanism, much like Napoleon undermined the First Republic.

An ongoing tension thus exists between the ideals of republicanism and the impulses of authoritarianism. Authoritarian impulses acquire shape and sturdiness when reinforced with technologies, whether those of warfare, transportation and communication, surveillance, or social media. Just as an active republican stance was required to hold back the Bourbons and their successors in nineteenth-century France or the PRI (Partido Revolucionario Institucional) in twentieth-century Mexico, so too in the twenty-first century, whether in America, the European Union, or non-European nations, resisting the encroachments of Facebook, Google, and others on personal autonomy and the common good will require not simply passive resistance but active measures.[6]

It is clear that it is possible to match institution-building with technological advance, but only under very special circumstances. At the top of the list is a realistic understanding of technology—neither as magic nor the wonders of "high tech"—but as a critical understanding of the standards on which it rests, the issues of scale, portability, and translation, and the intersection of these with Ostrom's (1990) eight criteria for governing the commons. Ironically, the emphasis in many schools on "STEM" (Science, Technology, Engineering, and Mathematics) disciplines often excludes a critical perspective on technology, questioning its character and its hidden implications, thus reinforcing what David Noble (1999) characterized as the "religion of technology."

Equally important is social cohesion: small, cohesive countries such as Estonia are better able to use technology to advance the common good than large, racially divided nations such as the United States. The "social construction of technology" is mirrored both by the problems and groups that it brings together, and by the social fractures that technology frequently glosses over or reinforces, including racial, geographical, and class divisions.

Estonia, although having multiple ethnic and linguistic communities, has been able to "punch above its weight" technologically because the total size of the country (over 17,000 square miles including 1,520 islands in the Baltic Sea and a population of 1.3 million [approximately the population of Detroit] with four cities with populations over 100,000) facilitates face-to-face interaction unavailable in larger polities.

Only under certain, identifiable conditions has technology contributed to the common good. Among these are the existence of an underlying community, whether a small nation like Estonia or an international brotherhood like the flight community, both of which can provide conflict resolution mechanisms that Ostrom identifies as part of governing the commons. Also important is the commitment of public resources (i.e., social infrastructure), so that the commons can grow. Ostrom's fourth criterion, "monitoring," is satisfied by the transparency of arrangements and industries such as air traffic and regional industries like power grids, and "clearly designed boundaries" (Ostrom's first criterion) are most easily realized when there is a congruence between the natural environment (e.g., the sky) and the institutional subdivision (e.g., airspace).

The "race between education and technology" (Goldin and Katz 2008) is one particular instantiation of a more general race between institutions and technology. Other instances are the regulation of pollution, assaults on privacy, and even literacy. Technological advance, in the absence of institutional guidance, can only undermine the common good, as we see in the breakdown of governance in the international finance community or in social media's exploitation of private information and attention. More generally, in a democratic society there needs to be protections against the undemocratic tendencies of technologies, whether those of corrupted political parties with massive databases, demagogues with Twitter megaphones, or antisocial media deploying armies of bots and trolls. The "technological society" otherwise replaces living, breathing, sentient masters with an array of invisible, automated autocrats. Conversely, republican impulses can be supported by social media, but they can also be dissolved into tribal squabbling. To avoid this tribal squabbling, we need to find a new narrative for the technological society.

In sum, building institutions for a technological world is feasible and not impenetrable, but only if the *community* sees technology in its rightful place as a *servant*, not a god. How a community might reclaim the commons in a technological world is a subject to which we now turn.

## Notes

1. For the poem "Ode, Inscribed to William H. Channing," see https://emersoncentral.com/texts/poems/ode-to-william-h-channing/ (retrieved 1 September 2021).
2. From the perspective of the utilities this is not quite accurate, but through decades of experience utilities have been able to plan production and share loads so that no domestic customer worries about "running out of electricity" if the lights are left on.
3. For the full song, see https://www.woodyguthrie.org/Lyrics/This_Land.htm (retrieved 1 September 2021).
4. Pilots speak of "pushing the envelope" as testing the aerodynamic limits of an airplane. In flight, one must maintain certain limits of attitude (nose up or nose down) and airspeed; otherwise, the airplane falls out of the sky. These limits are called the "flight envelope." Technologies likewise have performance envelopes, the boundaries of which we are still discovering: bandwidth defines the performance envelope of the internet, and the well-known trade-offs between reach and richness (Evans and Wurster 2000) of electronic communication, and the disappointment of Facebook users in remote areas (i.e., beyond the reach of broadband) in downloading videos may redefine relationships. Similarly, conference applications such as Zoom or WeChat stumble when too many users are online simultaneously, pushing the envelope of acceptable discourse.
5. Cf. https://e-estonia.com/wp-content/uploads/eestonia-guide-2018.pdf.
6. "Active measures" (Активные меры) is a term used by the KGB to promote political agendas outside of Russia, most notably the Russian interference in the 2016 US presidential election. In the current digital arms race (see above, Chapter 6), the forces of republicanism will also have to take active measures against encroaching authoritarianism, whether originating at home or abroad.

Conclusion
# Reclaiming the Commons

We have thus seen that it is possible to shape institutions to tame the machine that Jacques Ellul (1954, 1964) feared, but only under very specific cultural circumstances. The intertwining histories of technology and the commons, ever since the Industrial Revolution, show that just as technologies (such as radio transmission or air travel) open up new commons, technologies (such as social media) undermine and splinter existing commons. New institutions, whether branding or industrial parks, have a technological foundation, as existing institutions, notably educational institutions, are threatened by technologies such as MOOCs. Understanding and reclaiming the commons in a technological age requires us to have a clear-eyed assessment of these challenges.

At the top of the list, and perhaps providing a figure for the others, is an absence of colonial domination, the repression of one people by another. Colonialism, strictly speaking, is the domination of one people or nation by an imperial power, and it is clearly antithetical to the common good. More broadly, colonialism can be understood as a figure for class and race relationships as well as geographic domination, although frequently it involves all three. "Internal colonialism" (Hechter 1975) has been used to characterize the difference between cultural, racial, and linguistic majorities and minorities within single nations (or more accurately single nation-states).

Colonialism and imperialism are the opposite of republicanism, the mutual respect and citizenship of all within a nation. Ideals of republicanism contrast to the imperialistic tendencies within large-scale technologies, even if the technological empires are "accidental" (Cringely 1992). These imperialistic tendencies include aggregations of power and the domination of consciousness, only now not the consciousness of *subjects* but rather of *users*. The way millions of people are tethered to their smartphones is adequate testimony to this. A consequence of these empires and their global reach is the creation of new peripheries within the modern world system based less on military conquest and more on technological domination, a concept that I will examine below.

In this concluding chapter, I will examine both the new, twenty-first-century empires that now dominate the globe, their instabilities in terms of core and periphery, and how pioneers and creoles on the technological frontier are reclaiming the commons. I will focus on the role of educational institutions, notably universities, in creating a seedbed for a new commons in the technological society. In the New Worlds of the eighteenth and nineteenth centuries, as Benedict Anderson observes in *Imagined Communities* (1983), it was the "creole pioneers"—settlers whose ancestry was from the mother country yet who were born in the colony—who pushed back against imperial domination and created new nations, first among the Thirteen Colonies in North America and later in Latin America, Africa, and Asia. Creoles in Revolutionary America included John Adams and Thomas Jefferson. Today, creole pioneers are found in the arts and technology, including Jeff Bezos (the adopted son of a Cuban immigrant), Juan Lin Manuel Miranda, and many other second-generation immigrants who have made notable contributions both to the arts and to industry. Whether working to build new institutions in democracies like Estonia or on social media, or global supply chains, these individuals are less the technological pioneers than they are the second generation, the successors of the original pioneers. Just as was the case in the New World, some creoles created republics that have prospered, and others have created political entities that disguised their compromises with colonialism. Reclaiming the commons in a technological society will require a concerted effort by creoles such as Henry Ford and Thomas Edison (both of whom were children of immigrants), and the pioneers of the computer industry such as Vinton Cerf, who were technological pioneers yet who had a clear-eyed assessment of technological possibilities.

In Chapter 1, "Worlds without Technology," I examined the tools and institutions of societies prior to the Industrial Revolution. The Industrial Revolution was less a technological revolution than it was a social revolution, upsetting a social order that had provided stability for hundreds of years, and providing the coinage of a new term, "technology," for its new instrumentalities. Chapter 2, "Goods, and the Common Good, in a Liberal Society," considered the new configuration of society and its self-understanding or its cosmology as private goods became ascendant. Chapter 3, "Technology and the Commons," presented multiple case studies of technology creating and threatening the commons. The "commons" is understood as a figure of speech for shared goods in general, including public goods, club goods, and common pool resources, all of which are fundamental to the common good. This crisis of the commons results in a cosmological crisis and a collapse of sensemaking in societies focused on private goods. Chapter 4, "Beyond the Traditional Commons," presents three case studies of new commons created by technological advance, including identity, desire, and creativity, all of which are both technologically enabled and threatened. Identity and desire, I documented, are central to the economy today, as much as private goods and services. As technology advances into cyberspace, it creates new commons (Chapter 5) and new enclosures.

Chapter 6, "Democratic Vistas," considers both the civic "-scapes" and the finance"-scapes" of contemporary life, noting how these are intertwined with technological developments, yet also creating new moods and motivations of contemporary life ("The poetry of the commons"). Chapter 7, "Building Institutions for a Technological World," presents six examples, including regional and industrial development, air traffic, and social media, where new institutions have been built to govern the emerging commons of industries, airspace, finance, and the high seas. In this concluding chapter, I examine how we might reclaim the commons as a common heritage, noting that education should be at the forefront of efforts at reclamation.

## Technological Empires

Traditionally, an "empire" referred to an aggregation of territory under a monarch or emperor. As noted above, such empires are largely a thing of the past, but are being replaced by corporate and technological empires, within which an array of enterprises or industries are aggregated together. Google, for example, which started in 1998 as a useful search tool for exploring the World Wide Web, quickly discovered that its users' search history was a valuable resource, which could be mined for consumer data including lifestyles, preferences, and networks. Similarly Facebook, whose origins are described in Chapter 4, is now an empire. The "boys of Silicon Valley," in Robert Cringely's 1993 account (*Accidental Empires*), stumbled into their imperial role, abetted by the eager submission of millions of would-be subjects, who are only now called "users." Empires like these are conquered and maintained not by legions marching under the emperor's banner, but by armies of bots and trolls guided by algorithms and by seductive images and capabilities that colonize the conscience of communities. Silicon Valley began as a rebellion by tech upstarts against staid firms such as IBM, upstarts who took greater pleasure in hacking than in solving real-world problems. Most recently companies like Cambridge Analytica have discovered how to hack entire elections through micro-targeting based on user demographics and internet profiles.

The ability of these technologies to colonize the conscience, both of users and of society as whole, is an untold story. "Technology" occupies a larger and larger space in our daily lives and in our imaginations, crowding out both other concerns and other solutions (such as institutional reform) to pressing societal problems. For example, the search for technofixes for problems such as border security, public health, or public safety crowds out debates on institutional reform, such as rethinking immigration law or the role of the police. Similarly, we might suggest that text messaging and Facebook have become the dominant medium of sociability. There is no question that it is easier to send a text message than to lean over the fence and chat with a neighbor, and asynchronous communication (text messaging and email) crowds out synchronous channels of voice telephony and face-to-face conversation, but when the convenience of text messaging eclipses other forms of social interaction, something is lost.

The United States, which had its founding in a revolution against colonialism, now maintains perhaps the largest empire, albeit a hidden one as noted in the previous chapter, combining both territorial possessions around the world, such as Puerto Rico and Micronesia and American Samoa, military bases on every continent, and enterprises such as Facebook that now bestride the narrow world. Colonization in the twenty-first century is not merely a matter of military occupation. By colonizing the conscience of wider and wider parts of the world, harvesting users' attention, users' desires, social networks, and browsing and shopping history to promote the consumer economy, this empire extends its reach in ways far deeper than any monarch might have imagined. Users thus become subjected to the demands of technological imperialism. The surveillance of millions of users, for example, is at the core of Facebook's business model, as described in the previous chapter; Amazon—the "everything store"—uses massive data to anticipate consumer desires, and Twitter presents itself as the new public square, now with a global reach. Earlier tech giants, as I will describe below, similarly found a profitable business in extending their reach, both geographically and into more and more corners of their users' lives.

In sum, today's technological empires have a reach beyond the wildest imagination of the British, French, or even Chinese emperors, not only extending into villages and households around the world, but also engrossing friendships, attention, political opinions, and consumer preferences. These empires penetrate into civic institutions, demonstrably undermining democracy.

## Core and Periphery

Immanuel Wallerstein, in *The Modern World-System* (1976), argued that relationships between imperial powers and colonial possessions had largely been replaced by relationships between core states such as the United States and most of Europe, on the one hand, and peripheral states such as much of Africa and Latin America, on the other, with a semiperiphery, perhaps exemplified by Brazil or Mexico or mid-twentieth-century China. His model was a dynamic model—semiperipheral states could move into the core (China, for example, backward in the mid-twentieth century, has in the current century emerged as a technological powerhouse) and core states, through corruption and mismanagement, could slide into the semiperiphery (Greece, for example, or southern Italy).

Relationships between core and periphery are also defined by technologies. In terms of technological invention and adoption, this is a complex story, yet one that is now critical for our exposition. For most of recorded history, technologies and their precursor toolkits were at best regional or national systems confined to environments or the standard-setting of the nation-state. Technologies that probed these boundaries, whether railways or electric power transmission in the nineteenth century, had to make adjustments as they approached the boundaries of their accustomed context, typically in the adoption of regional standards: before the Civil War, trains traveling from the North to the South required a "break in gauge," an adjustment of the wheels, as they crossed the Mason–Dixon Line. Similar patterns occur all over Europe, Africa, and Asia. Likewise, standards for electric power transmission (110 vs. 220 volts, 50 or 60 cycles per second, and several other variables) had to respect national jurisdictions.

In the twentieth century, as we have seen, two new technologies burst these bonds: air transport and radio communication were both able to leap over national boundaries, and hence create a new species of adaptation, the large-scale technological system. In the twenty-first century, the internet has been added to this ensemble, reproducing the issues that earlier large-scale systems worked through in the twentieth.

Alain Gras, in *Les Macro-Systèmes Techniques* (1997), argues that large-scale technological systems are now the infrastructure for daily life, embracing all objects from portable telephones to aircraft to motor cars to broadcast communication. In contrast to eighteenth-century and nineteenth-century infrastructures, which were rooted in regions and localities, these new technologies span the entire world. Renate Mayntz and Thomas Hughes (1988) describe multiple large-scale systems, beginning with railway networks in America, France, and Germany, telephone systems in these countries, air traffic control, and electrical power systems, all of which probe the boundaries of core and periphery. The large-scale technological system is a new thing in human history.

These large-scale systems inevitably create peripheries, regions at some distance from the core of invention where the systems take on a different and often malign meaning (Batteau 2010). This is an inevitable consequence of their scale and the mismatch between rates of invention in the core and diffusion out to the periphery: "Moore's Law," a description of technological acceleration, describes a geometric progression in device performance. Originally identified by Gordon Moore, founder of Intel, "Moore's Law" states that the memory capacity of microchips double roughly every 18 months. Moore observed in 1965 that in addition to the acceleration of processing power, the price fell in half in approximately the same time period (Moore 1965). In the years since Moore made this observation, it has held up quite well: in 1965 when he wrote the article, 50 components per microchip was the upper limit; today, roughly 26 cycles later, components per chip number in the hundreds of millions.[1] Henry Adams had observed a similar dynamic in horsepower back in 1895: awestruck at the Machinery Hall at the Columbian Exposition, Adams sketched out an equation that the amount of energy harnessed by humans doubled roughly every ten years. He based this calculation on an observation of a 4,000 watt dynamo at the Exposition, tracing it back to the first locomotives earlier in the century (Adams 1900). Two decades later, the Titanic, with its two Olympic-class triple-expansion 16,000 horsepower steam engines, was on the leading edge of this curve of doubling horsepower, just as the 1,000 megawatt reactor at Three Mile Island was 65 years later.[2]

Relations between core and periphery are not simply a matter of how technologies perform; they are also a matter of the technologies' social role and acceptance. Technologies can be seen as useful tools, a magical force, or a malign presence. Must technology be *seen* to have agency? Non-technologists often accept new systems such as cloud computing without fully understanding either their limitations or the hazards that they pose, or how they subtly inflect the culture. User acceptance is now recognized as essential for any new technology, and research on user experience or UX is a new technological frontier where explorers such as Jeff Bezos, Mark Zuckerberg, and many others probe the ambient commons of social media, exploring for resources (such as attention or personal data) that can be harvested, aggregated, and monetized.

## Pioneers and Creoles on the Technological Frontier

In the twentieth and twenty-first centuries, "virgin lands" are no more, and the "frontier" is now a technological frontier, the outer limit of "civilization," beyond which the Wild West of what was once called the "electronic frontier" remains. Beyond the frontier is a lawless territory, which is now defined less by lines on a map or by indigenous tribes and more by goods and capabilities that are beginning to be explored. These "goods" include the "friendships" that Facebook has monetized, the networks of affiliation that Google exploits, and the ambient commons of the new public square that garish displays pollute. The pioneers exploring and exploiting this new territory are creoles who came of age in the internet era, and who, feeling at home on the electronic frontier, are now creating new settlements.

A strict definition of a creole is a first-generation descendent of the European pioneering settlers, but a more general definition is a descendant of settlers of European ancestry born in the colony. We might say that anyone whose heritage combines both a colonial power and a stake in a New World is a creole, who is prepared to build a new society.

In America, perhaps more so than any in other nation, as noted in Chapter 3 with reference to the sense of American national identity, "the frontier" is a commons, a common pool resource beckoning explorers. Although the original meaning of "frontier" was a border, in America it meant "virgin land" awaiting settlement. Substantial mythmaking has been invested in the American frontier, beginning with Daniel Boone and Davy Crockett, and going through scholarly accounts by Henry Nash Smith (1950) and Frederick Jackson Turner (2014), thus making the "frontier," and themes associated with it (cowboys, gunfighters, "Indians," wilderness areas, virgin land), a core element of American identity. When John F. Kennedy proclaimed the "New Frontier" facing America, he was drawing on powerful themes in American culture. Similarly, the "electronic frontier," a concept that took off at the end of the twentieth century, promised a new Wild West for internet pioneers to stake out their claims.

Benedict Anderson (1983) observed that in the Americas nationalist movements were led by creoles, descendants of the colonial powers who had been born in the New World. Creoles have an advantage—a firm sense of "we belong here"—which, when combined with the rich traditions of their ancestors whether of the Enlightenment or earlier traditions, give them a cultural force that propel them to create new nations. In America today, the creoles are the children of recent immigrants, whether from Latin America or Asia, who, as has been amply documented, make greater contributions to the economy than old-line Americans. Sergei Brin, co-founder of Google, was the son of Russian immigrants, while Alexander Graham Bell was a Scottish immigrant. Nikola Tesla, the inventor of several electrical innovations, was an immigrant from Croatia. Enrico Fermi, the architect of nuclear power, was an Italian immigrant who signed on with the Manhattan Project. This combination of Old World heritage and New World opportunity is perhaps unprecedented in world history.

On the technological frontier, the first explorers were inventors like Thomas Edison and Henry Ford, who created twentieth-century industry. David Lilienthal, who was discussed in the previous chapter, was a pioneer, as was Vannevar Bush, President Roosevelt's science advisor and the author of *Science, the Endless Frontier* (1945). After a stint supervising war production and the Manhattan Project, Bush went on to create the National Science Foundation, the premier sponsor of scientific research and inquiry in America. Since its inception in 1945, the National Science Foundation has sponsored billions of dollars in academic research, making American universities the leading institutions in the world for science and technology. In America, as noted in Chapter 3, the "frontier"—the boundary between civilization and pristine nature—is a commons, a figure that Bush drew on, making science and subsequent technological development not simply a laboratory exercise but a challenge for all Americans.

In *Science, the Endless Frontier*, Bush (1945; see also Bush 1985) laid out a progression from basic science to applied science to invention to commercialization, which has largely served as a charter for public investments in scientific research ever since. Some, however, have called into question the totemic character of these distinctions, noting for example that practical inventions such as the steam engine often preceded discovery of the laws of thermodynamics, a matter of basic science. In general, though, the distinction between science and technological development has largely stood the test of time.

In the shadow of these pioneers came the architects of today's technological world. These creoles include Bill Gates, the founder of Microsoft, Vinton Cerf, sometimes called the "father of the internet," and Mark Zuckerberg, the creator of Facebook and at one time the richest man in the world. They also include Jeff Bezos, who is noted less for any original invention than for scaling up distribution chains to create Amazon, the "everything store," including cloud computing (where computing power is housed on server farms), video streaming, entertainment, and video production and distribution. A *summa cum laude* graduate of Princeton in electrical engineering, with an innate love of tinkering, Bezos as an entrepreneur was perfectly situated to ride the dot-com boom in the late 1990s. Amazon's beginning as an online bookseller coincided with the appearance of the internet in the public consciousness in 1995. Some of these innovations have unquestionably advanced the common good, whereas the contribution of others is far more problematic. Facebook, in the words of one of its original sponsors, is a "catastrophe" less in its technology and more in its strategic decision to monetize information on its users. Facebook, for example, has created filter bubbles and preference bubbles that tear society apart and destroy democracy (McNamee 2019). *Any* commons can be monetized (i.e., enclosed), subject either to the safeguards of privacy laws or common sentiment. Technological developments, most notably the internet but also such matters as facial recognition technologies and data-mining algorithms, create new opportunities for monetizing the commons.

Perhaps America's most notable creole was Henry Ford, whose Highland Park Assembly Plant transformed manufacturing from a craft into a scalable industry. The son of Belgian and Irish immigrants, Ford observed in the Chicago stockyards how cattle were disassembled into component parts (steaks, roasts, etc.), and had the insight that the process could be reversed in the *assembly* of horseless carriages. Fifty years later, Ford was a vertically integrated empire, including iron mines in Minnesota, coal mines in Kentucky, rubber plantations in the Amazon, and manufacturing plants across America and around the world. "Fordism" became a template for numerous industries. The geographic reach of Ford, with operations on every continent, was matched by its industrial reach, making it a true industrial empire.

Notably missing in the efforts of these pioneers is any initiative to create public goods or common pool resources. Although earlier pioneers such as David Lilienthal created a prosperous region, and Vinton Cerf, a graduate of Stanford University, created the protocols that are the foundation of the internet, and Henry Ford arguably created the American middle class, the focus of Bezos and Zuckerberg and similar entrepreneurs has been exclusively on creating and distributing private goods that can be monetized (i.e., sold). The idea of harvesting billions of dollars through producing and distributing public goods or common pool resources is totally nonsensical. The closest they have come is in creating a new sort of club good, the "filter bubble," as described in Chapter 5.

In other words, technological pioneers such as Lilienthal, Bush, Cerf, and others created a new national narrative of heroic technological accomplishment that brought America together as evidenced by the "tech boom" at the close of the twentieth century. This boom came crashing down in 1999. By contrast, the filter bubbles and preference bubbles of Facebook are tearing the nation apart. Perhaps the gravest threat to American democracy today is the devolution of the polity into competing factions. This splintering has been with America since the beginning but now, with the internet, acquires new force and vigor.

## The Educational Commons

The biggest initiatives to extend the commons in modern society have been through the expansion of public education. As described in Chapter 3, the common school movement extended public education to all citizens, although "separate but equal" would remain the fate of education for minorities for more than a century. Similarly, the land-grant universities supported higher education throughout the country, including some leading institutions such as Cornell. Both the land-grant universities and the Transcontinental Railway emerged from the Louisiana Purchase, a vast 828,000 square mile tract of land acquired from France in 1803, which in the nineteenth century provided the foundation for critical public goods. In the Louisiana Purchase, one square-mile section out of every township (64 square miles) was set aside to support what eventually became the land-grant universities under the Morrill Act. Half of the Louisiana Purchase was also set aside to support a transcontinental railway, with railroads being given odd-numbered sections to sell and settle. The Louisiana Purchase and the two major institutions that it supported—land-grant universities and the Transcontinental Railway—were the major episodes of nation-building in the American nineteenth century, which was celebrated in 1869 by the driving of the "Golden Spike" in Promontory Summit in Utah, as described in Chapter 3. Both the Transcontinental Railway and the land-grant universities, major episodes in America's nation-building, would have to wait until the slave states seceded from the union.

A century later, the GI Bill of Rights supported higher education for servicemen who were veterans of World War II, thus leading to the explosive growth of higher education throughout the country. As a consequence, American colleges and universities attract students from all over the world, outcompeting universities in other OECD countries, in part because the American scientific establishment is recognized as a world leader, with more Nobel Prize winners than any other country. America has replaced Britain at the pinnacle of global higher education. As America starves its public universities (Newfield 2016), it shorts its future generations.

For more than a century, educators and scientists have been at the forefront of advancing the common good in America. This comes from an acceptance that education and knowledge generally are public goods, and that all benefit from an educated citizenry. Democracy depends on educated citizens, and recent efforts to starve the schools are a direct assault on democracy.

One consequence of the unique place of higher education in America has been the creation of several new technology-based industries and industrial regions, whether in Silicon Valley or along Route 128 around Boston. Route 128 became the home of a post–World War II commons, the industrial park, where startups could find offices and room to expand. Eventually, Route 128, anchored in higher education institutions (MIT, Harvard), became the seedbed of technology leaders such as Raytheon and Digital Equipment Corporation, which built the first digital computer. Later, other knowledge-intensive industries such as biotechnology, software, and fiber optics followed. Similarly, Silicon Valley was the seedbed of Apple, Google, and Facebook. The next frontier may well be found in human-centered design, where design firms in partnership with higher education institutions are blazing new trails. "Human-centered design," a discipline that was practically nonexistent before the tech boom of the end of the twentieth century, is now a new frontier in the design world.

Industrial parks are in fact the new commons of the technological society. An industrial park is a piece of real estate, typically adjacent to a large city, set aside for the development of light industry. They enable their tenants to share several advantages, including zoning restrictions, infrastructure, and transportation access, and they mirror the "campuses" of many leading firms, such as Microsoft, Raytheon, and Intel. Industrial parks, which were practically unknown before the 1950s, took off as industry transitioned away from heavy, smokestack industries to technology-oriented industries that depended on proximity to urban centers and higher education institutions.

This rapid rise of technology is reflected in the organization of Silicon Valley. The people who began or were employed in these new firms considered themselves technological trailblazers, and the formal and informal "communities" that they developed are in some ways akin to the pioneers who settled the West in the nineteenth century. The residents of this technological society were, originally at least, a strongly homogeneous group: white, male, Stanford- or MIT-educated engineers who migrated to California from other regions of the country. As modern-day pioneers, they were especially responsive to risky ventures that had the potential for great rewards.

The enclosures and privatization of public schools can be considered a tragedy of the twenty-first-century commons, in which the seedbeds of the economy of the future are overharvested to meet the demands of today's industry. In the view of *A Nation at Risk*, discussed in Chapter 3, schools at all levels were for training human parts for the industrial machine; universities were reduced to trade schools; and the liberal arts took a backseat to the STEM disciplines. Reclaiming the educational commons will require the efforts of men and women of vision who understand that the greater value of education is not simply in job training, as important as that is, but more in cultivating character for creativity and critical thinking and democratic souls. The frontiers of this effort are not only in classrooms and boardrooms, but in living rooms and dining rooms as parents explain to their children the importance of an education.

It is widely recognized that an educated and engaged citizenry is more prosperous than an uneducated one. Creativity and critical thinking are necessary to imagine the world of the future, and to build its economy. It is not difficult to imagine a viable business model where college tuition would be free at public institutions; indeed, this was the business model at the City University of New York for most of its history. Other notable experiments in tuition-free higher education include Berea College, founded by abolitionists as the first integrated college in the South in 1855, and Alice Lloyd College in Pippa Passes, Kentucky, which offers its students a tuition-free higher education in exchange for work on campus. The University of California was tuition-free for most of its history, moving away from tuition-free for California residents only in the 1970s. Current debates over higher education are not simply debates about bookkeeping: they are debates over the character of higher education, whether as a private or a public good. Although this debate was settled nearly two centuries ago for primary and secondary education, with the common school movement (see above, Chapter 3, Section 3, "Technologies and Institutions of Nation-Building"), current proposals to privatize public education are the latest form of enclosure.

The City University of New York, like universities in many European countries, was tuition-free until the city's near-bankruptcy in 1975. The austerity politics of the 1980s, beginning with New York City and spreading to the rest of the country, was not simply a matter of bookkeeping, but a matter of imperial assertion. New York City's financial difficulties followed years of neglect as multiple interests, notably the financial interests represented by Wall Street, pressed for lower taxes and less government in an increasingly complex and overcrowded city.

The financial collapse of New York City, like the actual bankruptcy of Detroit in 2013, is an urban version of the "tragedy of the commons," where mismanagement in the form of inattention (a lack of monitoring), a lack of clearly designed boundaries, and the crippling of conflict resolution mechanisms (i.e., government) permitted special interests (notably real estate speculators) to plunder the urban commons. In current times, it was not so much illiterate peasants, as it was some of the leading families, living in suburbs such as Greenwich, Connecticut, and Grosse Pointe Woods, Michigan, that picked the urban commons bare. Also plundering the urban commons were city leaders who found it easier (in the short term) to buy off the municipal unions, buying labor peace at the expense of future generations. The tragedy of the urban commons mirrors closely Garrett Hardin's 1968 morality tale, only updated for contemporary institutions, most notably financial institutions as they shifted their business priorities in the era of neoliberalism from funding new businesses and residences (their traditional purpose) to amassing unearned piles of wealth through private equity and rent-seeking, in the process nearly wrecking the American economy.[3]

Although the tragedy of the commons as described by Garrett Hardin played out in limited quarters over many years, the tragedy of the urban commons plays out on a global scale in a compressed time frame. Instead of overharvesting a mountain meadow over several decades, financial interests in the Cayman Islands and Luxembourg overharvested cities around the globe in a matter of just a few years: New York City went from being a glittering metropolis to a focus of the "urban crisis" in the 1970s. This difference in scale has made it difficult for the government institutions that normally protect the urban commons to rise to the challenge, as evidenced by cascading urban crises at the end of the twentieth century and the beginning of the twenty-first.

## This Land Is Our Land

We should not paint an idyllic picture of the commons prior to the enclosure movement and the Industrial Revolution. Illiterate peasants scratched out a living under the supervision of local lords whose vision scarcely extended beyond the valley over which they ruled. While the enclosure movement drove peasants off the land and into factories, the Industrial Revolution opened up new avenues for wealth and mobility. The world they lost, as described by Peter Laslett in *The World We Have Lost* (1965), combined both domestic security and limited horizons.

Is it possible to reclaim the commons in a technological society, or is humanity doomed to be under the surveillance of closed-circuit televisions dictated by distant algorithms? Are CCTV systems and surveillance technologies a new enclosure, or a new tool for monitoring the commons? More pointedly, can technological empires such as Google, Twitter, and Facebook be reconciled with a democratic society?

Just as the TVA successfully reclaimed the exhausted land of the Tennessee Valley (Lilienthal 1944), creating a dynamic and prosperous regional economy that has served as a model for other regional development efforts, it should be possible to reclaim the corrupted public square that Facebook, Amazon, and social media have given us. This requires a new vision of the common good.

Originally, the concept of "reclamation" referred to restoring lands worn out from overcultivation, whether by letting them lie fallow or by positively fertilizing, seeding, and cultivating them to gain back their productivity. The original "tragedy of the commons" specifically referred to the overuse of common pool resources such as meadows and forests, but it can be applied to technological and civic commons as well: the well-known neglect of infrastructure in the United States[4] is a tragedy of the commons, in which succeeding generations free-ride on the investments of their predecessors, and pay the price with contaminated water or rough roads. Cities such as Detroit and Chicago, for example, have lived off of their past prosperity, neglecting investments for the future. The underfunding of education at all levels is a tragedy of the commons, condemning future generations to careers and civic lives of semiliterate drones as they struggle to pay of college debts.

The concept of reclamation can be extended to all forms of shared resources under assault from these latter-day enclosures, whether the privatization of public services including education and law enforcement, the fencing in of copyright restrictions (see Chapter 6, Section 3), or the corruption of public discourse by bots and trolls. These earlier reclamation initiatives required a forward vision and affirmative efforts and political leadership; so too, today, reclamation must begin with a vision of the new commons of a technological society.

At the top of our list might be the urban commons, the neighborhoods, enterprises, institutions, factories, and surface resources that give cities their vitality. In the second chapter of *A People's Atlas of Detroit* (Campbell et al. 2020), "This Land Is Ours: Toward a New Urban Commons," Diane Feeley, Kezia Curtis, Jessi Quizar, Cecily McClellan, and other authors map out changing patterns of land use in Detroit neighborhoods, including community gardens, housing, and small retail stores, and the cross-border commons connecting Detroit and Windsor, Ontario. The authors stress the vitality of on-the-ground Detroit, in contrast to the abandoned city narrative that supported bankruptcy, and they focus on three interrelated themes: the image of Detroit as an "urban wilderness," the ongoing displacement (we could read "enclosure") of Detroiters from their neighborhoods, and the coming together of neighbors around grassroots projects such as neighborhood gardens and fishing in the Detroit River.

*A People's Atlas* is part of a movement of "counter-cartography" that seeks to uses the power of maps to imagine new social and economic relationships and create a new imaginary of shared struggle and alternative worlds. The counter-cartography movement has created new maps, in addition to Detroit, in the San Francisco Bay Area, Raleigh-Durham, North Carolina, Argentina, Ecuador, Palestine, and other countries and regions around the world, creating visual representations of such issues as life expectancy, education, and industrial vitality. Through creating new geographic images of these countries and regions, the counter-cartography movement re-imagines and reclaims the landscape commons. As noted above, shared representation is essential for imagining the common good. Counter-cartography grew out of the oral history movement in the 1970s and 1980s, where local historians sought to reclaim their heritage from the authoritative statements of academic and official histories. Both counter-cartography and oral history are a push back against twentieth-century and twenty-first-century enclosures, reclaiming both history and geography in the name of those who live it.

Both counter-cartography and oral history are based on a vision, the idea that a shared heritage can be reclaimed from the forces of colonization. The land, for example, which counter-cartography reclaims, is more than just real estate; it is, first and foremost, a commons or, more precisely, a common pool resource that citizens cannot be excluded from but that can become polluted through misuse or neglect. As residential real estate, it is a private good, yet as an urban commons it is a public good, neither depletable nor excludable. And finally, it is also a club good, as echoed in Woody Guthrie's folk song "This Land Is Your Land."[5]

The bankruptcies of Detroit and New York had a similar dynamic: the middle class abandoned a vibrant city, turning it over to slumlords and fly-by-night businesses. Municipal schools, services, and government also abandoned the city, turning it over to drug dealers and real estate speculators. In today's society, the degradation of the commons is less a gradual deterioration by illiterate peasants and more an active plundering of a shared good by some of the leading figures in society.

Earlier empires eventually met resistance in the form of nationalist movements as they colonized. Creoles led these movements, as exemplified first by the American Revolution and later independence movements in Latin America, Africa, and Asia (Anderson 1983). A century later, as industry engrossed leisure time and domestic spaces, union movements pushed back, eventually achieving a balance of power between the forces of capital and the common people. The shared prosperity of the 1950s was a consequence of this, although subsequent declines in trade unions have undermined this shared prosperity. Today, a growing tribe of technological creoles—entrepreneurs, scholars, advocates, and educators who have come of age in the technological world—is now, inchoately at first, pushing back against the arrogance of technological empires.

Finding a similar pushback in a technological society is now the challenge before us. Although earlier resistance movements—the "Luddites"—are often dismissed as being opposed to technology, in fact their opposition was not to factory production per se, but rather to the degraded quality of production and diminished quality of life that the factory system created in the English Midlands (Thompson 1963). Domestic production, whether by blacksmiths or housewives, was replaced by factory production with rigid supervision, turning skilled craftsmen such as smiths and weavers into "hands," appendages of the machine. Similarly, the trade-union movement was less opposed to business per se, than it was opposed to the oppressive power relationships that nineteenth- and twentieth-century industry brought. More recent movements, whether the environmental movement or the Civil Rights Movement, have had a narrower focus while still offering similar potential for societal transformation that earlier pushbacks to imperialism offered.

What might reclamation look like in our contemporary environment of digital globalism? It might begin with a recognition that private goods are not simply an alternative form of wealth, different from public goods, and that they are in many situations opposed and antithetical to the common good. Grouping different forms of value under the label of "goods" (private goods, club goods, public goods, etc.), while a convenient economic shorthand, completely erases the social character of each, whether the civic-mindedness of public goods, the belongingness of club goods, the natural sharing of common pool resources, or the greed associated with private goods. The hyper-emphasis on consumption in all aspects of life—the media, the public square, and commonplace conceptions of the "good life" promoted by some of the most powerful, industrial interests in society—is not only about gluttony, but also about a devaluation of the common good.

Can we imagine the world we have lost to private consumption? Can we reclaim the common good from today's economy? The answer might begin with an understanding that there are powerful forces arrayed against the common good, be they corporate, financial, or technological empires, and that these empires are free-riding on the public good. American prosperity and innovativeness, for but one of many examples, is based on America's long-standing reputation as a nation of laws, sound currency, and an educated citizenry. When these are undermined, whether through budget-busting deficits, imperialistic adventures overseas, official corruption, the privatization of schools, or the financialization of all aspects of life, the foundations of that prosperity are eroded. No amount of flag-waving can disguise the fact that nationalistic leaders all over the world are actively shorting their nations, betting against their future, and hoping for their failure, whether by disenfranchising minorities, colluding with technological empires such as Facebook, or corrupting the national government, all while they shout slogans about becoming "great again."

To reclaim the commons of our postindustrial society, we first must recognize that education is the central institution of the information age, and that diatribes against "government schools" are a rhetorical defense of today's enclosure movement. Although the common school movement, as described in Chapter 3, dates back to the 1820s, the derisive characterization of public schools as "government schools"—that are contrasted, for example, with charter schools—is a more recent, late-twentieth-century phenomenon reinforced by a neoliberal rhetoric that disparages all forms of government, replacing personal responsibility and future vision with free-riding and shorting, by some of the most powerful in society.

As *the* central institution of the information age, education not only trains students for sophisticated jobs, it also instills the values of a free and prosperous society. These values include an awareness of other peoples and ways of life around the world, a tolerance for different points of view, and a curiosity about new possibilities. In a globalizing world, knowledge of other cultures and customs is more essential than ever. New industries, in manufacturing, entertainment, and technology, are built not by illiterate drones but by young men and women whose innate curiosity and creativity was cultivated and encouraged by their teachers. In a globalizing economy, knowledge of both technologies *and* cultures is essential both for individual success and for national prosperity. This has been the story of America for most of its history.

Reclaiming this heritage could begin with a recognition that the United States was founded in a revolution against colonialism, albeit with an asterisk: for its first hundred years, more than 10 percent of the American population lived in colonial subjection, and even after enslaved people were freed, the country sought to build an empire with colonial outposts in the Pacific, the Caribbean, and the Far East. Even well into the twenty-first century, America's melting pot was built on the backs of immigrant laborers whose ambiguous status continues to disguise the corrupt stalemate between republicans and free-riding imperialists.

America's original sin of chattel slavery in an egalitarian society would require hundreds of years of ongoing effort to correct, and it has not yet been completely expunged. More recently, countries with a history of colonialism, notably France and Great Britain, are struggling to reconcile their colonial past with contemporary republican ideals. Great Britain (more accurately the United Kingdom of England, Wales, Scotland, and Northern Ireland) grew out of the union of Scotland and England (including Wales) in 1707, with Ireland added in 1800. The United Kingdom was not *united* by religion, language, law, or even territorial contiguity after 1800. Born of the industrial revolution, the United Kingdom is a perfect example of an "imagined community," which now threatens to become disunited as the United Kingdom exits the European Union, and this jury-rig of an empire threatens to come apart as Scotland threatens to leave the United Kingdom. France, which regarded its colonial possessions in Northern Africa as part of metropolitan France (hence *not* colonies), struggles with accommodation with immigrant communities, which have made France, more than any other European nation, a "nation of immigrants," even while multiculturalism is anathema to French ideals of republicanism. One might suggest that every contemporary empire, including technological empires, must struggle with ideals of republicanism.

The American construction of citizenship combines birthright, ancestry, and naturalization in an uneasy combination that periodically threatens to come apart. Notable events in the unraveling include the internment of American citizens of Japanese ancestry during World War II, the protests of the Civil Rights Movement, and contemporary debates over the rights and entitlements of children bought to the America by migrant parents. Stated simply, the original conceptions of citizenship—legal attachment to a territorially defined political entity—come apart in the contemporary world of global transportation and communication, with predatory interests probing the boundaries. Technological developments necessitate a renegotiation of ideals of citizenship, a larger project than current discussions over immigration reform. To analyze citizenship as a commons, in the terms that Ostrom (1990) used for *Governing the Commons* would be an instructive exercise, not the least because it would reveal the interests that are exploiting or free-riding on this commons. Similar stories could be told in every nation with a global reach, whether the former Soviet Union, China, or Brazil. In Russia, oligarchs prey on a corrupt economy, while in China visions of past imperial glory hold together increasingly fractious territorial and ethnic minorities.

Personal identity consists of those components of the individual that identify him or her as a unique person. They include their society's schema of classification (gender, race, etc.), occupation, and totemic objects, things that confer a unique identity. Although "totemism" is typically associated with the clans of tribal societies, the increasing tribalism of our society suggests that we have not outgrown this. Guns, for example, are no longer simply tools for foraging or self-defense; more importantly, today they are emblematic of identity, of *who I am*, at least for a large segment of American society. Richard Slotkin's book, *Gunfighter Nation* (1992), captures this totemic identification well, and the growing attention in recent years to the Second Amendment, in contrast to earlier, less tribalist years, suggests that gun-toting protesters are making a statement about "who we are" that was almost invisible for the first half of the twentieth century.

Similarly, many reject the idea that anyone with dark skin can be a citizen. Although the civil rights laws of the 1960s firmly rejected skin color as a marker of the legal status of citizenship, the fact that tens of millions of Americans 50 years later rejected Barack Obama, inventing a myth of Kenyan ancestry, suggests that this idea has not disappeared. Gun sales boomed after Obama's election, not out of any reality-based concern for personal safety, but rather out of a concern that people's American identity was being threatened.

We should recognize education in an industrial society, at all levels, as *the* ultimate public good, combining low subtractability with difficult exclusion. Education as an institutional complex has demonstrated its ability to scale up, through the common school movement in the early nineteenth century, the land-grant universities in the late nineteenth century, the GI Bill after World War II, and today with proposals for free college at public institutions, which would turn higher education from a toll good into a public good. There have been missteps along the way, whether in treating higher education as a business (a private institution producing private goods), or devaluing the community of scholars that Cardinal Newman (1982) described as the essence of the university, making it into more an assemblage of trade schools. Higher education in America is the envy of the world for its openness and excellence, and students from every continent come to universities throughout the United States. Although some private universities and prep schools are exclusive, that is a matter less of their educational mission than of their social character. Thus any effort to reclaim the commons will be led by educators and educational institutions, and the coming school wars will indeed be a conflict over the character of an advanced industrial society: is it a cage or a commons?

Reclaiming our heritage as a nation of immigrants should start with a recognition that, as the "first new nation," the United States was an early harbinger of globalization, bringing together peoples literally from all over the world. Efforts to reverse this trend, whether in the form of the Alien Exclusion Act of 1924 or the construction of border walls, are more than simply legal or architectural missteps: they are assaults on the soul of the nation. By contrast, as is easily demonstrated, extending the global reach of the American soul contributes not only to the prosperity of the American nation, but to the common good of all humanity.

The world of higher education is a commons, although one that is increasingly threatened by predators in the form of for-profit universities and free-riding legislators cutting university budgets. As a community of scholars (in contrast to a trade school), expecting a university to turn a profit is totally illogical. With the neoliberal turn in the 1980s, however, with its endorsement of free-riding and rent-seeking from the public good, this vision of a public good was increasingly eclipsed as more and more states shrank their support for higher education.

Educators are the creoles of a technological society. Having grown up in a world that was being shaped by technology, they imagine new possibilities of creativity and invention whether on the platforms of social media or at the forefront of climate action. The Green New Deal, for example, building on the legacy of Roosevelt's New Deal, confronts the issues of climate change and economic inequality as *the* challenges of the twenty-first century. As a consequence, universities are on the frontlines between free-riding elites on the one hand and the next generation of America's leaders on the other. They are shaping new possibilities for industries, communities, institutions, and entire regions. Like any other pioneering effort, there will be false starts and many efforts that are wildly successful: Facebook, as described above, grew out of a student experience at Harvard, and Amazon went from a bookseller to an "everything-seller." By contrast, nearly all of the startups of Silicon Valley grew out of the nexus of Stanford University and the University of California at Berkeley, arguably *the* incubators (along with Route 128 in Massachusetts) for the information economy. When politicians starve the schools for funds, they are not simply attacking the teachers' unions; they are shorting the entire nation, betting against its future.

Reclamation of the commons in a technological society must begin with educators and educational leaders who can articulate a vision of the interplay between education and technology in today's society. Education is *less* about the STEM disciplines, and more about a creative, global, and critical perspective on the common good. Just as technology has expanded our horizons to include other peoples, religions, and ways of life around the world, and has demonstrably enriched America by so doing, we must expand our understanding of the common good as far broader than personal consumption.

In sum, we can see that some of the greatest advances in American society have been with efforts to reclaim the commons, whether through the TVA, which created a prosperous region; the creation of the land-grant universities; the Homestead Act, which created thousands of yeoman farmers; the creation of industrial parks and the tech boom for which they provided a seedbed; or the revitalization of major cities such as Detroit, Chicago, and New York City. Conversely, some of the biggest setbacks came from predators, often in the highest positions in government, industry, and society, who plundered the commons.

The tragedy of the commons in a technological society, like the original "tragedy of the commons" that Garrett Hardin (1968) prophesied, comes from a narrowness of vision from and short-term thinking that substitutes immediate, private gratification for the long-term good of the society. The tragedy of the technological commons is a result not only of predation and free-riding, but also more from a misapprehension of the nature of the technological society by some of its leading figures, both in government and in industry.

Reclaiming the technological commons might begin with an acceptance that we must tame the things that are currently, in Ralph Waldo Emerson's words, "in the saddle and ride mankind."[6] This entails returning information technology to its original purpose of tabulating information for social purposes, or transportation technology and infrastructure to unite, rather than divide, communities. An active effort must be made to assure that technology serves human purposes, rather than the other way around. In the past two centuries, America and other industrial countries have made incredible progress in creating devices that conquer time, distance, and other impediments to shared prosperity. The challenge before us is a concerted effort to turn these devices toward conquering social divisions and fostering the common good.

### Notes

1. A cartoon accompanying the Moore (1965) article, which must have seemed wildly humorous in 1965, showed a smiling department-store salesman, in between the notions and the cosmetics counters, selling "handy home computers." This almost perfectly illustrates an important dynamic as technologies go from science-fiction novelties to laboratory breakthroughs to office appliances to daily necessities. The 1943 remark attributed to Thomas Watson, who grew IBM to be a dominant information technology company, "I think there is a world market for maybe five computers," while probably apocryphal, provides a context for this humorous concept of "handy home computers." A better-documented statement to the same effect came in 1951 from the Cambridge mathematician Douglas Hartree, in whose opinion "all the calculations that would ever be needed [in England] could be done on ... three digital computers." (q. in Bowden 1970).

2. In fact many well-known industrial accidents result from similar efforts to push devices beyond the limits of familiar operating regimes (Batteau 2003). Once other elements of the assemblage, including operator skills, management practices, and regulation, catch up with the improved device capability, the assemblage stabilizes. Technologies, in other words, are not simply clever devices, but rather embrace an array of social practices including user skills and community attitudes.
3. See above, Chapter 6, Section 2, "Wealth and Poverty," on the role of technology and institutional corruption in creating the "finance curse."
4. The American Society of Civil Engineers has estimated that an investment of $3.6 trillion is needed to upgrade America's roads, ports, bridges, wastewater, inland waterways, airports, dams, drinking water supplies, railways, and flood control. The investments in these common pool resources are not being maintained by the current generation.
5. For the full song, see https://www.woodyguthrie.org/Lyrics/This_Land.htm (retrieved 1 September 2021).
6. For the poem "Ode, Inscribed to William H. Channing," see https://emersoncentral.com/texts/poems/ode-to-william-h-channing/ (retrieved 1 September 2021).

# References

Adams, Henry. [1900]. 1961. "The Dynamo and the Virgin." In *The Education of Henry Adams*. Boston: Houghton Mifflin, 379–90.
Adams, Robert M. 1996. *Paths of Fire: An Anthropologist's Inquiry into Western Technology*. Princeton, NJ: Princeton University Press.
Anderies, John M., Marco A. Janssen, and Edella Schlager. 2016. "Institutions and the Performance of Coupled Infrastructure Systems." *International Journal of the Commons* 10 (2), 495–516.
Anderson, Benedict. 1983. *Imagined Communities: Reflections on the Origin and Spread of Nationalism*. London: Verso.
Ansary, Tamim. 2007. "Education at Risk: Fallout from a Flawed Report." *Edutopia*, 9 March. https://www.edutopia.org/landmark-education-report-nation-risk.
Appadurai, Arjun. 1996. *Modernity at Large: Cultural Dimensions of Globalization*. Minneapolis: University of Minnesota Press.
Arnold, Matthew. 1869. *Culture and Anarchy*. London: Smith, Elder, & Co.
Aronczyk, Melissa. 2008. "'Living the Brand': Nationality, Globality, and the Identity Strategies of Nation Branding Consultants." *International Journal of Communication* 2, 41–65.
Atwood, Margaret. 2013. *The MaddAddam Trilogy*. New York. Anchor.
Baradaran, Mehrta. 2017. *The Color of Money: Black Banks and the Racial Wealth Gap*. Cambridge, MA: Belknap Press of Harvard University Press.
Barber, Benjamin. 1995. *Jihad vs. McWorld*. New York: Times Books.
Batteau, Allen. 2003. "Un Siglo de Desastres Industrialies: Una Extensión de la Antropología Frazierana." In Carmen Bueno and María Josefa Santos (eds.), *Nuevas tecnologías y cultura*. Barcelona: Anthropos, 211–228.
———. 2010. "Technological Peripheralization." *Science, Technology, and Human Values* 35 (3), 1–21.
———. 2011. "Negations and Ambiguities in the Cultures of Organization." In Mats Alvesson (ed.), *Classics in Critical Management Studies*. Cheltenham, UK: Edward Elgar, 235–249.
———. 2012a. "The World of Finance." In Anne Jordan and Douglas Caulkins (eds.), *Companion to Organizational Anthropology*. Malden, MA: Wiley-Blackwell, 381–398.
———. 2012b. "The Changing Rhetoric of Corporate Culture." In Anne Jordan and Douglas Caulkins (eds.), *Companion to Organizational Anthropology*. Malden, MA: Wiley-Blackwell, 56–74.

Bell, Daniel. 1947. "The Study of Man: Adjusting Men to Machines." *Commentary*, January, 79–88.
Benjamin, Ruha. 2019. *Race after Technology: Abolitionist Tools for the New Jim Code*. Cambridge: Polity Press.
Benjamin, Walter. [1936]. 2015. *Kunstwerk im Zeitalter seiner technischen Reproduzierbarkeit*. Berlin: Suhrkamp.
———. 1968. *Illuminations: Essays and Reflections*. New York: Harcourt, Brace, and World.
Benkler, Yochai. 2006. *The Wealth of Networks: How Social Production Transforms Markets and Freedom*. New Haven, CT: Yale University Press.
Berger, Peter, and Thomas Luckmann. 1966. *The Social Construction of Reality: A Treatise in the Sociology of Knowledge*. Garden City, NY: Anchor Books.
Berman, Marshall. 1982. *All That Is Solid Melts Into Air*. New York: Penguin Books.
Bledstein, Burton. 1978. *The Culture of Professionalism: The Middle Class and the Development of Higher Education in America*. New York: Norton.
Blomkvist, Pär, and Jesper Larsson. 2013. "An Analytical Framework for Common-Pool Resource Large Technical System (CPR-LTS) Constellations." *International Journal of the Commons* 7 (1), 113–139.
Boas, Franz. 1940. *Race, Language, and Culture*. New York: The Macmillan Company.
Bollier, David, and Silked Helfrich (eds.). 2012. *The Wealth of the Commons: A World beyond Market and State*. Amherst, MA: Levellers Press.
Borgmann, Albert. 1984. *Technology and the Character of Contemporary Life: A Philosophical Inquiry*. Chicago: University of Chicago Press.
Bowden, Lord. 1970. "The Language of Computers: The Man Who Sold the First Digital Computer on the Commercial Market Describes the Explosion in Programming." *American Scientist* 58 (1), 43–53.
Bower, Joseph, and Clayton L. Christensen. 1995. "Disruptive Technologies: Catching the Wave." *Harvard Business Review* 73 (1), 43–53.
Boyle, James. 2002. "Fencing off Ideas: Enclosure and the Disappearance of the Public Domain." *Daedalus* 131, 13–25.
Braverman, Harry. 1974. *Labor and Monopoly Capital: The Degradation of Work in the Twentieth Century*. New York: Monthly Review Press.
Bromley, Daniel W., ed. 1992. *Making the Commons Work: Theory, Practice, and Policy*. San Francisco: Institute for Contemporary Studies.
Bryce, James. 1888. *The American Commonwealth*. London: Macmillan.
Burke, Kenneth. [1941]. 1973. *The Philosophy of Literary Form*. Berkeley: University of California Press.
———. 1961. *The Rhetoric of Religion*. Boston: Beacon Press.
Bury, J. B. 1932. *The Idea of Progress*. New York: Macmillan.
Bush, Vannevar. 1945. *Science: The Endless Frontier*. Washington, DC: Government Printing Office.

---. 1985. *Modern Arms and Free Men: A Discussion of the Role of Science in Preserving Democracy.* Westport, CT: Greenwood Press.

Campbell, Linda, Andrew Newman, Sara Safransky, and Tim Stollman. 2020. *A People's Atlas of Detroit.* Detroit: Wayne State University Press.

Castells, Manuel. 1996. *The Rise of the Network Society.* Malden, MA: Blackwell Publishers.

Chrisomalis, Stephen. 2010. *Numerical Notation: A Comparative History.* Cambridge: Cambridge University Press.

Coles, Thomas. 1836. "Essay on American Scenery." *The American Magazine*, NS, 1, 1–12.

Conca, James. 2018. "It's a Horrible Idea to Try to Privatize the Tennessee Valley Authority and Other Public Energy Assets." *Forbes Magazine*, 18 March 18.

Cornes, Richard, and Todd Sandler. 1986. *The Theory of Externalities, Public Goods, and Club Goods.* Cambridge: Cambridge University Press.

Cringely, Robert X. 1992. *Accidental Empires: How the Boys of Silicon Valley Make Their Millions, Battle Foreign Competition, and Still Can't Get a Date.* New York: HarperCollins.

Darwin, Charles. 1859. *The Origin of Species.* Oxford: Oxford University Press.

De Tocqueville, Alexis. [1835/1840]. 2000. *Democracy in America.* Ed. and Tr. Harvey C. Mansfield and Delba Winthrop. Chicago: University of Chicago Press.

Diamond, Jared M. 2005. *Collapse: How Societies Choose to Fail or Succeed.* New York: Viking.

Douglas, Mary. 1986. *How Institutions Think.* Syracuse, NY: Syracuse University Press.

Durkheim, Émile. [1893]. 2013. *The Division of Labour in Society.* Tr. Steven Lukes. Houndmills, UK: Palgrave Macmillan.

---. [1912]. 1965. *The Elementary Forms of the Religious Life.* Trans. Joseph Swain. New York: The Free Press.

Ellul, Jacques. 1954. *La Technique ou l'Enjeu du Siècle.* 1954: Paris: Armand Colin.

---. 1964. *The Technological Society.* Tr. John Wilkinson. New York: Basic Books.

Etzioni, Amitai. 2004. *The Common Good.* Malden, MA: Polity Press.

Evans, Philip, and Thomas Wurster. 2000. *Blown to Bits: How the New Economics of Information Transforms Strategy.* Boston: Harvard Business School Press.

Ewen, Stuart. 1976. *Captains of Consciousness: Advertising and the Social Roots of Consumer Culture.* New York: McGraw-Hill.

Farmer, Stephanie, and Sean Noonan. 2014. "The Contradictions of Capital and Mass Transit: Chicago, USA." *Science and Society* 78 (1), 61–87.

Feenberg, Andrew. 1999. *Questioning Technology.* New York: Routledge.

Ferguson, Niall. 2018. *The Square and the Tower: Networks, Hierarchies, and the Struggle for Global Power.* New York: Allen Lane.

Fiedler, Leslie. 1968. *The Return of the Vanishing American*. New York. Stein and Day.
Fisher, Max, Amanda Taub, and Dalia Martinez. 2018. "Some Mexican Towns Are Effectively Seceding." *New York Times*, 8 January.
Fitzgerald, F. Scott. [1936]. 1945. The Catch-Up. Ed. Edmund Wilson. New York: New Directions.
Florman, Samuel. 1976. *The Existential Pleasures of Engineering*. New York: St. Martin's Press.
Foucault, Michel. 1975. *Surveiller et Punir: Naissance de la Prison*. Paris: Gallimard.
———. 1977. *Discipline and Punish: The Birth of the Prison*. Tr. Alan Sheridan. New York: Vintage Books.
Friedman, Jonathan. 1994. *Cultural Identity and Global Process*. Thousand Oaks, CA: Sage Publications.
Frischmann, Brett M. 2012. *Infrastructure: The Social Value of Shared Resources*. Oxford: Oxford University Press.
Galbraith, John Kenneth. 1958. *The Affluent Society*. Boston: Houghton Mifflin.
Geertz, Clifford. 1973. *The Interpretation of Cultures*. New York: Basic Books.
Gell, Alfred. 1988. "Technology and Magic." *Anthropology Today* 4 (2), 6–9.
Gellner, Ernest. 1983. *Nations and Nationalism*. Ithaca, NY: Cornell University Press.
George, Andrew. 2008. "Avoiding the Tragedy of the Wiki-Commons." *SSRN*, 19 March. https://ssrn.com/abstract=975096.
Goldin, Claudia, and Lawrence Katz. 2008. *The Race between Education and Technology*. Cambridge. MA: Belknap Press of Harvard University Press.
Graan, Andrew. 2013. "Counterfeiting the Nation? Skopje 2014 and the Politics of Nation Branding in Macedonia." *Cultural Anthropology* 28 (1), 161–179.
Grandin, Greg. 2009. *Fordlandia: The Rise and Fall of Henry Ford's Forgotten Jungle City*. New York: Henry Holt.
Gras, Alain. 1997. *Les Macro-Systèmes Techniques*. Paris: Presses Universitaires de France.
Gras, Alain, Caroline Moricot, Sophie L. Poirot-Delpech, and Victor Scardigli. 1994. *Face à l'Automate: Le Pilote, le Contrôleur et l'Ingénieur*. Paris: Publications de la Sorbonne.
Grotius, Hugo. 1609. *Mare Liberum; sive, De jure quod Batavis competit ad indicana commercia dissertatio*. Trans. Richard Hakluyt. Lugduni Batavorum, Ex officina L. Elzevirii.
Hackett, Edward J., Olga Amsterdamska, Michael E. Lynch, and Judy Wajcman (eds.). 2008. *Handbook of Science and Technology Studies*, 3rd ed. Cambridge, MA: MIT Press.
Hardin, Garrett. 1968. "The Tragedy of the Commons." *Science*, New Series, 162 (3859), 1243–1248.
Harris, Marvin. 1968. *The Rise of Anthropological Theory*. London: Routledge & Kegan Paul.

Hayek, Friedrich. 1944. *The Road to Serfdom*. London: George Routledge and Sons, Ltd.

Hechter, Michael. 1975. *Internal Colonialism: The Celtic Fringe in British National Development, 1536–1966*. Berkeley: University of California Press.

Hess, Charlotte, and Elinor Ostrom, eds. 2007. *Understanding Knowledge as a Commons*. Cambridge, MA: MIT Press.

Hess, David. 1995. *Science and Technology in a Multicultural World*. New York: Columbia University Press.

Ho, Karen. 2009. *Liquidated: An Ethnography of Wall Street*. Durham, NC: Duke University Press.

Hobsbawm, Eric. 1969. *Industry and Empire*. Harmondsworth, UK: Penguin Books.

———. 1990. *Nations and Nationalism since 1780*. Cambridge: Cambridge University Press.

Hoffman, Samantha. 2018. "Social Credit: Technology Enhanced Social Control with Global Consequences." *ASPI International Cyber Policy Centre*, 28 June. https://aspi.org.au/report/social-credit.

Hofstede, Geert. 1997. *Cultures and Organizations: Software of the Mind*. New York: McGraw-Hill.

Hubert, Henri, and Marcel Mauss. [1899]. 1964. *Sacrifice: Its Nature and Function*. Trans. W. D. Halls. Chicago: University of Chicago Press.

Hughes, Thomas P. 1983. *Networks of Power: Electrification in Western Society, 1880–1930*. Baltimore: Johns Hopkins University Press.

———. 1998. *Rescuing Prometheus: Four Monumental Projects that Changed the Modern World*. New York: Pantheon Books.

Immerwahr, Daniel. 2019. *How to Hide an Empire: A History of the Greater United States*. New York: Farrar, Straus and Giroux.

Jacobs, Jane. 1961. *The Death and Life of Great American Cities*. New York: Random House.

———. 1984. *Cities and the Wealth of Nations: Principles of Economic Life*. New York: Random House.

Jasanoff, Sheila, and Sang-Hyun Kim. 2015. *Dreamscapes of Modernity: Sociotechnical Imaginaries and the Fabrication of Power*. Chicago: University of Chicago Press.

Jennings, Thomas A., and Don Wyckoff. 2009. "San Patrice Technology and Mobility across the Plains-Woodland Border." R. E. Bell Monographs in Anthropology #5. *Lithic Technology* 34 (2), 127–130.

Kubiszewski, Ida, Robert Costanza, Carol Franco, Philip Lawn, John Talberth, Tim Jackson, and Camille Aylmer. "Beyond GDP: Measuring and Achieving Global Genuine Progress." *Ecological Economics* 93 (C), 57–68.

Kubrick, Stanley, dir. 1964. *Dr. Strangelove or: How I Learned to Stop Worrying and Love the Bomb*. London: Shepperton Studios.

Kuhn, Thomas. 1962. *The Structure of Scientific Revolutions*. Chicago: University of Chicago Press.

Kuznets, Simon. 1934. "Report to the U.S. Congress." Reprinted at http://www.beyond-gdp.eu. Retrieved 1 September 2021.
Laslett, Peter. 1965. *The World We Have Lost*. New York: Scribner.
Latour, Bruno. 2005. *Reassembling the Social: An Introduction to Actor-Network Theory*. Oxford: Clarendon Press.
Leach, Edmund. 1954. *Political Systems of Highland Burma*. Cambridge, MA: Harvard University Press.
Lepenies, Philipp. 2016. "Why GDP?" *Project Syndicate*, 16 August. https://www.project-syndicate.org/commentary/why-gdp-by-philipp-lepenies-2016-08.
Lessig, Lawrence. 2004. *Free Culture: The Nature and Future of Creativity*. New York: Penguin Books.
Lévi-Strauss, Claude. [1952]. 1968. *Race and History*. Paris: UNESCO.
———. [1962]. 1969. *Totemism*. Tr. Rodney Needham. London: Penguin Books.
———. [1966]. 1969. *The Savage Mind*. Chicago: University of Chicago Press.
Levitsky, Steven, and Daniel Ziblatt. 2018. *How Democracies Die*. New York: Crown Publishing Group.
Lilienthal, David. 1944. *TVA: Democracy on the March*. New York: Harper & Brothers.
Lipset, Seymour Martin. 1973. *The First New Nation: The United States in Historical and Comparative Perspective*. New York: W. W. Norton.
Locke, John. [1689]. 1968. *Two Treatises of Government*. London: Dent.
Lury, Celia. 2004. *Brands: The Logos of the Global Economy*. London: Routledge.
Maraniss, David. 2015. *Once in a Great City: A Detroit Story*. New York: Simon & Schuster.
Marx, Karl, and Friedrich Engels. [1848]. 2014. *The Communist Manifesto*. London: Penguin Books.
Marx, Leo. 1964. *The Machine in the Garden: Technology and the Pastoral Ideal in America*. New York: Oxford University Press.
Mayntz, Renate. 2008. "Von der Steuerungstheorie zu Global Governance." In Gunnar F. Schuppert and Michael Zürn (eds.), *Governance in einer sich wandelnden Welt*. Wiesbaden: VS Verlag, 43–60.
Mayntz, Renate, and Thomas P. Hughes, eds. 1988. *The Development of Large Technical Systems*. Frankfurt am Main: Campus Verlag.
McCarter, P. Kyle, Jr. 1975. *The Antiquity of the Greek Alphabet and Early Phoenician Scripts*. Missoula, MT: Scholars Press.
McCullough, Malcolm. 2013. *Ambient Commons: Attention in the Age of Embodied Information*. Cambridge, MA: MIT Press.
McLuhan, Marshall. 1989. *The Global Village*. Oxford: Oxford University Press.
McNamee. Roger. 2019. *Zucked: Waking up to the Facebook Catastrophe*. New York: Penguin Books.
Miller, Perry. 1956. *Errand into the Wilderness*. Cambridge, MA: Harvard University Press.
Moore, Gordon. 1965. "Cramming More Components onto Integrated Circuits." *Electronics* 38 (8), 114–117.

Morgan, Lewis H. 1877. *Ancient Society*. Chicago: Charles H. Kerr & Company.
Mumford, Lewis. 1961. *The City in History*. New York: Harcourt, Inc.
Mylonas, Harris. 2012. *The Politics of Nation-Building*. New York: Cambridge University Press.
National Commission on Excellence in Education. 1983. *A Nation at Risk: The Imperative for Educational Reform: A Report to the Nation and the Secretary of Education*. Washington, DC: Government Printing Office.
National Research Council. 2002. *The Drama of the Commons*. Ed. Elinor Ostrom. Washington, DC: National Academies Press.
Newfield, Christopher. 2016. *The Great Mistake: How We Wrecked Public Universities and How We Can Fix Them*. Baltimore: Johns Hopkins University Press.
Newman, Andrew. 2013. "Gatekeepers of the urban commons: Vigilant Citizenship and Neoliberal Space in Multiethnic Paris." *Antipode: A Journal of Radical Geography* 45 (4), 947–964.
———. 2015. *Landscape of Discontent: Urban Sustainability in Immigrant Paris*. Minneapolis: University of Minnesota Press.
Newman, John Henry. 1982. *The Idea of a University*. Notre Dame, IN: University of Notre Dame Press.
Noble, David. 1997. *The Religion of Technology: The Divinity of Man and the Spirit of Invention*. New York: A. A. Knopf.
Nonini, Donald M., ed. 2007. *The Global Idea of "The Commons."* New York: Berghahn Books.
Novak, Barbara. 1980. *Nature and Culture: American Landscape and Painting, 1825–1875*. New York: Oxford University Press.
Olson, Mancur. 1965. *The Logic of Collective Action: Public Goods and the Theory of Groups*. Cambridge, MA: Harvard University Press.
Orwell, George. 1949. *1984*. New York: Signet Classics.
Ostrom, Elinor. 1990. *Governing the Commons: The Evolution of Institutions for Collective Action*. Cambridge: Cambridge University Press.
Ostrom, Elinor, Thomas Dietz, Nives Dolšak, Paul C. Stern, Susan Stonich, and Elke U. Weber, eds. 2002. *The Drama of the Commons*. Washington, DC: National Academy Press.
Overton, Joseph P. 2013. "The Overton Window – Mackinac Center." https://mackinac.org/OvertonWindow. Retrieved August 3, 2021.
Packard, Vance. 1957. *The Hidden Persuaders*. New York: D. McKay Company.
Pelto, Pertti J. 1973. *The Snowmobile Revolution: Technology and Social Change in the Arctic*. Menlo Park, CA: Cummings Publishing Company.
Perrow, Charles. 1974. *Complex Organizations: A Critical Essay*. Glenview, IL: Scott, Foresman.
———. 1984. *Normal Accidents: Living with High-Risk Technologies*. New York: Basic Books.
Petroski, Henry. 1985. *To Engineer Is Human: The Role of Failure in Successful Design*. New York: St. Martin's Press.

———. 1995. *Engineers of Dreams: Great Bridge Builders and the Spanning of America*. New York: Knopf.

Petzinger, Thomas. 1995. *Hard Landing: The Epic Conquest for Power and Profits that Plunged the Airlines into Chaos*. New York: Three Rivers Press.

Pfaffenberger, Bryan. 1992a. "Technological Dramas." *Science, Technology, and Human Values* 17 (3), 382–312.

———. 1992b. "The Social Anthropology of Technology." *Annual Review of Anthropology* 21, 491–516.

Pinch, Trevor, and Wiebe E. Bijker. 1984. "The Social Construction of Facts and Artefacts: Or How the Sociology of Science and the Sociology of Technology Might Benefit Each Other." *Social Studies of Science* 14 (3), 399–441.

Preda, Alex. 2017. "Machineries of Finance: Technologies and Sciences of Markets." In Edward J. Hackett, Olga Amsterdamska, Michael E. Lynch, and Judy Wajcman (eds.), *Handbook of Science and Technology Studies*, 4th ed. Cambridge, MA: MIT Press, 609–634.

Putnam, Robert D. 1995. "Bowling Alone: America's Declining Social Capital." *Journal of Democracy* 6 (1), 65–78.

Rauch, Jonathan. 2021. *The Constitution of Knowledge: A Defense of Truth*. Washington, DC: Brookings Institution Press.

Reich, Robert. 2018. *The Common Good*. New York: A. A. Knopf.

Rogers, Everett. 1995. *Diffusion of Innovations*. 4th ed. New York: Free Press.

Ross, Michael L. 1999. "The Political Economy of the Resource Curse." *World Politics* 51 (2), 297–322.

Sachs, Jeffrey, and Andrew Warner. 1995. *Natural Resource Abundance and Economic Growth*. NBEC Working Paper. Washington, DC: National Bureau of Economic Research.

Sharp, Lauriston. 1952. "Steel Axes for Stone Age Australians." *Human Organization* 11 (2), 17–22.

Shaxson, Nicholas. 2019. *The Finance Curse: How Global Finance Is Making Us All Poorer*. New York: Grove Press.

Shelley, Mary Wollstonecraft. 1818. *Frankenstein, or the Modern Prometheus*. London: Lackington, Hughes, Harding, Mavor & Jones.

Sinclair, Upton. [1906] 1980. *The Jungle*. New York: Penguin Books.

Skocpol, Theda. 1994. *Social Revolutions in the Modern World*. Cambridge: Cambridge University Press.

Slotkin, Richard. 1992. *Gunfighter Nation: The Myth of the Frontier in Twentieth-Century America*. New York: Atheneum.

Smith, Adam. [1776]. 1970. *The Wealth of Nations*. Ed. Andrew Skinner. Harmondsworth, UK: Penguin Books.

Smith, Henry Nash. 1950. *Virgin Land: The American West as Symbol and Myth*. Cambridge, MA: Harvard University Press.

Stern, Paul C. 2011. "Design Principles for Global Commons: Natural Resources and Emerging Technologies." *International Journal of the Commons* 5 (2), 213–232.

Stilgoe, John R. 2007. *Train Time: Railroads and the Imminent Reshaping of the United States Landscape.* Charlottesville: University of Virginia Press.

Strathern, Marilyn. 2004. *Commons and Borderlands.* Herefordshire, UK: Sean Kingston.

Suskind, Richard. 2004. "Faith, Certainty and the Presidency of George W. Bush." *New York Times*, 27 October. https://www.nytimes.com/2004/10/17/magazine/faith-certainty-and-the-presidency-of-george-w-bush.html.

Tett, Gillian. 2009. *Fool's Gold: The Inside Story of J. P. Morgan and How Wall St. Greed Corrupted Its Bold Dream and Created a Financial Catastrophe.* New York: Free Press.

Thompson, E. P. 1963. *The Making of the English Working Class.* New York: Random House.

Turner, Frederick Jackson. [1893] 2014. *The Frontier in American History.* Mansfield Centre, CT: Martino Publishing.

Van Maanen, John. 1991. "The Smile Factory: Work at Disneyland." In Peter J. Frost, Larry F. Moore, Meryl R. Louis, and Craig C. Lundberg (eds.), *Reframing Organizational Culture.* Thousand Oaks, CA: Sage Publications, 58–76.

Wachowski, Lana, and Lilly Wachowski, dirs. 1999. *The Matrix.* Sidney, Australia: Fox Studios.

Wallerstein, Immanuel. 1976. *The Modern World-System.* New York: Academic Press.

Weber, Max. [1905]. 1930. *The Protestant Ethic and the Spirit of Capitalism.* New York: Scribner.

———. 1946. "Class, Status, Party." In *From Max Weber: Essays in Sociology.* Ed. H. H. Gerth and C. Wright Mills. London: Routledge, 177–193.

Weick, Karl. 1993. "The Collapse of Sensemaking: The Mann Gulch Disaster." *Administrative Science Quarterly* 38 (4), 628–652.

———. 1995. *Sensemaking in Organizations.* Thousand Oaks, CA: Sage Publications.

White, Leslie. 1959. *The Evolution of Culture: The Development of Civilization to the Fall of Rome.* New York: Grove Press.

Whitman. Walt. [1855]. 2019. *Leaves of Grass.* Ed. Bridget Bennett. London: Macmillan.

Williams, Raymond. 1983. *Keywords: A Vocabulary of Culture and Society.* New York: Oxford University Press.

Winston, Clifford. 2010. *Last Exit: Privatization and Deregulation of the U.S. Transportation System.* Washington, DC: Brookings Institution Press.

Wu, Tim. 2016. *The Attention Merchants: The Epic Scramble to Get Inside Our Heads.* New York: A. A. Knopf.

Zaloom, Caitlin. 2006. *Out of the Pits: Traders and Technology from Chicago to London.* Chicago: University of Chicago Press.

Zuboff, Shoshana. 1988. *In the Age of the Smart Machine: The Future of Work and Power.* New York: Basic Books.

———. 2019. *The Age of Surveillance Capitalism: The Fight for a Human Future at the New Frontier of Power.* New York: Public Affairs.

# Index

Acela, 77
*Accidental Empires* (Robert Cringely), 186
Adams, Henry, 188
Adaptation, local, 16, 19
Advertising, 85, 125, 126
Agora, 8, 133, 156
Air Commerce Act, 95, 97
Airspace, 97, 98, 160
Alice Lloyd College, 194
Alien Exclusion Act (1924), 152, 202
Amazon, 109, 116, 126, 133, 146, 156, 175, 186
Ambient commons, 29, 109, 124, 141, 149, 189
American Society of Civil Engineers, 163, 205
Anderson, Benedict (*Imagined Communities*), 43, 72, 73, 74, 115, 121, 128, 137, 184, 190, 198
Appadurai, Arjun, 118, 127, 131, 132, 137
Archimedes screw, 18, 19
Arnold, Matthew, 127
Athabaskan, 13, 16
"Attention merchants" (Tim Wu), 70, 86, 124, 126
Authoritarianism, 180
Aviation Safety Reporting System (ASRS), 162, 164, 170

Benjamin, Ruha, 121
Benjamin, Walter, 94, 106, 131, 161
Berea College, 194
Bezos, Jeff, 184, 189, 191

Bonneville Power Administration, 166, 169
Bot farms, 137
Boundaries, 33, 38, 39, 69, 70, 95, 96, 98, 99, 101, 103, 114, 122–125, 139, 154, 163–165, 170, 173, 178, 181, 187, 188, 195
Boundary markers, 168
"Bowling Alone," 38
Boyle, James, 110, 150
Brand equity, 86, 97, 104, 107
Brands, 19, 95, 97, 104, 105, 107, 108, 114, 124, 129
Braverman, Henry, 56
Bretton Woods, 175, 176
Burke, Kenneth, 36, 158
Bush, Vannevar, 3, 159, 190

CCTV (Closed-circuit television), 156, 106
Cerf, Vinton, 184, 191, 192
Charter Schools, 44, 69, 80–83
Chicago, 139, 140, 157, 158, 196
Cities, 20, 24–29, 42, 50, 73, 76, 118–119, 139–141, 156–158, 195–197
*Cities and the Wealth of Nations*, 28, 139, 157
Citizenship, 42, 49–50, 80, 82, 98, 112, 119, 133, 135, 139, 151–15, 156, 179, 201, 202
City of Big Shoulders, 140, 158
City University of New York, 195
Civic commons, 25, 26, 28, 41, 50, 57
Civic participation, 56, 80, 119, 120, 126

Civic spaces, 27, 35, 36, 41, 49, 50, 119, 120
Civil society, 23, 25, 27, 84
Click bait, 70
Club goods, 8, 9, 25, 26, 41, 42, 46, 47d, 49, 55, 69, 84, 86, 88, 94, 95, 98, 101, 103, 106, 114, 142, 143, 144, 158, 160, 173, 175, 184, 199
Collective conscience, 120
Colonialism, 56–58, 76, 78, 179, 180, 183, 184, 186, 200
Colonialism, internal, 183
Colonization, 29–32, 121, 159, 160, 186
Colonizing the conscience, 113, 186
Columbus, 30
Common pool resources, 8, 9, 29–34, 38, 39, 41–44, 47, 50, 55, 64, 68, 69, 94, 95, 110, 111, 114, 124, 125, 143, 144, 150, 158, 161, 163, 165, 167, 184, 191, 192, 196, 199
Common school movement, 79, 81, 82, 192, 195, 202
Commons, ambient, 29, 70, 109, 124, 141, 189
*Communist Manifesto, The*, 35
Conflict resolution, 39, 70, 124, 125, 164, 181, 195
Copyright, 29, 44, 47, 105, 109, 110, 149–151, 197
Core, 128, 184, 187–188
Corruption, 31, 129, 172–174
Cosmology, 37, 41, 42, 49, 59, 90, 184
Costs, hidden, 42–43
Counter-cartography, 197
Creation science, 63
Creative commons, 109, 111, 114
Creole, 115, 184, 189, 191
Cult value (*Kultwert*), 106
Cultural production, 131, 133
Culture Industry, 109, 110, 149
*Culture of Professionalism, The* (Burton Bledstein), 26
Cyberspace, 9, 92, 118, 121

da Vinci, Leonardo, 2, 21, 35
David Lilienthal, 165, 166, 190, 192, 196
Deepwater Horizon, 71
Defense Advanced Research Projects Agency, 24
*Democracy in America* (Alexis de Tocqueville), 75
De-skilling, 56
Detroit, 140, 141, 181, 195, 197, 198, 204
Diasporic public spheres, 118
Digital globalism, 108, 120, 121, 128, 130, 132, 139, 140
Diploma mills, 49
Disney, 104, 105, 110
Disruption, 6, 54, 55, 123, 155
Durkheim, David Emile, 120

Education, 28, 44, 47, 56, 57, 69, 70–72, 75, 79, 80–82, 83, 85, 91, 110, 115, 127, 134, 150, 152, 153, 181, 185, 192–194, 195–197, 200, 202–203
E-Estonia, 163, 171, 172, 181, 184
Ego-centric cosmology, 59, 64
Ellul, Jacques (*The Technological Society*), 162, 184
Emerson, Ralph W., 92
Empires, 31, 116, 119–121, 169, 172, 179, 185, 186, 191, 200, 201
Enclosure, 26, 28, 29, 48, 50, 55–58, 69, 80, 81, 84, 85, 104, 105, 107, 108, 110, 111, 120, 121, 134, 146, 149, 150, 157, 161, 166, 169, 173, 174, 180, 195, 196, 197, 200
Ethnoscape, 138, 139, 141, 143, 151, 160
Etzioni, Amatai, 36
Eurocontrol, 163, 169–170
European expansion, 9, 14, 89
Ewen, Stewart, 124
Exhibition value (*Ausstellungswert*), 106

Externalities, 42, 102, 143, 148

Facebook, 31, 42, 47, 57, 59, 60, 70, 108, 109, 112–113, 119, 122, 125, 126, 131, 133–134, 142, 154–155, 173, 174, 180, 185, 186, 191–193, 196, 203
Facial recognition, 48, 70, 112, 123, 125, 149, 155, 156, 191
Factory system, 9, 35, 55–57, 72, 198
Feudal society, 24, 25, 27, 29, 55–89
Fiedler, Leslie, 30
Filter bubbles, 43, 112, 125, 132, 134, 173, 191, 192
*Finance Curse, The* (Nicholas Shaxson), 147
Financial engineering, 145
Financial technology, 47, 146, 176
Fintech, 47, 90, 176
Fitzgerald, F. Scott, 161
Ford, Henry, 5, 184, 190–192
Fordism, 191
Foucault, Michel, 93, 123, 156
Free rider, 37, 39, 98
Free Software Foundation, 151
Friedman, Milton, 42
Frontier, 7, 74, 102, 105, 159, 171, 184, 189, 190, 193
Frontinus, 22, 23
*Futurist Manifesto, The*, 155
Futurist, futurism, 155, 6, 62, 123

Galbraith, John Kenneth, 65, 142
Gates, Bill, 191
General Data Protection Regulation, 175
Genuine Progress Indicator, 148
Gerrymandering, 152
GI Bill of Rights, 193, 202
Gig economy, 131
Glass-Steagall Act, 154
Goods, private, 8, 26, 29, 41, 49, 54, 64, 65, 69, 83, 87, 88, 94, 95, 105, 112–114, 116, 120, 138, 142–144, 147, 150, 155, 158, 159, 184–185, 192, 199, 202
Google, 31, 70, 108, 113, 126, 155, 174 // 169, 173, 174, 175, 180, 185, 195, // 189, 190, 196
*Governing the Commons* (Elinor Ostrom), 8, 9, 29, 36, 38, 69, 95, 111, 123, 125, 164, 180, 181, 201
Gras, Alain, 17, 188
Green New Deal, 203
Gresham's Law, 91, 119
Gross Domestic Product, 143, 144, 146–148
Gross National Product, 74, 140
Grosvenor Square, 156
Grotius, Hugo, 177
Guilds, 14, 22–25, 26–27, 46–47, 53, 149

Harden, Garrett, 38, 195, 204
Harley-Davidson motorcycle, 51, 108
Hayek, Friedrich, 48, 144
Health Insurance, 86, 87
Hedonic calculus (Jeremy Bentham), 59, 60
"High Flight" (John Gillespie McGee), 160
High tech, 123, 180
High-speed rail, 77
Ho, Karen, 47
Hobsbawm, Eric, 115, 116
Home ownership, 144–145
Homestead Act, 78, 203
Horace Mann, 79
Hudson River School, 45, 95, 101, 102, 105, 159
Human-centered design, 193

Identity tokens, 49, 50, 52, 86, 105, 117
Ignorance, 63, 64, 71, 88–92
*Imagined Communities* (Benedict Anderson), 8, 160, 200, 73, 115, 121, 139, 184

Imperial domination, 32, 92, 116, 128, 183–185
Imperialism, 36, 179, 183, 186
Individualism, 34, 37, 38, 47, 75, 144
Industrial parks, 183, 193, 194, 204
Industrial Revolution, 1, 9, 11, 14, 30–32, 48, 50, 56, 58, 62, 68, 72, 74–75, 83, 94, 96, 114–116, 131, 153, 183, 184, 196, 200
Industry as a commons
Infrastructure, 44, 66, 76–77, 144, 157, 163, 167, 172, 181, 188, 194, 196, 204
Inhofe, James, 71
Innuit, 16, 17
Insider information, 46
Intellectual property (IP), 106, 107, 151
Interior universalism, 74
International Civil Aviation Organization (ICAO), 97, 171
International Law of the Sea, 163, 164, 176, 178
Internet, 23, 63, 65, 74, 89–90, 91, 96, 111, 118, 121, 122, 124, 126, 128, 130, 132, 133–135, 137, 138, 146, 149, 150, 154, 159–165, 171–176, 187, 189, 190–192
Interstate Highway System, 77

Jacobs, Jane, 28, 139, 156–157
Jardin d'Eole, 148, 150

Knowledge, 18, 26, 29, 41, 45–46, 59, 63, 83, 88–92, 100, 101, 110–111, 137, 149–151, 158, 168, 193, 200
Knowledge, tacit, 5, 46
Ku Klux Klan, 130
Kuznets, Simon, 148

*Laissez-faire*, 58
Land-grant universities, 78, 79, 167, 192, 193, 202, 203

Landscape, 44, 75, 86, 101–106, 149, 167, 168, 169, 176, 197
*Landscape of Discontent* (Andrew Newman), 139, 148
Large technical systems, 40
Laslett, Peter, 196
Leach, Edmund, 15
Libertarianism, 37
Libraries, 40, 41, 69, 93, 121, 158
"Library Ode" (Philip Larkin), 158, 161
Lifestyle, 85, 86, 105, 107, 108
Lilienthal, David, 165, 166, 190, 192, 196
Locality, independence of, 9, 65, 66, 68, 99, 154
Locke, John, 57, 58, 60, 61
Louisiana Purchase, 77, 192
Luddites, 56, 198
Lury, Celia, 105, 126

*Macro-Systèmes Techniques, Le* (Alain Gras), 188
Magic, 48, 67, 68, 90, 96, 123, 126, 165, 176
Manuel Miranda, Juan Lin, 184
Marx, Karl, 32, 34, 58, 123
Marx, Leo, 101–103
Massive Online Open Classrooms (MOOCs), 83, 183
Mayntz, Renate, 140, 188
Media, 9, 29, 35, 39, 41, 46, 48, 49, 54, 57, 58, 59, 70, 83, 85, 91, 92, 111, 112, 114, 116, 119, 120, 121, 128, 131, 133, 137, 138, 139, 141, 149–151, 153, 160, 162–164, 172–174, 176, 179, 180–181, 184, 185, 189, 196, 203
Mediascapes, 9, 118, 132, 137, 160, 161
Merchandising, 95, 106
Modernism, 65, 67, 123, 155–156
Monitoring, 9, 33, 39, 68–70, 112, 124, 125, 133, 149, 156, 163–165, 170, 171, 178, 181, 196

Moochers, 38
Moore, Gordon, 188
Moore's Law, 54, 123, 152, 188
Morgan, Lewis Henry, 47, 127
Morrill Act, 79, 192
Moses, Robert, 157
Mumford, Lewis, 76
Myanmar, 15

Narrative, 2, 4, 6–7, 9–10, 23–25
Nation-branding, 107, 134
Nation-building, 72–83, 115, 193, 195
National Commission on Excellence in Education, 81
National parks, 45, 102
National road, 77
National Science Foundation, 3, 190
Nationalism, 73–75, 101, 114–116, 121, 128, 130, 139, 153
Nation-state, 2, 8, 72–76, 91, 111, 114–117, 131, 147, 183, 187
Neighborhood speculation, 159
Neoliberalism, 38, 48–49, 83
Nested enterprises, 39, 70, 125, 164, 170
Network society (Manuel Castells), 128
New nations, 75, 184, 190
New World, 6, 30–32, 55, 89, 101, 115, 177, 189, 190
New York City, 77, 156, 165, 195, 204
Newman, Andrew, 139, 148–149
Newman, Cardinal, 202
Normal accidents, 147

Obama, Barack, 87, 91, 202
Office of Technology Assessment, 10
Olson, Mancur, 37
Open source movement, 100
Open-field system, 55
Oral history, 197–198
Organized culture, 128, 135
Orwell, George, 4, 5, 112, 133
Ostrom, Elinor, 29, 38–41, 46, 69, 70, 85, 88, 89, 95, 100–101, 107, 111, 137, 142, 143, 153, 158, 165, 178, 181, 201
Othering, 44, 90
Overton window, 109

Packard, Vance, 125
Panopticon, 108
Paris, 6, 28, 74, 115, 139, 140, 141, 149, 158, 163
Path dependence, 4
Patrimonial authority, 20, 108, 111, 128, 135, 139, 154
People's Atlas of Detroit, 197
Periphery, 128, 184, 187–188
Perrow, Charles, 147, 167
Pfaffenberger, Bryan, 3, 68
Platform, 112, 131, 133, 134, 172
Pont du Gard, 22–23
Power grids, 163, 165–167, 181
Prep schools, 80, 202
Print capitalism, 73, 120, 121, 128, 130, 139, 149
Private equity, 145, 195
Private goods, 8, 26, 29, 41, 44, 49, 54, 64, 65, 69, 83, 85, 87, 88, 94, 95, 104, 105, 112, 113, 114, 116, 120, 138, 142–144, 147, 148, 150, 155, 158–159, 184–185, 192, 199, 202
Privatization, 8, 26, 28, 29, 40, 44, 45, 47, 48, 54, 57, 80, 81, 87, 157–158, 194, 197, 199
Progress, idea of, 74
Ptolemaic universe, 59, 64
Public goods, 8, 9, 26, 29, 33, 41, 42–44, 47–50, 55, 59, 64, 66, 69, 77, 80, 84–85, 94–95, 103, 111, 118–136, 137, 138, 139, 142–144, 147–151, 158, 159, 184, 191–193, 199
Public hazards, 85–86, 89, 147, 158
Public health, 63, 84, 87, 139, 186
Pure Food and Drug Act, 84, 142
Putnam, Robert, 38

Race between education and
  technology, 70, 71, 91, 152, 163,
  181
Railways, 78, 99, 101, 102, 187
Reach and richness, tradeoff, 91, 122
Real estate speculation, 145
Reality-based community, 91, 92
Reclamation, 9, 166, 185, 196, 197,
  203
Recontextualization, 18, 65
Regions, 165–169, 188, 193, 197, 203
Reich, Robert, 37
Religion of technology, 29, 180
Rent-seeking, 80, 203
Representation, 62, 138, 144, 150,
  159, 161, 197
Representation, autonomous, 65, 66,
  94, 122, 123, 138, 164
Republic, republican, 34, 36, 41,
  64, 77, 107, 113, 119, 138, 162,
  179–180, 181, 200
Republicanism, 28, 138, 152, 179–
  180, 183, 201
Reputation, 145
Resource curse, 84, 146, 172
RF Spectrum, 9, 40, 95, 97, 99–100,
  114, 124, 125
*Road to Serfdom, The* (Friedrich
  Hayek), 48–49
Roosevelt, Franklin, 3, 141, 159, 167,
  190, 203
Rural Electrification Administration
  (REA), 165

Sacred value, 43, 59
Sacrifice, 43, 74
Safety culture, 170
Sanctions, 39, 70, 112, 125, 164, 170
Sandburg, Carl, 158
Scalability, 9, 62, 65, 66, 68, 156, 164,
  178
Scale-free network, 129, 131
School to prison pipeline, 93

*Science: The Endless Frontier*
  (Vannevar Bush), 3, 9, 10, 159, 190
Scientific management (Frederick
  Taylor), 129
Second enclosure movement (James
  Boyle), 150
Sensemaking, 35, 54, 64, 68, 91–92,
  185
Short selling, 147
Silicon Valley, 23, 166, 168, 185,
  193–194, 203
Single European Sky, 169
Slavery, 52, 56, 58, 78, 87, 200
Slotkin, Richard, 201
Smith, Adam, 26, 30, 57, 59–60, 142,
  144
Social capital, 38, 80, 129, 131
Social class, 49, 52, 175
Social construction of knowledge,
  63–65, 88
Social construction of technology
  (SCOT), 6, 10, 35, 88, 180
Social credit system (China), 70, 112
Social media, 9, 29, 35, 39, 41, 46, 48,
  54, 57, 58, 59, 70, 85, 91, 92, 111,
  112, 114, 116, 119, 120, 121, 128,
  133, 137–141, 163, 173–175, 176,
  179–180, 183–185, 189, 196, 203
Social status, 4, 5, 14, 86
Social status of engineers, 6, 11, 23
Socialism, 48, 86–87
Sonny Bono Copyright Act (1998),
  110, 149
Speculation, 145, 159
Stadt Luft Macht Frei, 24, 50
Standardization, 6, 115, 122
Standardized tests, 72, 81, 82
Standards, 20–22, 26, 42, 52, 56, 66,
  76, 81, 82, 122, 143, 153, 180, 187
Statute of Anne (1710), 149
STEM (Science, Technology,
  Engineering, Mathematics), 1, 80,
  180, 194

Stern, Paul, 39
Stonemason's hammer, 15
Structure of Scientific Revolutions (Thomas Kuhn), 59
Sunlight rights, 42, 69
Supply chains, 72, 125, 165–167, 184
Surveillance capitalism, 108, 124

Tax avoidance, 38, 153
Tax havens, 146, 154
Taxes, 42, 50, 76, 84, 153, 195
Technocratic authority, 111, 154
Technological drama, 68, 173
Technology, character of, 5, 65–68
Technototemism, 51
Tennessee Valley Authority (TVA), 165–167, 169, 203
Thompson, E. P., 56
Thoreau, Henry David, 45
Tiananmen Square, 156
Times Square, 156
Toll goods, 9, 29, 43–46, 69, 94, 99, 113, 173, 175
Totems, totemic objects, 16, 50–51, 53, 60, 88, 114, 149, 151, 175, 190, 201
Trade studies, 144
Tragedy of the commons, 33, 38, 57, 95, 159, 195–196, 204
Transcontinental railway, 77, 78, 162, 193
Tribalism, 9, 48, 74, 90, 180, 201
Turner, Frederick Jackson, 159, 189
Twitter, 42, 53, 57, 99, 119, 133, 154, 164, 169, 173, 186, 196

United Kingdom (UK), 200–201
Universalism, 36, 47, 74
University of California, 194, 203
Urban commons, 99, 138, 139, 141, 148, 149, 156, 157, 159, 195–196, 197–198
Urban crisis, 195
Urban renewal, 157
Urbanites, 141
User acceptance, 189
User experience (UX), 189
Utilitarianism, 10, 30, 59, 70

Vector-centric cosmology, 59, 64
Vitruvius, 5, 20–21, 22, 65–66, 76
Voter suppression, 152

Watt, James, 5, 35, 56
Weber, Max, 86, 128
Weick, Karl, 17, 54, 64
White, Leslie, 35
Whitman, Walt, 45, 75
Wiki-Commons, 100
Wilderness Road, 77
Woody Guthrie, 169
*Work of Art in an Age of Mechanical Reproduction, The* (Walter Benjamin), 94, 101, 109, 121
World Economic Forum (Davos), 176
World War II, 3, 31, 36, 48, 75, 77, 86, 154, 165, 175, 193, 202
Wu, Tim, 124, 126

Yir Yoront, 17

Zaloom, Caitlin, 46–47
Zuboff, Shoshana (Surveillance capitalism), 108, 124, 129
Zuckerberg, Mark, 189, 191, 192